THE 6D ASCENSION JOURNEY

"Once again Judith Corvin-Blackburn has given birth to a truly multidimensional masterpiece. Her new book is destined to become a shamanic map between worlds and a guiding light for the great shift and awakening of our of ka consciousness that humanity may finally be ready for."

LINDA STAR WOLF, PH.D., FOUNDER OF VENUS RISING ASSOCIATION FOR TRANSFORMATION AND AUTHOR OF *THE AQUARIAN SHAMAN*

"As always, Judith is ahead of the pack—traversing the unmapped wilderness to show us the next step in our evolution. We can no longer deny, hide from, or feign ignorance of our power as sole creators of our lived experience. Judith illuminates this power and gives us a vocabulary and understanding of just how potent and effective we are."

REV. STEPHANIE RED FEATHER, AUTHOR OF *THE EVOLUTIONARY EMPATH* AND *EMPATH ACTIVATION CARDS*

"*The 6D Ascension Journey* is crucial reading at this juncture to understand the metaphysical science and emerging truths of how the physical body, the spiritual body, the collective body of the Earth, dimensional truths, DNA, and healing are linked. This is a great work for our time!"

JOSHUA REICHMANN, AUTHOR OF *THE REALIZED LIGHT OF THE TWELVE DIMENSIONS*

"In *The 6D Ascension Journey*, Judith Corvin-Blackburn masterfully elevates our awareness to embrace all parts of our psyche in order to activate the light codes held within our 12-stranded DNA. It's a beautiful work!"

TAMMY BILLUPS, PIONEER ON THE ANIMAL-HUMAN SACRED SOUL PARTNERSHIP AND AUTHOR OF *YOUR ANIMAL—YOUR SOUL MIRROR*

"Uplifting and consciousness-expanding! We're blessed to have this truly wise elder explain how to transform personal and planetary challenges into radiant reality. Judith's life-changing revelations and meditations will accelerate your personal healing and awakening and co-create the New Earth!"

BENJAMIN BERNSTEIN, AUTHOR OF *INSTANT DIVINE ASSISTANCE*

"Powerful, timeless, ancient wisdom! *The 6D Ascension Journey* is a mystical portal into our multidimensional consciousness to activate the light codes of our dormant DNA. If you are prepared to release your wounds, traumas, and shadows, to heal, and to reclaim your limitless self, then dive in."

EVA MARQUEZ, AUTHOR OF *ACTIVATE YOUR COSMIC DNA*

"*The 6D Ascension Journey* is magnificent! Judith's synthesis merges the 5D fields of love and unbridled creative vision, enabling us to create a new future and birth the Divine Human on Earth."

CARLEY MATTIMORE, COAUTHOR OF *SACRED MESSENGERS OF SHAMANIC AFRICA*

"Judith Corvin-Blackburn explores the relationship between 5D and 6D while offering readers the opportunity to participate in the creation of a new Earth reality. This is exciting beyond words, and Judith finds the words to explain this process in a very accessible way. I highly recommend this book!"

RUBY FALCONER, COAUTHOR OF *SHAMANIC EGYPTIAN ASTROLOGY*

"In *The 6D Ascension Journey*, Judith offers a timely roadmap to a much greater reality. With Judith's clear, step-by-step guidance, we have a high-frequency opportunity to evolve ourselves and our world together."

AMRITA GRACE, AUTHOR OF *RECLAIMING APHRODITE*

"Enjoy this beautiful and intriguing read—an inspiring adventure among the dimensions and a guidebook for all wishing to birth life from a higher vibrational reality. I highly recommend!"

CAROLINE OCEANA RYAN, AUTHOR OF *THE SPIRIT OF THE DRAGON TRIBES*

THE ASCENSION JOURNEY

ACTIVATING THE LIGHT CODES IN OUR 12-STRAND DNA

JUDITH CORVIN-BLACKBURN,
LCSW, DMin

Bear & Company
Rochester, Vermont

Bear & Company
One Park Street
Rochester, Vermont 05767
www.BearandCompanyBooks.com

Bear & Company is a division of Inner Traditions International

Copyright © 2025 by Judith Corvin-Blackburn

All rights reserved. No part of this book may be reproduced or utilized in any form or by any means, electronic or mechanical, including photocopying, recording, or any information storage and retrieval system, without permission in writing from the publisher. No part of this book may be used or reproduced to train artificial intelligence technologies or systems.

Cataloging-in-Publication Data for this title is available from the Library of Congress

ISBN 978-1-59143-546-4 (print)
ISBN 978-1-59143-549-5 (ebook)

Printed and bound in the United States by Lake Book Manufacturing, LLC

10 9 8 7 6 5 4 3 2 1

Text design by Kenleigh Manseau and layout by Priscilla Harris Baker
This book was typeset in Garamond with Bookmania, Caredrock, Futura, Gill Sans, Legacy Sans, and Quasimoda used as display typefaces

To send correspondence to the author of this book, mail a first-class letter to the author c/o Inner Traditions • Bear & Company, One Park Street, Rochester, VT 05767, and we will forward the communication, or contact the author directly at empoweringthespirit.com.

Scan the QR code and save 25% at InnerTraditions.com. Browse over 2,000 titles on spirituality, the occult, ancient mysteries, new science, holistic health, and natural medicine.

To my planetary and celestial family—
Deep gratitude for our collaboration

Contents

Foreword: Activating Our 6D Powers   xi
by Barbara Hand Clow

INTRODUCTION
6D: The Key to Personal and Collective Evolution   1

PART ONE
Reality Creation and the Sixth Dimension

1 The Big Picture   8
  * Connecting with Your Soul Mission   37

2 A Deeper Look at Sixth-Dimensional Consciousness   41
  * Rogue Cell Dialogue: Meeting and Transforming Rogue Beliefs and Fears   74

3 The Creation of Our Personal Reality   78
  * Meeting Your Ka   101

4 We Really Can Change the World 104
  * Planetary Healing:
    Planting Portals of Light 122

PART TWO
Reclaiming and Living in Expanded Sacred Connection

5 Sacred Geometry and Other Light Languages 128
  * Messages from Metatron's Cube 145

6 Sacred Architecture, Sacred Sites, and the Frequency of Our Structures 148
  * Visiting Advanced Civilizations 174

7 Time, Timelines, and Timelessness 177
  * Cellular Journey to Deactivate Our Trauma DNA 197

PART THREE
Pathways to New Earth through Empowerment and Compassion

8 Steps to True Empowerment: The Antidote to Control 202
  * Reclaiming Empowerment and Authenticity 221

9 A Joyful New World 225
  * Stepping into a Higher-Frequency World 235

✲✲✲

Acknowledgments	237
Notes	239
Bibliography	243
Index	245
About the Author	255

FOREWORD
Activating Our 6D Powers

Barbara Hand Clow

You have chosen to read a very significant book. *The 6D Ascension Journey: Activating the Light Codes in Our 12-Strand DNA* describes how to maintain your sanity and thrive during the current evolutionary leap. Judith Corvin-Blackburn's latest book zeroes in on the sixth dimension (6D)—the world of ideal forms that inspire us while we navigate life in 3D. As a brilliant psychotherapist, she guides us skillfully on the healing path as we all endure this chaotic moment in time.

My most important book on the dimensions, *Alchemy of Nine Dimensions*, inspired Judith to write her previous book, *Activating Your 5D Frequency*. While reading that book, I was excited by her deep understanding of my hypothesis describing the vertical axis, a user-friendly model for being in nine dimensions of consciousness. Now, after activating nine-dimensional consciousness for fifteen years, I'm so grateful that teachers like Judith are carrying on, each in their own unique way.

Her book about 5D has done well and has encouraged me to update my thoughts about the vertical axis for my twentieth-anniversary edition of *Alchemy of Nine Dimensions*. In her excellent foreword for the new edition, she noted that "we both realized we had complementary planetary assignments that included bringing awareness of the Nine-Dimensional Vertical Axis back to help humanity in this next stage of our evolution." Like me, Judith knows we are *bringing something back*. She's right because I've recently found evidence for the use of these dimensional tools by humans as far back as fifty thousand years! Fundamental to our evolutionary leap, these consciousness-expansion tools also can be detected in the work of physicists describing string theory.

I was delighted when Judith dove into the rapidly accelerating comprehension of 6D, my favorite dimension because it inspires our human intentions and actions in 3D. The great value of Judith's 6D work is her gentle guidance as a therapist as she leads you skillfully into 6D's formative intensity. She'd already grappled with its strong force by opening her mind to the agony and ecstasy of its divine power. For example, the records of all time are in 6D, and remembering the forgotten past can be overwhelming at first. Yet, when you shine light into your unconscious to claim your primordial inner knowing, the universe awaits you.

I am also honored to write this foreword because my comprehension of 6D is deeply sourced in some of the psychotherapeutic methods she uses. For example, when *The Pleiadian Agenda* came out in 1995, I was worried that the intense Pleiadian material might trigger kundalini risings in the participants. My partner and husband Gerry Clow was training in various healing modalities and is very calming and available, so I thought he could help students become comfortable in their bodies when I opened the dimensions. The workshops provided one bodyworker for every ten students to facilitate the dimensional forces coming in. Around the same time, Judith was intensifying her therapy skills by adding dimensionality to her client sessions.

In 2012, Gerry and I completed our *activations* (workshops to open nine dimensions of consciousness) because now it was time for students to create their own. And I needed time to write new material. I wanted to write about fictional characters healing their shadows; I created a group of courageous initiates shining light into their unconscious minds in order to find many new worlds. My new storytelling excited the emotions of readers in the *Revelations Trilogy* that came out from 2015 through 2021. Readers report they feel the qualities of the dimensions, so this is a new therapeutic pathway for awakening dimensional consciousness.

I first heard from Judith while I was writing the third novel, *Revelations from the Source*, when I felt a dimensional triangle forming. When Gerry and I taught activations, he was *body*, I was *mind*, and now with Judith's latest book, we can add the *therapist*. Judith's clearance and shadow work in written form allows you to explore many dimensions safely, anchoring yourself in 6D.

Well, what does 6D have to do with therapy? Judith's book addresses this extensively, and here are my own reflections. When I was forty and my youngest child was in preschool, it was time for my career. I was thinking about training as a Jungian analyst when I heard about Matthew Fox's master's program in creation-centered spirituality at Loyola University in Chicago. It was deeply influenced by Jungian ideas, so I enrolled in 1982. Matt accepted me even though I insisted I wanted my master's thesis to be a comparison of Jungian psychotherapy and past-life regression under hypnosis. Now, as you read Judith's new book, you will see that exploring past lives and Jung's insights are central to dimensional access for Judith.

Also, during the 1980s, I admired Stanislav and Christina Grof's work using breath techniques to move people through trauma—Holotropic Breathwork. Jung's body of work, the Grofs' birth-trauma research, and Judith's insights are comprehensive, deep, and compelling pathways into our unconscious—*that are linked to the perfected forms in 6D*. Deep trauma therapy opens us to 6D powers. *The 6D Ascension Journey* is Judith's gold mine. She breathes with you as you read, subtly encouraging you to rebirth yourself. Much like the Grofs' rebirthing therapy, her book holds you in a form of *active trauma release*.

Judith insists *we were designed to be 5D/6D humans*, and at this time we are bringing these dimensions fully into our lives. This is happening because cosmic light codes are activating us. She offers personal descriptions of facing her own shadow and discovering visualization methods to contact 6D. This helps you accept that in 3D there is really no way out of facing the shadow to find the light—all you can do is go through it. The Grofs used this method to help people heal birth trauma for many years and to release ancient memories of suffering and trauma. Now these ancient shadows are engulfing the collective mind amid constant wars; we have to embrace our resistance to reach joy and higher consciousness.

When we are in timeless bliss in 5D, we let old baggage go, fly, and our hearts open fully. At that point the marvelous 6D tool chest is available to us. This is genius—using visualization to create things in 3D—and it works! Visualization is a potent tool because 6D is the Land of Platonia, as described by the Oxford physicist Julian Barbour, based on Plato's world of forms. According to Barbour's *The End of Time*, mathematically the Land of Platonia is filled with magical triangles that hold all the thoughts of humans in 3D. The triangles in this world of forms hold the positive and negative aspects of all the 4D dilemmas that exist for us in 3D. We can actually go there in our minds to decide what we want to create in 3D. For example, do we seek joy and peace or pain and aggression? Barbour says what is in our minds creates the rising or lowering of the mists in Platonia inside the triangles. Once enough of us figure out how to do this, our world will change for the better; and if we do not, the path to destruction is unavoidable. In other words, *what is in our minds is creating the world out there.* Right now the world is dark and traumatic because of our fear, anger, and loss of faith.

I could write pages more about dimensionality, but it is your time for Judith's book. She takes you through the issues—the condition of the world, the reasons why humans are perpetuating it instead of improving it—and then all the therapeutic techniques she combines with dimensionality in a way that opens you up to change in the slow, wise, and professional style of an excellently trained psychotherapist. This level of energetic balance and flow is waiting for you as you move along, page by page, gradually widening your dimensional band. This book is going to greatly intensify your shadow clearing to awaken you to higher levels. This will be happening all around you, dear reader, during these intense times. You will find it is all so much easier if you commit to your own clearing work. Enjoy this wonderful book. Someday we will all be together in a world of peace, joy, and love. The time is coming.

BARBARA HAND CLOW is the author of *The Pleiadian Agenda: A New Cosmology for the Age of Light*, *The Alchemy of Nine Dimensions: The 2011/2012 Prophecies and Nine Dimensions of Consciousness*, and *Awakening the Planetary Mind: Beyond the Trauma of the Past to a New Era of Creativity*.

Introduction

6D: The Key to Personal and Collective Evolution

Our planet is in chaos as the old world burns to the ground. Yet this is not the time to lose heart. Rather it is the time for us to step up and together birth the new, higher-consciousness world that has been waiting behind the dimensional veil to be born. It is the time to own who we are as creators of our reality and to choose the reality we most wish to create.

We are on the precipice of a great evolutionary shift where we will reclaim both our true nature as divine humans and the higher-frequency world we are meant to live in. Over the last twelve thousand years, much of our genetic prowess has been shut down as the DNA strands that hold our higher-dimensional gifts became dormant. This has kept us stuck in the duality of the third and fourth dimensions, creating a world of suffering and struggle.

Going through millennia of this dimensional descent, and having lost much of the story of what life was like on this planet before this descent, we have created a world filled with pain, violence, and distress. It is now time to reverse this, to re-ascend, reclaiming our birthright to operate out of our full genetic potential and live from the higher-dimensional frequencies and higher dimensions of consciousness that are our birthright.

Currently, we have entered a transitionary stage of this reclamation journey, a journey that will ultimately restore peace, love, and justice globally, and create a vibrant world where all beings can thrive. People around the globe are waking up. Numerous souls have returned to Earth now to help, having signed up to be pioneers in this transition and to go through a personal evolutionary process that in turn will shift the energy field of the collective.

Those of you who are drawn to this book are part of this early wave of humans who have agreed to lead the way. We have come in with a sacred mission and with the intent to activate the courage needed to carry our mission out, no matter how challenging it may be. We are not alone; there are millions of us on this New Earth team. The guidance and wisdom we need are inside of us, waiting to be excavated. Our star ancestors, too, are here to help us remember and to ease our way once we free ourselves enough to listen.

As I wrote in my book *Activating Your 5D Frequency*, when all our DNA is fired up, we have access to at least nine dimensions of consciousness. This is part of the ancient star wisdom that Barbara Hand Clow has brought into our modern awareness through her channeling with her Pleiadian guides, and shares in detail in her book *Alchemy of Nine Dimensions*, written with her husband, Gerry. As our dormant DNA strands and the light codes within them begin to refire, they can absorb even more of the information in the higher-dimensional light codes now coming to us from the photons hitting and being absorbed by our planet. In *The 6D Ascension Journey*, we revisit this 9D vertical axis and focus on utilizing the magic of the sixth dimension, blending it with our 5D frequency to co-create a loving, higher-dimensional world.

Our current evolutionary imperative is to move from the limits and pain of the third and fourth dimensions and instead operate out of our fifth and sixth-dimensional consciousness, integrating the 5D qualities of love, Oneness, and unbridled creative vision with the New Earth energy blueprints that already exist in 6D. When enough of us use clear and focused intent and disempower our fears, limited beliefs, and resistances, we will manifest and transform our planet by consciously reclaiming these creative abilities. This is how we reconnect with our true selves and how we change our world.

The sixth dimension, which Plato called the *world of forms* and which physicists have labeled *the quantum field*, holds every idea, quality, object, and being that we can imagine, including us, in a geometric energy form. These forms are essentially light bodies. There is an interactive relationship between 3D and 6D so that whatever we envision and energize while in our bodies in 3D, shows up in these energy forms in 6D, and whatever energy forms reside in 6D, have the potential to manifest here. Manifestation occurs when we energize an intent or idea strongly enough. Thus, this is the dimension where we directly create what we perceive as reality in 3D.

Everything we experience, everything that has shown up in our lives has been of our own creation and soul agreements, but with those DNA strands shut down, we have created most of our 3D reality from unconsciousness. This has left us to be easily manipulated because we have lost our critical connection to our divine core. As we reclaim who we are, we step out of a very limited bandwidth of conscious perception and gradually step into our higher-dimensional consciousness, where we can fully own our role as reality creators and together choose a new reality from the wisdom of our hearts.

Writing this book has taken me through my own journey, as reading it and working with the material will take you through yours. You will journey both to understand and increase your awareness of how we consciously can use our fifth- and sixth-dimensional abilities to shift our reality, as well as to find and develop more tools to help you shift out of your old conditioning into a new empowered version of yourself in this process.

From birth, we have been programmed to operate out of an extremely limited perceptual bandwidth, made to believe that much of the abilities we are genetically designed to have access to do not exist. This is like looking at the world with blinders on that allow you to only see a fraction of what is there. Additionally, we have been conditioned to believe that anyone who removes these blinders is crazy or, at best, misguided. At various times over these past millenniums, the dangers of breaking through these limiting societal norms, to see and speak the truth, have led to traumatic repercussions, causing those who were brave enough to do this to be literally or figuratively burned at the stake. This has created fears and other forms of trauma that we carry on the cellular level. To carry out our soul missions, learning how to quiet our fear and disempower our trauma response is an important part of this journey and one that this book addresses as you read it.

This is my fourth book, and I have found that writing books is a bit like raising children; each has its unique gifts, demands, and growth process. I wrote the first few pages of this book in 2021, then came to an abrupt stop. Old doubts and fears arose, as did many questions. Was I really up to this endeavor? Did I know enough about the sixth dimension to lead others? But despite this, this book never went away, and I began to study more about sacred geometry, a primary characteristic of 6D structure, despite not knowing how or even if it would interface with the book. Over a year later, at the ocean that invariably expands my consciousness, I unearthed those few beginning pages and made myself write an hour a day, whether it seemed like gibberish or not. I returned to my mountain home having written a few chapters, but after having a few friends read it, I received feedback that let me know it needed a lot of revision. And so it went into pause mode again for almost another year. I spent much of that year learning and experiencing more about sacred geometry and, from this, more about the structure of the universe as it was showing up in the 9D vertical axis. Then an oracle reading in June 2023 by Shama Viola from Damanhur confirmed this book was finally ready to be written, which energized me to rewrite what I had started. Within eight months, with a contract from Inner Traditions in hand, the main text was completed. My guides had stood at the ready, downloading me with much of the concepts you will find as you go along. My own bandwidth of perception has expanded from this experience, and my 6D creative prowess, while still developing, has grown as well. I believe the same will happen for you.

Chapter 1 will give you more background and understanding of where we've been and where we are going in this evolutionary process. It will also help you understand why this journey brings up our fears, old limited beliefs, and resistances, and give you a preview of ways to work with these. It will also help you connect with how our personal growth can reconfigure our collective reality.

Chapter 2 introduces you to the 9D Vertical Axis, and how to consciously use its wisdom to release victim consciousness and take full responsibility for what you create. You will understand the sixth dimension in more depth and how it is an important part of the current ascension happening on our planet.

In chapters 3 and 4, we delve deeper into how we create personal and collective reality. You will be able to meet and strengthen your connection to your *ka*, the energy blueprint of your realized self as it resides in its geometric configuration in 6D. You will also become more attuned to how to create the frequency match needed for your intentions to manifest. Chapter 4 focuses on how we shift our world to create a higher-dimensional planet. This includes understanding and integrating the collective shadow, as well as activating our starseed memories to provide us with models of awakened civilizations.

Chapters 5 and 6 will deepen your experience of sacred geometry and light languages to help expand your perceptual bandwidth and deepen your connection to universal wisdom. As we create this new world, we will relearn how the energy emitted from structures we create on the planet can help us collectively hold a higher-dimensional energy field.

Chapter 7 explores this odd thing we call time, and how to understand and utilize various aspects of it. This includes helping us work with other lifetime traumas that may be making it more difficult to carry out our current mission, and ways to deactivate these old traumas on a cellular level.

Chapter 8 draws most on my decades of experience as a transpersonal psychotherapist, where I have guided clients into the personal empowerment needed to become fully aligned with their soul potential. When we reach this level of empowerment, we are no longer vulnerable to manipulation and control, whether from people in our lives or from society at large. We know how to connect with the Divine wisdom we carry within us and allow it to be our guide.

Finally, chapter 9 brings us into our transition to a joyful new world, to connect with this planet we all deserve to live on, where the pain and trauma of current life in 3D becomes a thing of the past.

The meditations at the end of each chapter are designed to help you experience and integrate the information shared from your inner guidance and wisdom. The journal questions and exercises will aid you in uncovering what may be holding you back and and will provide you additional support on your journey.

Remember, you hold the awareness, the answers, and the solutions within you. My mission, my job here, is to help you access this and become more fully aware when something resonates as truth for you and when it doesn't. We can no longer count on, nor should we count on, information that is being blasted through our airways. Rather we must step into our own inner authority, remembering who we truly are, and learning to trust that with the help of our guides, we will lead ourselves and humanity out of the darkness and into a loving and enlightened world that supports the well-being of all.

Enjoy the journey and know we are walking this together.

PART ONE
Reality Creation and the Sixth Dimension

1

The Big Picture

What we thought we could count on, even definitions of who we are, are rapidly morphing. Contradictory narratives arise everywhere. Consensus reality seems to be dissolving. We find ourselves in an era where opposing facts have become the norm, and what and whom to trust in terms of what is true lacks any solid foundation. Even our sense that 3D reality is solid shifts as the old guideposts disappear.

Simultaneously, there is an evolutionary movement going on across the globe. People are waking up to a new awareness of who as humans we really are. And although we are often in a state of collective discomfort as we struggle to keep our balance, release old-paradigm beliefs, and commit to being ever more loving, conscious, and co-creative, this collective awakening is heartening news.

Large numbers of us are seeking to become more conscious and open dormant light codes within our DNA. These light codes give us access to our multidimensional nature and higher-dimensional information. This allows us ultimately to transform life on Earth, creating a loving, peaceful, just, and healthy planet for all who live on it.

As humans, we are designed to operate out of our twelve strands of DNA. Ten of those strands have been dormant within most of us for millennia. Our twentieth-century scientists called those ten dormant strands *junk DNA*, with the assumption they had no purpose. If one takes a moment to think about this, this is absurd. Our bodies are efficient systems. There is no way we have ten random strands of DNA that serve no important function.

Light codes are embedded in these ten DNA strands, and many of us have now begun to reactivate them. These codes, which are currently being amplified from the photons hitting our planet, hold incredible talents and gifts, including empathy, telepathy, and clairvoyance. They are our passage to full empowerment and our co-creative abilities, as well as to cosmic wisdom. They allow us to expand the bandwidth of our perception so we can plug into this higher wisdom and experience reality in a way that allows us to both see and live in a much bigger, more conscious picture.

The chart below (fig. 1.1) provides a visual representation of our

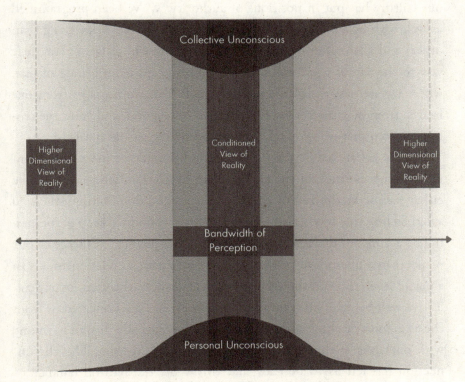

Fig. 1.1. Bandwidth of Perception chart

perceptional bandwidth. The horizontal line in the middle of the chart represents our potential to see reality from an unlimited, higher-dimensional perspective. The two vertical lines in the center represent the limited bandwidth that we have been traditionally trained to use to determine what is real. As we reactivate our dormant DNA strands, we move into a much larger view of reality until, ultimately, we live consistently in this expanded perception. The other thing that happens is that both what is held in our personal unconscious and our collective unconscious rise more and more into our awareness. Simply put, the more we expand our bandwidth, the more conscious we become.

From birth, we have been conditioned with beliefs that limit our perceptions and essentially keep us in a state of disempowerment, conflict, and suffering. Beliefs such as life is unfair, that we are inherently shameful or sinful, that we cannot trust ourselves or anyone else except those our culture has put in positions of authority. We've been programmed as well with beliefs that some groups of people are more deserving than others and that suffering is inevitable for those who cannot claw their way to the top of the social structure. This keeps us in a state of fear, where we are easily misled and controlled. It disconnects us from our hearts, from our interconnection with all of creation, and from the cosmic wisdom that we all carry but have been taught does not exist.

These beliefs have created wounds and trauma for most of humanity, keeping us stuck in the energy of victimization, with most people either feeling victimized or else persecuting and dominating others to avoid feeling this way . This is the collective wound we keep perpetuating by acting out dysfunctional dramas on the physical 3D stage of our planet. On a micro level, this can show up as painful relationships. On a macro level, this can show up as wars and leaders, threatening our collective well-being. This trauma consciousness has disconnected us from the awareness of our true potential, where we naturally live in harmony with ourselves, with each other, and with all of creation. This disconnection has led us to policies that throw off the natural balance of Mother Earth and could ultimately wipe out humans from the planet.

Our DNA and the Fall: How It All Began

Some years ago when I was teaching a workshop on reclaiming our multidimensionality and talking about what I've coined the *dimensional descent*, it suddenly dawned on me that the biblical story of the Fall was in fact a patriarchal interpretation of how we came to shut down most of our DNA and got ourselves kicked out of the Garden. Or more accurately, how we kicked ourselves out of the Garden.

Before the Fall, we were operating out of multidimensional consciousness. We were a lighter, brighter version of ourselves naturally accessing our higher-dimensional gifts, and living from our fifth-dimensional frequency, as we are genetically designed to do. The fifth dimension is all about unconditional love of self and others, unity consciousness, unbridled creativity, and the awareness of our interconnection with all of creation. We partnered with our sixth-dimensional expression to choose and anchor the reality that was most aligned with these qualities, so they could manifest in 3D on our planet.

After the Fall, with these important parts of our DNA shut down, we have been mostly operating out of third-dimensional consciousness, a denser version of our true nature, and partnering with the archetypes of the fourth dimension—unconsciously allowing them to play with our emotional and mental bodies.

Ironically, this information is embedded in our culture through philosophy, story, and myth, but we lost our ability to understand it. It also has been slanted in such a way to support a denser dimensional view of the world, blaming the feminine and sending us deeper into the separation consciousness that has become so pervasive over the last twelve thousand years. It disconnected us from our essence, our divine core, our heart, and we have become mere shadows of who we truly are.

The biblical story itself implies that seeking cosmic knowledge, which we do naturally when we are operating at our full twelve-strand DNA potential, is somehow sinful, and we should subvert ourselves to some "guy in the sky" image of divinity that, well, gives us some pretty dysfunctional rules to follow. Why we went along with this, of course, is open to vast speculation, but I think that what's most important is to understand that we had some collective agreement to explore living in this limited consciousness. Still, I suspect we had no idea of what a painful reality we would be creating.

Perhaps this pain was needed to propel us out of our limited beliefs and motivate us to throw off the shackles we put ourselves in. We now are living at a crisis point where if we don't change, if we don't reclaim our gifts, we may kick ourselves not just out of the Garden, but off the planet as well. And so now many of us are beginning to reawaken. More souls are showing up with the mission to reverse this dimensional descent and once again bring humanity into a golden age.

As Plato speaks of in his allegory of the cave, we are those who have broken free of our chains that had us living in a shadow reality, and we are facing the light of both what we have created and what we can create. It is not an easy journey, but it is an essential and satisfying one if we persevere.

Those ten strands of DNA hold the gifts of our star ancestors—beings from the advanced star civilizations who seeded humans on our planet long before our so-called history began. These beings operated from a fifth-dimensional frequency—a higher heart-based consciousness where all knew they were part of this beautiful web of creation and could work in harmony to expand cosmic love and wisdom throughout our galaxy and beyond.

Information about civilizations that existed on our planet before the Fall, which became erased from our cultural history, is now beginning to spread around the world. Memories of living in places like Atlantis and Lemuria are resurfacing at rapid speed, and many are teaching these things through books, classes, and podcasts. Remembering how we lived on Lemuria and on Atlantis when it was in its more evolved state, gives us much-needed models for what we can create here and now. We can then use the suffering of our recent past and current present as compost to grow an even more advanced version of evolved human civilization on Earth.

For those unfamiliar with Lemuria and Atlantis, they are legendary societies that thrived on our planet well over one hundred thousand years ago. They were both on continents that no longer exist and that conventional scientists still say don't exist, but too many people have memories of those societies to dismiss them. And many channelers keep bringing in more information. Plato talked of Atlantis in his dialogues, *Timaeus* and *Critius*. Edgar Cayce brought Atlantis back into our modern consciousness through his teachings as well.

Lemuria was on a continent located in the Pacific Ocean that is thought to have sunk from a series of volcanic eruptions. It has been suggested that the society began around five hundred thousand years ago. From my understanding and channeled information, it started as an experiment by a group of beings from the Pleiades, Arcturus, Sirius, and Lyra star systems with the intent of recreating advanced civilizations here on Earth.

Atlantis came later. It is believed to have been on a continent in the Atlantic Ocean near and including some of the East Coast of the United States. I sense that Atlantis and Lemuria were both happening here at the same time before Lemuria disappeared.[1]

Atlantis is said to have gone through three rises and falls, with the latest fall thought to be around twelve thousand years ago. Its golden age, or at least one of them, has been dated from 50,000 to 30,000 BCE. From my memories, Atlantis deteriorated before a massive earthquake, and ensuing floods fully destroyed it because it had become out of balance, with masculine energies overtaking the feminine. It was highly technologically advanced, unlike Lemuria, where its inhabitants lived in harmony with the natural world and were not drawn to creating advanced technology but rather simply created through their thought forms. Creating through thought forms is one of the gifts of partnering with our sixth-dimensional abilities. Atlantis did this as well, but because of its more masculine nature, it created a much more elaborate outer life.

Ancient Egypt, awakened Egypt, long before the pharaohs and our current recorded history—carried much of the frequencies and wisdom of Atlantis before its fall. The Emerald Tablets suggest that Thoth (whom Plato called Theuth) arrived in Egypt to bring Atlantean information there.[2] Thoth became part of the Egyptian Neturu, or pantheon of their gods and goddesses. When I traveled on a sacred journey in Egypt some years ago, not knowing about this legend, I could see Egypt had once been a higher-dimensional society and that it had gone through a long period of dimensional descent. All over the ancient temples are hieroglyphs and other clues to support this.

Our current journey of personal and collective ascension, which for me is the term for our reclaiming our higher-frequency potential, is much about expanding our bandwidth so that we can remember these societies and co-create them anew in an even more advanced state.

This is not for the weak of heart. Simply being a conscious human on our planet right now is fraught with challenges. Yet there's nothing like challenges to activate our highest level of creativity. There's nothing like challenges to allow us to reveal to ourselves our immense resourcefulness and strength.

This is a time like no other, a time that all of you reading this book have chosen to incarnate for, a time when all the souls who have agreed to be on the New Earth birthing team have shown up. Since all experience is an opportunity for growth, realize that finding ourselves now at the nadir of the dimensional descent is a collective opportunity to become wiser and more compassionate than ever before. And together to co-create miracles that transform ourselves and our world.

When the occurrences on this planet feel overwhelming, when the suffering of so many threatens to take us down, this is the time to remember that something hugely transformative is afoot. We are re-becoming the *divine human*, as Richard Rudd labels us in his book *Gene Keys*. My definition, as will become more clear as you read this book, involves us re-becoming 5D/6D humans—which is the new human or divine human—a renewal of our ancient selves with a modern twist.

The New Divine 5D/6D Human

Before the dimensional descent, before getting stuck in the frequencies of 3D and 4D, when we operated out of our twelve DNA strands, we naturally lived from our inner divinity, from our fifth and sixth-dimensional qualities. To deepen our understanding of our current journey to live from these qualities once again, it is useful to become familiar with the 9D vertical axis of multidimensionality because it provides us with a cognitive structure, a road map if you will.

Barbara Hand Clow first brought this information about the vertical axis into modern consciousness. This is a very ancient system that Barbara accessed from her Pleiadian guides and explains in brilliant detail in the book she and her husband wrote called *Alchemy of Nine Dimensions*. It impacted me so greatly, that I used it as a foundational theory for my book *Activating Your 5D Frequency*.

Because the third and fifth dimensions, unlike the fourth and sixth, are more physical dimensions, as we activate our higher-dimensional DNA, 5D becomes the physical world we live in. The physicality of 5D vibrates much faster and holds more light than 3D, but it is physical nonetheless. The fourth dimension deals with the emotional body, not the physical one. This is the dimension of archetypes, symbols, and the consciousness that holds the emotional themes of humanity—qualities we access through the right hemisphere of our brains. When we are in balance, when we are emotionally clear and healthy, our 4D frequency opens the portals to the light of the higher dimensions. If we can stay emotionally healthy, we will hold the energy of unconditional love of self and others that will naturally activate the higher frequency of 5D within us. If we have not worked on healing our emotional wounds and neutralizing our shadow parts, those parts we have stuffed into our unconscious because we have deemed them "unacceptable," we contribute to mucking up the 4D canopy, thus blocking higher-dimensional light.

Fig. 1.2 shows you a visual representation of how 4D works. This was an image that Hand Clow was given from the Pleiadians, who

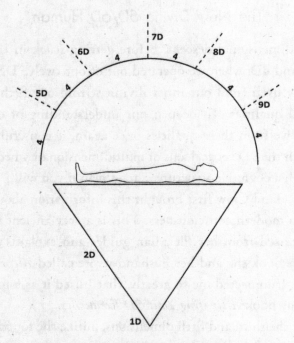

Fig. 1.2. Understanding the 4D canopy

stressed the importance of it. Energetically, 4D is like a canopy covering us in 3D. If we become emotionally clear, the canopy is filled with clear light, and the higher-dimensional portals become fully accessible. If we have not cleared the emotional body, it becomes murky and blocks our access. This is true both on a personal and a collective level. Clearing out stored-up emotions through identifying and expressing our feelings in a non-harmful way, and then releasing them, as well as continually integrating shadow issues that arise, is what we need to do for successful navigation. I've outlined this process of honoring feelings in detail in my book *Journey to Wholeness: A Guide to Inner Healing*. The main message here is that becoming emotionally healthy is an important part of the ascension journey.

From a left-brain/right-brain perspective, before the Fall we lived in a 5D world that had physical consistency (left brain) and utilized our 6D consciousness to envision that which we wished to see in the physical (right brain). Thus we co-created all we needed since the sixth dimension is where we create our reality from. We lived from the love and wisdom of our heart, naturally expressing our inborn divine nature, and created our outer life to reflect this. Our world was peaceful and kind, just and thriving.

To reclaim this, to reverse millenniums of trauma, suffering, and disharmony, we are asked to embark on both an individual and a collective journey to activate the higher-dimensional energies we are meant to hold. What is new is that we are making a conscious choice to re-ascend, which alters us as a species. The original 5D beings on this planet had not gone through this experience and had not come through the density of being stuck in lower-frequency energies.

Since most humans over the last several millenniums lived with ten of their twelve DNA strands shut down and saw reality from a very narrow and constricted bandwidth of perception, the divine balance of the feminine and masculine principles, the yin and yang, disintegrated. Patriarchy took hold, no longer honoring the feminine, and created great emotional imbalance. This gave us a world of suffering, inequality, and general misery for most on our planet.

As I said above, it thrust us into operating from the frequency of 3D/4D, unable to balance the polarity that is part of these dimensions, and threw us into separation consciousness, ultimately separating ourselves not just from all of creation but from our own heart, soul, and sense of personal empowerment. Our egos, which have been programmed for physical survival, ran our lives, and true inner peace, joy, and cosmic love eluded us.

This separation consciousness has kept us suffering and disconnected. This is true for both the victim and oppressor. Although we've been able to do much in the way of technological advances from our narrow bandwidth, even those of us who experience a relatively safe physical life are vulnerable to emotional trauma, mental anguish, and spiritual disharmony. We are stuck in not feeling good enough, worthy enough, loveable enough, and unless we have committed to healing this, we will project this onto others or drop into depression and anxiety.

Our emotional bodies are typically out of alignment as we are not taught how to process our feelings; often not even allowed to acknowledge, never mind honor our feelings. This clouds the fourth-dimensional canopy, which then continues to limit our access to the gifts of the higher dimensions.

We have been stuck in the energy of victimization, creating from the collective 4D wound where dysfunctional dramas get played out on the physical 3D stage of our world. As we actively work to heal our old emotional wounds, and in turn heal our hearts, we are not only in our fifth-dimensional vibration more frequently, but we understand in a new way that we are co-creators and what this means. We understand our connection to 6D, which empowers us to consciously, rather than unconsciously, create. We are always creating reality, but since the shutting down of our cosmic DNA, we create much of it through our unconscious rather than conscious intent.

The sixth dimension holds an energy blueprint of everything we can conceive of, whether it's an object like the computer I'm writing on, a quality like love or despair, or whether it is a soul, a being. The sixth dimension is a quantum field that holds all possibilities. Plato called it the world of forms. You and I have our idealized energetic blueprint in its most beautiful geometric form floating around in 6D.

There is ongoing interplay between 3D and 6D and vice versa. So if I want to create something in 3D, and all parts of me are aligned with this creation, I simply need to visualize clearly what I want to create and continually strengthen my vision: seeing it, feeling it, hearing it, smelling it, fully embodying it. When I can do this with enough power and intent—voilá!—it shows up. The caveat, of course, is having all parts of myself aligned enough to bring empowered energy and clear intent to what I want to manifest and simultaneously surrender my ego in the process.

We have been deeply programmed to believe that there is no way this could be easy, no way we are worthy enough, no way we can overcome human nature to be a conscious creator and to create a loving, just, harmonious world that honors all. These limiting beliefs live in our DNA and have been fed by our families, our education system, our religious institutions, and our media. They do not step aside easily. But we have the power to replace those beliefs with a much wider and truer version of what we call reality.

Some now will choose to remain in the lower dimensions, generally out of fear of the unknown or fear of breaking out of the old rules. Others of us have begun to awaken and are beginning to access higher-dimensional information. But if we have not cleared our emotional field and reprogrammed enough of our old beliefs, parts of us will remain separate from holding the higher-frequency energy, and this will interfere with our co-creative ability and with our ascension journey.

If our commitment to the journey is strong enough, through synchronicity and higher guidance, we will learn to help those parts catch up, but in the meantime, having one foot in 3D and the other in 5D is quite a challenge. I speak about this at length in *Activating Your 5D Frequency*, so I won't repeat myself here, but my intent is to help you envision what you and your life and our planet can become as we break free and allow ourselves to more fully open our 5D/6D frequencies, where we are operating from a significantly larger bandwidth and taking full responsibility for the reality we create.

We are creators. That is our birthright. We have allowed ourselves to be separated from this truth and have created a collective disaster. As we understand, reclaim, and live from these higher-dimensional energies, we can live without trauma and pain and become a beacon of light for all beings.

Avatars, Starseeds, Way-Showers, and Light Workers

It doesn't matter which, if any, of these names you identify with. You, like me, are one of the souls who have chosen to come back onto the planet now to help lead us into a 5D world. All these terms describe different ways of looking at our missions. We are the pioneers doing what we can and what we've agreed to before our current birth, to bring expanded consciousness onto our planet, to light up more of our own DNA strands, and to help others do the same.

Is this dimensional ascent predestined? Certainly, there are enough ancient prophecies to suggest this is the case. To me this means we agreed on the idea of exploring what it would be like to live with those DNA strands shut down for all those millennia, giving up our inner authority and awareness to see what would happen. Because we are all *one*, things don't happen without our agreement. All destinies are a choice, conscious or unconscious. That doesn't mean, however, that we had any clue about how awful it could get. Now though, it seems clear we have a collective agreement to re-ascend and, ideally, to ascend at a higher octave of awareness than we had before the Fall. We've made an agreement for humanity to be led back to the life it was designed for, and to create a loving, conscious, and healthy planet for all.

My definition of a starseed is a soul who came from highly conscious star civilizations, such as those that exist in the Pleiades and in the Sirius and Arcturus constellations. Although I believe all humans on the planet carry star DNA, those whose souls first came from the stars have directly experienced worlds that have been operating at a fifth-dimensional frequency and higher, and thus have a firsthand understanding of what New Earth could be like because we carry cellular memories of living on planets that have advanced, loving, and just societies. It is essential for us to have images and visions of what this is like so we can help manifest this here on Earth.

While I assume most avatars, light workers, and way-showers are starseeds, it is certainly possible that souls who originated on Earth, newer souls perhaps, are equally committed to helping and have unique qualities to support this ascension process. So, although they may not have as clear cellular memories as starseeds, they still have the inner drive and the sacred commitment to support this goal.

We are in the beginning stages of what might be a long, linear journey. We are the ones who have the courage and commitment to break free of the old conditioning, to consciously activate more of our star DNA, and to be the guides for others to wake up.

Many who have signed on to lead this way had to go through tumultuous childhoods. I suspect the reason for this was to give them a deeper level of compassion as they healed their wounds. It also may have provided them a way to heal wounds their soul has carried over many lifetimes. Those who have been blessed enough to have avoided much trauma still have major challenges: to learn to both honor our humanness, and thus our current limitations, while being consistently committed to breaking through these old barriers and healing our soul wounds, understanding that we are doing this not just for ourselves but for the good of all. This is so much larger than any of our individual experiences.

Although opening our hearts to become heart-centered rather than intellect-centered brings the potential of great joy, it also leaves us vulnerable to being misunderstood, ostracized, or even demonized. We will be called on to activate our courage again and again and again, so we must continue to step outside our comfort zone if we are to keep growing, evolving, and to essentially be able to do the job we've signed up for.

Many of us by now have become familiar with what it looks and feels like to be in our 5D expression whether we've experienced it through meditation, guided visualization, or some other method. Understanding how to consciously incorporate 6D takes us, well, quite literally to a new dimension. When we consciously incorporate our sixth-dimensional expression, we realize that we are fully responsible for everything that has happened in our adult lives. This leads us to understand more completely that not only are we creating everything that occurs, whether positive or negative, but that owning this power collectively allows us to shift and save our planet. More on this in chapter 2.

Fear, Freedom, and Reality Manipulation

Where we used to be able to count on some standardization of consensus reality, this has shifted drastically in recent years. Now, not only are we dealing with "fake facts," "fake news," and numerous examples of contradictory information blasting us through social media algorithms, we have added AI to the mix. With the development of AI, voices and images can be replicated and used to broadcast things that have never happened and that people have never said.

While of course our government and governments around the world have hidden many truths for decades, probably for centuries, from their populous, what is going on now moves far beyond this. Unless we see something ourselves or hear reports from a credible eyewitness, reality can be manipulated in ways that totally discredit what may have occurred in 3D.

Truly the only thing we can count on is what resonates in our hearts and souls as truth. And we can only fully access this once we have healed enough of our old wounds, cleared our emotional energy field, and stepped out of our conditioned perceptions enough to get a clear reading on what to trust and what to stay away from. Since we are human and fallible, this is not going to be 100 percent accurate, so releasing attachment to knowing, while doing our best to live from compassion and our inner and higher guidance, is what will help us through.

As all the guideposts fall away, and we have no clear idea of what is or isn't real, two simultaneous possibilities occur, and many of us experience both at the same time. They are fear and freedom, or as the Chinese word for crisis suggests, danger and opportunity.

A recurring collective belief is that change is threatening, that if we can't predict something, if we don't know the rules, if we don't even know what's really happening, then we are in grave danger. Since everything is in high-relief flux right now, and our media is set up for sensationalism, fear becomes a standard response.

It's important not to pretend there is no fear, because anything we deny, anything we push into the shadow gains rather than loses power. It is equally important not to be motivated by this fear but rather to recognize it, to pat it on its head, and then to go deep inside of ourselves to that eternal core, that piece of the Divine that lives within us all and that has no need for outward certainty and predictability. Opening more strands of our DNA increases our access to our inner divine spark. It is here we understand we are immensely powerful, immensely gifted. It is from this place that we understand we are creator-beings able to manifest our most treasured visions and that we know that we are interconnected with all of creation, so no matter what occurs in 3D, there is the bigger picture of our soul that is always safe and always embraced by divine love.

We can observe the confusion in the outer world that no longer provides us with any answers from a place of calm because we know and can access our answers from within.

True freedom is not about which rule we choose to follow, and certainly not about what we choose to believe, but rather it is about the awareness that we are creators. We can choose to give up this creative freedom whether through naïveté, ignorance, fear, or brainwashing. We might choose to stay shut down, to keep giving our power away, and to embrace beliefs that we know deep in our hearts are not true because this is what we have associated with safety and therefore these beliefs momentarily quell our fears. Or we can choose to live lovingly and courageously in the discomfort and uncertainty, continuing to strengthen our connection to inner wisdom.

Ultimately, this 3D human experience is impermanent, as the Buddhists so beautifully teach. Like all experiences, it is something that we simply pass through. But if we want humanity to thrive on this planet, we need to stay aware that this is a critical time for us and that we have the power to co-create a new version of reality different from any that's occurred before on this planet, building on the ancient 5D societies that were here before.

Adulting

An important part of our current evolution is to become spiritual adults. Spiritual adults take full responsibility and understand that whatever divine energy, whatever Prime Creator may exist outside of ourselves, is not here to deliver us, to save us, but rather as a model of what we truly are. Once we own this, we no longer look to others to tell us what is okay and what is not. We go within for direction and guidance. We run this information through our hearts, and from there we know how to proceed. Most importantly, we take responsibility for everything we create and for everything we have agreed to.

To truly be an adult is to own our power and to understand that any negative reality in which we find ourselves is something we unconsciously participated in creating. And since we created it, we can change it.

This is not to run a guilt or shame trip on ourselves or anyone else. There are all sorts of reasons we create negative realities. We're at Earth school, and perhaps we carry a belief that the curriculum needs to be hard. Perhaps experiencing tragedy and finding our way through it is important to our soul development. Maybe we just wanted an adventure, a new experience to try out. Maybe we thought of this as a quest to see how long we would allow ourselves to stay stuck before we could change our story. Or perhaps we got caught in a lower-frequency belief system and simply forgot there was a way out. We certainly aren't bad for creating a negative reality for ourselves—we are all doing the best we can. Our souls may even choose to experience collective negative realities such as war, famine, and persecution to test our ability to hold love and consciousness no matter how awful the outer conditions. I love the story of Saint Francis of Assisi who had his spiritual awakening and ecstatic experiences while imprisoned in a dungeon. Although we may not have the individual ability to change all our outer conditions, we always have the ability to change how we experience them. As humans, we need to honor our anger, fear, and grief, but once the feelings are processed, we can activate our higher frequencies to lessen our suffering and to live in a much bigger picture. Keep in mind anything can be changed because everything is energy. We just need to learn to step out of the way.

Another piece to keep in mind is that often we find ourselves in challenging realities because of the cultural lies we've been fed that have us believing we are not the powerful creators we really are. So yes, we've been lied to. But here's the rub: we also created the lie.

There is no doubt beings from star civilizations who have what we would call negative agendas have perhaps designed or at least perpetuated those lies, but those beings are also us. We are part of everything! As we consciously take responsibility and refuse to play the old games, we step into a whole new experience of being. We step into true adulthood.

Every aspect of creation is contained in fractals within our energy field. This is because we are holographic. For example, if you look at a holographic plate of a horse, which I did many decades ago at a New York City art show, and you break off a tiny piece of that plate, the whole image of the horse remains in that tiny piece. It is just much fainter than the original image. We are all tiny pieces of a giant holographic plate of creation, and we all hold this holographic plate within us. This is Oneness. This is the unified field defined by physics. The idea of us and them is an illusion caused by the collective illusion of separation. Spiritual adults get this.

There are numerous reasons why we resist owning who we are and activating our full adult potential. One reason is we're not sure that we really want to grow up because it means no more excuses. It means we can't play the blame or self-blame game. Maybe part of us believes it would be boring—no drama, no trauma. Then there's admitting we have all this co-creative responsibility—what if we keep screwing up?

This taking-responsibility view of things is so counter to everything we've been told that it rarely can be done without some ongoing internal struggle and self-doubt. But there's no time to waste if we want to raise the collective vibration of our planet. And raise the vibration we must if we are going to choose both to reactivate those strands of DNA to reclaim our 5D/6D design and to recreate a world that operates at the frequency of unconditional love (5D).

The more of us who step up to strengthen this expanded consciousness, including looking within to transform and heal any parts of us that either don't believe we can shift things, that fear this shift, or don't want it to happen, the more we strengthen the ascension energy. So, stay conscious of the fact that an important part of this journey is to continually increase our self-awareness. And the more aware we become, the more we can work with and integrate those shadow parts that want to hang on to the old, painful ways.

Balance Within/Balance Without

From working as a therapist and helping numerous people explore their psyches, it is clear to me that there are many variations on the theme of suffering and unworthiness that live within us all. This is not the natural balance of things. Our psyche has been distorted from generations and lifetimes of trauma. Our energy is off-kilter from centuries of patriarchy where the Goddess and therefore the energy of the sacred feminine have been in exile, leaving all humans at the mercy of a system that was never designed to support an evolved humanity.

Under patriarchy both the feminine polarity and masculine polarity, which we all carry within us, have been deeply wounded. When we kicked the sacred feminine, the highest expression of yin energy, out of the Garden, the sacred masculine was exiled as well and replaced by an out-of-balance version of masculinity. This disconnected us from the internal wisdom and intuitive awareness of the feminine that feels the interconnection with all of creation. While this disconnection has generally kept us insecure and ego focused, it has affected males most deeply. Women, while denied external power, have had more cultural permission to connect with their emotional and spiritual wisdom. Under patriarchy, emotional and spiritual wisdom are devalued, and thus have not been seen as a threat to the power structure. They've only been seen as unmanly and therefore not important.

No matter what our gender identity is, we all must reclaim the healthy, evolved expression of feminine energy and the healthy evolved expression of masculine energy. We must reclaim the heart in balance with the mind, and the mind in balance with the heart.

Part of this process is to continually meet the parts of us that are not committed to this evolution, and to teach these parts that we are powerful enough to create anything. We need to commit, the best we can, to help those parts heal, shift, and transform.

Helping our 3D/4D selves get fully aligned in this purpose is a big challenge. We are being asked to live from a belief system that is diametrically opposed to the one we've been brought up with in this lifetime and that we have carried in from other lifetimes as well. Large parts of our psyche have been programmed to believe that if we let these beliefs go, we cannot be safe and that we need them to survive. Thus, we've been programmed to believe these dysfunctional beliefs are important to our well-being. It's no wonder many want to bypass this part of the ascension process, but it will not be fully authentic without facing and transforming these internal beliefs.

Having some resistance to accepting these monumental changes is natural and, in some senses, healthy. It can make us more aware and more mindful of our 3D experience and of what we need to transform from this experience. It thus keeps us more conscious of the need to continually help these resistant parts of ourselves come on board with the new program.

Remember our resistance is often made up of fear and thus fear is likely to walk with us on this journey. Each time we overcome what is currently scaring us, we are likely to find another fear popping up. For some of us, this may happen frequently and sequentially. For others, we may have long periods of rest and integration before the next fear challenge occurs. Probably whether we rest or not depends on how much intensity we like in our lives. The most important point is for us to understand that this is the way we are designed to grow—not linearly, and not instantaneously. We can have a growth spurt that we experience as life-changing, which is wonderful, and then a year later find that old issues that occurred before this growth spurt have resurfaced to be dealt with yet again. Although this often feels like we lunged backward, we are now dealing with transforming those issues at a higher octave.

This is the spiral path. When we consciously walk this path, we circle around many of the same issues we have dealt with and transformed before, but never at the same place; rather always higher up the spiral. This means that in all healing there is always more to be addressed to deepen and expand the inner transformation.

The Right to Be Joyful

What if, just for a moment, we could instantly release any energy that holds us in individual and collective trauma and pain? Most of us would be delighted on the one hand to release the fear, sadness, anger, resentment, guilt, and shame. But then what? What purpose has this trauma response served for us? For you? What purpose has it served for humanity? Which parts of us are not ready to allow this kind of change? Are we truly open to being in joy?

For some of us, it might make us feel too privileged. How do we get to have all we desire while living a heart-based and joyful life? How do we justify being so different from others around us who are still stuck in some degree of struggle? How do we deal with the potential jealousy that might get projected on us?

For others of us, it could create too much uncertainty. We know what sadness, fear, guilt, and shame feel like. They have walked with us through many of our earthly lifetimes. To fully give them up before we feel assured that we know what we're doing—well that can feel just too scary as well.

And what about anger, which is the most misunderstood of our emotions? Those who lash out when feeling a sense of powerlessness would have to learn a whole new way of self-protection. People who repress anger and therefore become depressed and anxious would have to activate enough courage to break through old fears and programming to allow themselves a healthy, non-harmful expression and release of this emotion. Those who get stuck in blaming others would have to activate enough self-love to take responsibility for their part in things while also honoring their feelings.

As for humanity as a whole, the strangeness of giving up victim consciousness and giving up our childlike dreams of being saved by some force outside of ourselves asks us to take a collective leap of faith. And many on the planet are not yet ready or confident enough to do this.

What would it be like to get out of bed tomorrow and just be a radiating light being? What if our family and friends found that too blinding, too uncomfortable? Would we care? Would you care?

What if, just for a moment, we had to give up all our opinions, our treasured views of what is accurate perception and what is not? Are we ready to handle this? Are we ready to live in uncertainty and still be fine?

In order not to bypass these parts of our psyche, in order not to shove the old, scared, uncooperative parts of ourselves who are stuck in old-paradigm beliefs back into some compartment in our unconscious, we need to be willing to unearth all the opposing forces within us. If we aren't willing to take this on, we are not going to be able to fully carry out our mission to help humanity evolve. And we will continue to deny ourselves full access to the joyfulness that is our right.

There are not many models for true joy to show up in our world. Joyfulness is different from external success, from meeting goals, or achieving financial independence. It is not about winning a competition or in any way believing that we are more worthy than others. It's not even about connecting with our soulmate, although, of course, that's a wonderful experience. To be truly joyful is to be aligned with our souls, to keep opening our hearts, and to strengthen our commitment to serving higher love.

To do this fully, we must be willing to release struggle and allow ourselves to delight in our blessings and our challenges. After all, our challenges are just us taking an advanced Earth school curriculum. Remember, too, that we have no control over our loved ones' journeys. And if they are on difficult journeys, we need to release judgment and replace it with compassion and realize that any grief we feel does not preclude our right and our ability to feel joy.

Remember, being truly open to joyfulness is what brings the ease, grace, and flow that is natural for our 5D/6D selves. This is not a snap-your-fingers-and-it's-done sort of deal. But it is a process we can successfully commit to if we are ready to do ongoing self-assessment and the transformational work needed.

We Carry It All

As I said above, the resistance we are looking for inside ourselves is not just about our individual issues. For many who have already done a great deal of personal healing, transforming, and growing, personal issues become a smaller part of what we are dealing with. That is not to minimize the importance of getting in touch with and working with this smaller part, but to recognize there is the even larger task of healing the collective issues that are also within us.

Because we are holographic, we hold all the most wonderful and most terrible characteristics that exist in the collective experience of being human. We have been generally trained to avoid looking at the most terrible parts, learning to project them onto others, onto those we label "not us." So rather than learning how to identify, accept, and ultimately transform those inner parts of ourselves that hold the energy of liars, abusers, torturers, or any other qualities that we view as evil, we put them outside of ourselves and onto groups of people, fully disowning what lives in our own psyche. When we do this, we are not able to disempower these qualities. When we face them with compassion, we help to ultimately neutralize their energy and purge them from our collective experience.

Equally frequent is our projecting the most wonderful human attributes onto others rather than owning that we have all those attributes as well. We have been programmed to believe that we are not as good, worthy, loveable, or powerful as whomever we might admire. While perhaps this does less harm than disowning the negative attributes, it still feeds a field of powerlessness that holds humanity hostage. Although certainly there are individuals who are going to hold unique gifts, the qualities behind these gifts are shared.

As an example, I have friends who are amazing visual artists. There is no way that I can draw or paint like them. But the quality underneath the unique part of their gift is the ability to be creative and inspire various feelings in others. I can express that same quality in a way that honors my uniqueness. For me, it's through writing and facilitating growth in others. For you it might be through growing a beautiful garden or singing, chanting, dancing—just to name a few possibilities. There are a multitude of ways. What is essential to understand is that we all hold the ability to be creative and inspiring, so I can love my friends' artistic ability and simultaneously realize that I also hold the same qualities that give rise to it.

Notice if you can breathe into all your cells the awareness, the wisdom that because we are holographic, we hold all that exists in all of creation. What does it feel like to realize that everything that bothers you in the outer world also lives within you? What feelings arise when you become aware that whatever you love and admire in others is part of you as well? Notice what happens inside of you as you allow the idea to take hold that you are truly powerful and magnificent.

We hold an internal divinity that, if fully owned by enough of us, can shift our planet away from suffering, lack, abuse, and victimization and into a place of love, fairness, abundance, and safety for all.

Personal Intention and Your Rogue Cells

My friend Stephanie Red Feather has a card in her *Empath Activation Cards* deck that speaks to me repeatedly. It's called Master of Trillions. Red Feather points out that we have trillions of cells in our body, and each of them can have their separate awareness.[3]

Although her point is that we can shift our cellular responses by taking charge of those trillions of cells, I also came to realize that, just like different aspects of our psyche, not all our cells are likely to be in harmony with our positive intentions and may therefore stand in the way of our fully manifesting what we most seek in our lives. The messages from these rogue cells can move into our unconscious where, if they are not accessed, they can essentially prevent us from stepping into our self-authority, soul potential, and inner power. They therefore can simultaneously impair our ability to create what we most desire and our ability to take full responsibility for what we are creating.

When I teach, I often use the technique of asking students what percentage of themselves is still attached to various beliefs or fears that keep them from being fully conscious creators. In this kind of exercise, I ask that they pay attention to the first thing that pops into their heads, not to think about it but to be spontaneous. The percentages that show up correspond to these rogue cells inside of us. It doesn't need to be precise, just close enough. Seventy-five percent of my cells might be ready to create my ideal life and carry out my soul mission, but 25 percent of those rogue cells are standing in the way and need to be dealt with.

This technique helps us identify those inner parts that we use to sabotage ourselves. These are the parts that run old messages that say we are not worthy, not evolved enough, or that this is too weird, that it's too hard, and on and on. They send these messages to the sixth-dimensional part of ourselves, the part that creates what we manifest in our 3D lives. If their intensity is stronger than our positive conscious intention, then they will succeed in their sabotage. If their intensity is weaker but still pronounced, we'll create a compromise: we will get part of what we intend, but not all.

Imagine you could call those rogue cells forward, sit them in a room, and have a conversation with them. They hold a lot of valuable information. Listening to them and getting to know them gives you more ability to transform them. The meditation at the end of chapter 2 can help you with this.

Collective Intention

Although each of us can help neutralize the imbalances that create suffering for ourselves and others, we cannot change another's journey.

Soul lessons come in many forms, and some are quite painful. This is a hard reality to absorb. We can work our higher-dimensional magic to create new realities for ourselves, but for our loved ones and all those suffering on the planet, our ability to shift their individual outer reality is limited. We carry fractals of all who are suffering within us, but on an individual level, these fractals are very small.

Old collective belief systems hold a huge amount of power. Although large numbers of us are aware that many of our beliefs are inaccurate, they are very hard to fully release because much of our survival in the past depended on them to provide us with an illusion of safety.

In our current chaotic times, new, strange beliefs are surfacing because people no longer have an accurate sense of what to believe, of what is true. In the United States, there is rampant distrust of politicians on both sides of the political aisle. Where once we believed most of our leaders were here to carry out the wishes of the people, few if any believe this now. Ironically, different sides hold totally opposing belief systems, typically believing that the people they like, those they feel aligned with, are spouting truth while simultaneously believing those on the other side are not. Even things that seemed pretty much indisputable are being called into question. And although I always support healthy skepticism, what is going on now is incredibly extreme.

Some people believe they are getting free by only following one view and shutting out all others. To me, this is a very dangerous path. Yet, despite how this feels when I go within, I also know that I've been programmed to look at this current phenomenon from a relatively narrow bandwidth. When I expand my perceptual container, I can see we can hold all sorts of contradictory views. But if our hearts are truly loving, if we care about the well-being of all others in addition to the well-being of ourselves and our family without running the energy of judgment, we can ultimately unite to create the planet we all deserve to live on. For this to work, though, we need to be willing to hold all points of view with compassion and with the awareness that none of them might be fully accurate.

The way 3D and 6D reality connect makes this more complex. What we most feed into the sixth dimension through our intent and visions is what shows up most in our collective 3D reality. If there is no collective alignment in our beliefs, the confusion and chaos will continue. If instead there are enough of us who expand our psychic containers to hold an inclusive and bigger picture, who know that 3D reality is permeable rather than fixed, and who care deeply about the well-being of all on our planet, the easier and more quickly we will create a reality based on compassion and kindness.

If I hold a strong vision that we can have world peace, and enough others, no matter what their politics may be, also hold this vision, not just as an intellectual concept but also in their heart, and we all choose to energize this intent, we can create this almost instantaneously; we can reach a tipping point where peace will show up in our 3D reality. This is the power of collective intention. And although the current fragmentation of consensus about what is real keeps this from happening, we can override it if enough of us can hold onto the belief that our world can live in peace.

Pay attention to your thoughts. Pay attention to your judgments of who has the truth and who doesn't, and then do your very best to expand beyond this. Hold all the different ideas of truth and the people who have them in your heart. Keep imagining a planet where every person is loved and honored. Imagine a planet where resources are abundant and shared. A planet where everyone is making their contribution to the good of the whole, and where all of life can thrive. Hold those images and know that this reality already exists in the sixth dimension and is just waiting for enough of us to choose it so that it can show up here.

Reweaving Our Collective Fabric

As I said above, our world shifts when large enough numbers of us hold the same vision and continue to energize it. Although the divergent visions we are holding right now in 2024 seem insurmountable, this is a planetary dark night of the soul, and we will ultimately emerge changed and more unified. Unified enough to at least release more of the 3D density and expand higher-consciousness energy, thus activating more of the 5D and 6D frequencies to see their manifestation on the Earth.

This is an individual task and an inside job for all of us who wish to see peace, harmony, justice, love, and spiritual awareness be the essential characteristics on our planet. Remember, what is reflected outside of us is also part of our inner landscape. Since we are all interconnected, it cannot be any other way.

The teachers who offer global peace meditations understand this and help the process. The other side of the process is to find the contradictory beliefs and desires we are holding in our psyches. To take a brutally honest look at this part of our inner landscape is an important step in breaking through the old-paradigm structures that are still in place. We will find a lot of opposing beliefs and views living within us.

I deeply wish to live on a planet where love, peace, and harmony reign and where every living being is dealt with compassionately and respectfully. I came back in this incarnation to help open the way for this to show up in our earthly reality. But I have found a part of my shadow that feels this will be boring and will lack dynamism. There's a part, for instance, that is fascinated by severe weather even though I know the fear and suffering it can cause. There's another part of me that doesn't want to give up the us vs. them view, whether out of fear that things will get worse on the planet if I do, or because of my arrogant belief that I am more right than those who oppose my views. And if I look closely and honestly, I can find another part of me who could be violent and aggressive and likes feeling superior. Then there's the part who has bought into the belief that planetary transformation isn't possible. As I locate all these parts inside myself, I then can send them love and do my best to neutralize them so they will not have any power.

Each of us carries these beliefs, although each person may describe them with different words and images. If we don't allow ourselves to see them, we contribute, despite our best conscious intention, to keeping humanity operating at a lower frequency. To reweave the collective intent, each of us is asked to unearth the parts of our subconscious that feed this negative reality and interfere with lifting it into its higher manifestation.

This is not to deny that empowering and getting to know our higher selves is essential. Of course it is. But if we are here to ascend and to help humanity ascend, we need to not bypass those lower energies. We need to look for them, deal compassionately with them, and let them know that we are here to support their transformation—to release the old and to join the part of our psyche that is fully on board for this shift.

Utilizing Our Emotional Triggers

Notice if there are any emotional triggers for you as you read my words above about our shadow. Does this make you angry? Does it scare you? Does it go against your belief system in a way that your mind rebels against this process? Do you feel judgmental? Any response is fine. We've been intensely conditioned to believe that the only way we can be loveable and worthy is to be all good and eschew all parts of us that are not. However, if we truly intend to program a different Earth reality to manifest here, we need to find and clear these things within us.

Joe Vitale in the book *Zero Limits* written with Dr. Hew Len explains how *Ho'oponopono*, the reconciliation, forgiveness, and transmutation prayer from the Hawaiian tradition, works. He gives the example of how Dr. Hew Len, a psychologist who was hired to work in an institution for the criminally insane in Hawaii, shifted the consciousness of the inmates and ultimately the entire energy field of the facility. He did this by going through each inmate's file, finding the wounds and imbalances of that inmate within himself, and doing *Ho'oponopono*. The results were astonishing.

When Vitale asked Dr. Hew Len what he was doing when he

looked at his patients' files, he said, "I just kept saying 'I'm sorry, I love you' over and over again." When Vitale asked him if that was it, he said, "That's it."[4] Vitale goes on to say, "As Dr. Hew Len worked at the hospital, whatever came up in him he turned over to divinity and asked that it be released. He always trusted. It always worked. Dr. Hew Len would ask himself 'What is going on with me that I have caused this problem, and how can I rectify this problem in me.'"[5]

Hew Len's ability to do this suggests that he had cleared his internal blocks to locating unacceptable parts of himself. These inmates were dangerous and no doubt perpetrated some pretty terrible things. Yet they were, on another level, simply carrying out the shadow of the collective so that others didn't have to. And they were healed not through judgment, and not through psychiatry, but through acknowledgment that they were a part of us and that all of us deserve love, compassion, and respect.

Thus, any emotional triggers we have about shadow parts are ultimately helpful. They help us identify and clear their impact inside us. As we do this, we calm the ego and allow spirit to do its work. When enough of us on this path are willing to find the criminally insane part of ourselves, to deal compassionately with these parts while asking that they shift, this is when we can truly begin to create our 5D/6D world.

✵ MEDITATION ✵
Connecting with Your Soul Mission

Allow your eyes to soften and put all your attention on the act of breathing, taking several deep centering breaths. As you exhale release any distractions, any concerns, any tensions. Just let that all flow out with the breath. On the inhale imagine that you are drawing in tiny golden spirals of light filled with love and consciousness and allow those tiny spirals to spread to every cell in your body. Keep focusing on your breath as you begin to feel a deeper and deeper sense of calm and relaxation.

Now I would like you to imagine you are on a private deck by a beautiful ocean. Night has come with just a sliver of moon in the sky. The stars and planets shine above you in full relief, absorbing all your attention. Find somewhere comfortable to sit or lie upon, feeling the cool breeze on your skin, and listening to the rhythm of the ocean waves as they crash upon the shore.

Spend a few moments gazing up at the beauty of the sky and bathing yourself in its magical energies. You begin to sense it holds worlds upon worlds upon worlds as you gaze upward. Surround yourself with a circle of light that acts as a protective filter to allow only the most loving of the sky energies through. Feel yourself relax into this feeling of both vastness and safety. You might notice, too, that your heart feels lighter, and a sense of love permeates all your cells with every breath you take.

Take some time to luxuriate in this while continuing to gaze upward. There may be a particular star or constellation that draws your attention. If this is happening, just allow it.

As you are lying or sitting there looking skyward, you sense a being nearby that is coming to greet you. Although this may feel surprising, you can tell that this being is loving and is coming to help and support you. You feel a wave of love and familiarity travel through your heart.

You greet each other, and this being explains that they have come to you from a place in the stars, a place that your soul has spent much time upon. They let you know they are one of your guides, and they have an important message for you.

A shimmering box appears, which they give to you saying that the message within the box is guidance about the soul mission you have agreed to in your current earthly incarnation. Spend a moment looking the box over, noticing its shape and color, feeling its energy,

Whenever you feel ready, open the box and see what message it holds. It may be something clear or it might be just a symbol. You may immediately understand it, or it might be just giving you a hint or two. Just allow this all to unfold. Be aware that this being is waiting for you and is open to you asking for more clarity and guidance. Go ahead and have this conversation with your guide if it feels right.

Soon this guide will re-ascend back into the heavens, but before this happens, remember to thank them and ask if they would continue to support and communicate with you as you find ways to put this message, which contains your soul agreement to help planetary transformation, into action.

You watch as this being moves higher and higher, traveling back to where they started. Breathe deeply and feel into and ponder the experience you just had. Now slowly allow yourself to leave the deck and come back into the room you are in, perhaps wiggling your fingers and toes to help you more fully get back into your body and take some time to journal on your experience. The message you received can travel with you on this journey as you continue with this book.

Note: Find this meditation on my YouTube channel, Wisdom Within Us, in the "Meditations to Raise Your Frequency" playlist.

Journal Questions to Ponder

1. What have you noticed about your own awakening? Are you more empathic? Are you more intuitive? Do you experience your life more from a bigger-picture perspective?
2. How do you handle things when the intensity of the energies you feel from the outer world gets overwhelming?
3. Do you have any memories or images of advanced ancient societies on our planet? If so, do you trust these memories or images?
4. Do you pay attention to your emotional body, observing and processing feelings as they arise? Have you addressed old trauma and been on a healing journey for your old emotional wounds? If so, how has your life changed? If not, what beliefs or fears have kept you from doing this? What do you need to do to allow this to happen for you?
5. Do you have a sense of your soul mission? Journal on what you know about your gifts, talents, and interests that can help our collective evolutionary journey.
6. How do you deal with change? How do you deal with uncertainty?

What strategies do you have or can you develop, to make change easier?
7. What parts of you are attached to the drama of our current dysfunction?
8. How do you allow the perceptions of others to hold you back?

2

A Deeper Look at Sixth-Dimensional Consciousness

> *[The Pleiadians] say the great feline gods from Sirius periodically come to Earth to build their temples and found new cultures that can discover the vertical axis. This includes the ancient Egyptians.*
>
> BARBARA HAND CLOW AND GERRY CLOW,
> *ALCHEMY OF THE NINE DIMENSIONS*

The vertical axis Barbara's referring to above is the nine-dimensional axis. To make 6D more intelligible, it's useful to have at least a cursory understanding of this theory of multidimensionality. This also provides us with important guidance in our ascension journey as we shift from the limitations of being 3D/4D humans to becoming the 5D/6D humans we are designed to be.

I included the sentence about the ancient Egyptians in the Hand Clow quote above because I believe they were the most recent large

5D society to exist on our planet. This was around twelve thousand years ago, after the fall of Atlantis and before the dimensional descent that occurred there.

I find it interesting that there are not many teachers of multidimensionality who are teaching about the vertical axis right now. I do believe that as more of us make this journey, this model will regain popularity. It's an elegant system and can deepen our understanding of what is happening as we access more of our multidimensional nature.

Fig. 2.1 below will give you a visual understanding of this vertical axis. The first dimension, which is at the base of the axis, is in the heart of our Earth inside its crystal iron core and the center of the golden pyramid within that core. (The idea of the golden pyramid is from the teachings of African shaman Credo Mutwa and resonates strongly with me.) The ninth dimension is in the galactic center, so it might be helpful to visualize a straight line from within our Earth extending up and ending there. Both the first and the ninth dimensions hold different types of gravity that interact with each other and help create the frequencies of the additional seven dimensions within them. All the dimensions interact with one another, but understanding them sequentially will yield the most understanding.

We hold these nine dimensions within our consciousness like Russian nesting dolls. Each doll contains the energy and perspective of one of the dimensions, with the first dimension being held by the innermost doll while the ninth is held by the outermost doll. From 4D–9D, the dolls surround us outside our physical body. Once we fully ascend to 5D, the 3D and 4D dolls will be within us.

We have the capacity to view reality from the eyes of each of these nesting dolls. And like windows on a computer, we can have more than one view open at the same time. For example, we can be seeing from the perspective of our 5D nesting doll and our 3D nesting doll simultaneously. Fig. 2.1 also gives you some key words that convey the characteristics of each of these dimensions.

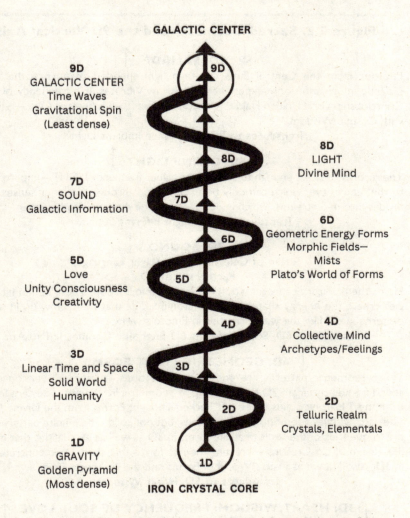

Fig. 2.1. The Nine-Dimensional Human, adapted from *Alchemy of Nine Dimensions* by Barbara Hand Clow and Gerry Clow

(A meditation to help you understand this, "Experiencing Your Multidimensionality," is on my YouTube Channel, Wisdom Within Us, in the Meditations to Raise Your Frequency playlist.)

This next chart, 2.2, is more detailed, and I urge you to spend a bit of time with it. Notice the arrows go both up and down to give you a stronger sense of the ways the dimensions interact.

Figure 2.2. Sacred Geometry and the 9D Vertical Axis

↓ **9D: SAMADI** ↑

Photons from the Central Suns create a light-encoded resonance that holds Galactic information only experienced inwardly. Vibrates at a frequency of Unity Consciousness or a Unified Field of Consciousness... All is/feels as ONE—Vibrates with Cosmic Wisdom.

Transduces to 8D. Resonance informs Light.

↓ **8D: DIVINE LIGHT** ↑

The resonance slows enough to show up as higher frequency LIGHT—imperceptible to the human eye, which can only be experienced through the inner senses. Light divides into 4–5 streams, which in 3D becomes the 4 elements plus ether.

Transduces to 7D. Light informs Sound.

↓ **7D: SOUND** ↑

Realm of Celestial Music. (Light Language)
Partners with 8D.

Holds the Auditory representation of Galactic information. These sound frequencies create the energy shapes of the Platonic Solids that then show up in myriad patterns in 6D like the water crystals in Emoto's work.

Transduces to 6D. Sound informs 6D Energetic Geometric Patterns.

↓ **6D: GEOMETRIC LIGHT FORMS** ↑

These geometric patterns are energy configurations, a "denser" version of the sound frequencies from 7D that show up as geometric light forms. They are formed from the 5 Platonic solids that hold "Packed Thought Forms from the Divine Mind." They are "visible" geometric configurations, but not solid. The infinite patterns hold the frequencies of the souls of all life forms in 3D as well as all qualities that exist in 3D. Realm of Co-Creation—creating thought forms that show up in concrete form in 3D. Also known as Plato's World of Forms and the Quantum Field.

Transduces to 5D. Heart Wisdom.

↓ **5D: HEART WISDOM: FREQUENCY OF SOUL LOVE** ↑

Partners with 6D.

Adds the frequency of what we experience as Unconditional Heart LOVE to the geometric energy patterns of 6D as well as the opening of higher creativity that can include visions that show up in 3D. Collaboration and synergy are qualities of this realm.

Transduces to 4D. Archetypes and Polarity.

↓ **4D: ARCHETYPES, EMOTIONAL POLARITY REALM,** ↑
RIGHT HEMISPHERE OF HUMAN BRAIN

Higher and Lower ASTRAL PLANE.
All Time is Simultaneous.

Energy from Higher Dimensions shows up as Archetypes. Geometry shows up in the emotional realm as dark and light. (YIN/YANG). As painful emotions are cleared, emotional field becomes diaphanous so higher dimensional frequencies can be accessed. All the Platonic Solids have a 4D representation—for example, the cube becomes the HYPERCUBE or TESSERACT.

Transduces to 3D.

↓ **3D: PHYSICAL REALITY** ↑
Partners with 4D.

Created through the 5 PLATONIC SOLIDS that show up in our DNA as well as in all visible creation. Star Tetrahedron can become the Merkaba. Polarity realm. Visions in 3D can show up as energetic light patterns in 6D.

Transduces to Crystals, Elementals, Viruses, etc.

↓ **2D: GEOMETRY of CRYSTALS** ↑

Based on the cube that can connect to all the Platonic Solids. 2D holds and emits higher dimensional information embedded in dense physical form.

↓ **1D: CENTER OF THE EARTH** ↑

According to African Shaman, Credo Mutwa, in the center of the iron crystal core is a golden pyramid. I see the center of this pyramid as the heart of the Earth. It holds CREATOR ENERGY and ABSORBS Photonic Information. Starts at zero point, which holds all creation, then radiates out and back in, with each heartbeat.

The frequency of the ninth dimension is that of total unity or Oneness. It is here we lose the sense of being in an individual body and experience a feeling of both vastness and interconnectedness with all that is. This frequency at a slightly slower vibration transduces into 8D, which is light, divine light, which we can only experience on a feeling level at this stage rather than see through our human eyes.

From the eighth dimension, the slower vibration of the seventh dimension converts this light into sound. From there, sound transforms into the energetic configurations of geometric light forms in the sixth dimension, much like Emoto's experiment, where he showed how various words create various patterns in water crystals. The meaning of the word is held in the vibration of its sound and from there it can show up visually in formations of crystalized water. Words like *peace* formed beautiful patterns. Words like war created fragmented, visually unappealing patterns.

Throughout the book, we'll be looking more at 6D to understand how essential it is for our current ascension process, but for now just understand that everything in 6D holds energetic patterns that can manifest in form in 3D.

From 6D, the light frequencies will vibrate at a slower rate where they activate the human heart, bringing us to the vibration of unconditional love, the central quality needed to step into our 5D frequency. As 5D/6D humans we will be working with 6D configurations and infusing them all with the frequencies of fifth-dimensional love.

Once the energy of 5D transduces to 4D, we have a slightly different ball game. Polarity arises in 4D (and 3D), which means that to successfully hold those frequencies in expanded awareness, we need to learn to balance the opposing forces rather than identifying with one pole or the other. We also need to both master our human emotions and own and integrate our shadow as I explain in greater detail in my book *Activating Your 5D Frequency*.

When we heal our emotional wounds, and thus no longer participate in unhealthy emotional dramas and traumas, we clear the fourth dimension to become the diaphanous arc of light it is meant to be. Once the canopy is relatively cleared, the light of the higher dimensions can then reach the lower dimensions. You might want to refer back to fig. 1.2.

Each dimension serves an essential purpose, and although we tend to think of higher dimensions as holding more intelligence, this is not accurate. They hold different types of intelligence, and they vibrate more quickly, so they have a higher frequency and hold more light. When the nine dimensions are in harmony, however, one of the jobs of the higher dimensions is to bring their light frequencies into the lower ones. Once this happens, we become fully able to experience the gifts of the lower dimensions. If 4D is filled with uncleared energy and is thus murky, then the light cannot get through, and we are sorely out of balance. There is much awareness right now that an important part of the ascension process is to become fully embodied. This happens as we heal the emotional body enough to let more light into our physical cells.

The third dimension is physical and self-explanatory. It still holds the challenge of polarity, but if we have cleared enough of our 4D emotional field, all should be well.

The first dimension and 2D are inside the Earth. The second dimension is just below the Earth's crust and holds the crystals, gems, and metals, much of which store the data of higher-dimensional wisdom and can interact with all the higher dimensions. As an example, Lemurian seed crystals have been buried in the Earth by ancient 5D cultures to hold information for humans to use in this current ascension journey. To unlock these gifts inside of us, we need to bring in higher-dimensional light.

The first dimension seems to be a microcosm for everything that exists in all nine dimensions, but because of its slower vibration, it holds these energies uniquely, grounding them in Mother Earth. This, in turn, helps us ground higher-dimensional information. And again, 1D needs the light from the higher dimensions to give us access to it.

Remember the arrows in this chart are pointing in both directions. Mastering the lower dimensions opens us up for moving into the higher dimensions and provides us with the foundation necessary to operate at higher-dimensional frequencies in the human body.

The Structure of 6D

Plato called it the world of forms. Quantum physics talks about it as the morphogenetic field or quantum field. Native American elders referred to it as *the field of plenty*. When I visualize 6D, I see energy configurations filled with light and color forming an infinite number of patterns using the structure of the Platonic solids (see fig. 2.3 on p. 48).

This dimension holds all potential creations. Everything you can feel or imagine is in its energy form here, and we can tap into all of it. What will ultimately manifest in 3D form is what has been activated most strongly, both consciously and unconsciously through our beliefs and our intent in 6D.

Like the structure of the light configurations in 6D, everything in

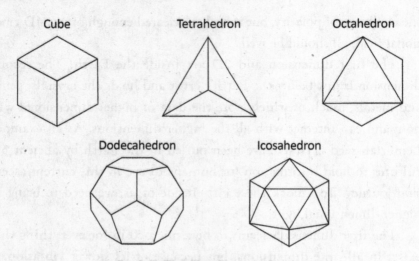

Fig 2.3. The Five Platonic Solids
Illustration by DepositPhotos.com/Iryna Anashkevich

3D, including our 3D bodies, is also formed from the Platonic solids. These are part of the light symbology or light language that connects the dimensions. Their structure is magical, as it is designed to connect humans and all other life forms in the cosmos to Divine Source.[1]

Each one of us has an energetic configuration. The Egyptians called it our ka body. It is the idealized energetic blueprint of our soul, and it resides in the sixth dimension. As we evolve, we are strengthening our connection to our ka.

When I tune into the visual appearance of my 6D soul configuration, I see a radiant multidimensional star with many points that emit more strands of light. It has a slightly bluish color. And in its center sits an energy being in a lotus position. That energetic shape is informing and holding in place my physical 3D body. If I were to toxify my 3D body, if I were to disconnect from my heart and lower my frequency, although my ideal potential would still exist in 6D, the visual experience of it would be dimmer and lose some potency. If I detoxify and reopen my heart, I can re-energize this soul configuration, bringing myself closer to my true nature. Thus, there is always interaction between the physical as it manifests in the third dimension and the amount of light emitted from my 6D form.

Your ka might look quite different from mine, but it will still be made up of recognizable shapes that are made of and emit light. You, too, are always interacting with this 6D part of yourself.

Qualities have energetic configurations in 6D too. Any quality you can think of exists there. If we take the quality of love, while I personally cannot see the form it is taking, I know it is some form of radiating light, and I can feel the quality that it emits. It feels wonderful.

If I tune into the quality of hatred, the configuration lacks any sense of harmony (again you may want to refer to Emoto's water crystals), and when I feel into it, it manifests in 3D as heavy and dark and evokes sadness in me.

Anything we can think of or imagine has its own energy configuration in 6D. The sixth dimension holds infinite space and infinite expandability. While all potentiality is already there, as we imagine something in a new way, we form new energy configurations there as well.

For example, I hold the belief that all humans are born of equal value. Because I have this belief, it exists in an equality configuration in the sixth dimension. However, how much of that shows up in 3D depends on how energized it becomes. If 40 percent of people do not believe that all humans are born of equal value, and 30 percent of people have no point of view, the remaining 30 percent can only make equality show up globally if they focus and energize it more intensely than the beliefs held by the other 70 percent of folks on the planet.

Using the example of world peace, it has its own energy configuration in 6D. However, the concept that war is inevitable also has its own energetic configuration. If enough of us feed the world-peace configuration, war will no longer manifest on our planet. If enough of us feed the war-is-inevitable belief in 6D, we will continue to experience war.

Thus we keep our world as it is or change it by which beliefs have the most energy in 6D. If we energize the concept of peace strongly enough, it manifests globally, but this does not mean that the war-is-inevitable belief disappears. Its potentiality is always there on this energy plane, but if we are not feeding it, not energizing it, it will not manifest in 3D.

You might want to ponder how the wars we have here connect to our current collective beliefs and our 6D energy configurations. Although the configuration of peace was being actively energized in the 1960s and 1970s, it was not being activated strongly enough to create peace around the globe. We did manage, however, to end the Vietnam War and perhaps avoid larger destruction. As I'm writing this now in 2024, however, a horrendous war is taking place between Israel and Gaza, with Israel brutally retaliating for brutality that ended up killing a lot of people and taking hostages. The retaliation is creating a horrible humanitarian crisis in Gaza affecting most of its citizens. Each side believes that they are victims and therefore justify these actions as important for their well-being. This is clearly a perspective stuck in 3D victim consciousness, which is why collectively shifting out of this old paradigm view is so vital.

Once war takes center stage again, fear arises in the 3D/4D dimensions, which energizes the belief there will be more wars because people have been manipulated into thinking that we must have wars to make us feel both safer and freer. This belief, in turn, de-energizes the belief that peace can prevail. As long as this fear and these beliefs remain strong, peace becomes impossible to manifest here. But the energetic configuration of peace prevailing still exists in 6D.

Once you gain an understanding of both the nature of the sixth dimension and the reciprocal relationship that it has to 3D manifestation, it becomes clear that changing our consciousness is how we can change both our lives and our world.

Your Life in Higher Frequencies

When we have activated and are living from our 5D expression, we have opened our hearts to hold unconditional love and compassion for ourselves and all others. We understand viscerally that we are interconnected with all of creation. We are each like a cell in this great tapestry of consciousness, an essential cell. Each of us, with our individual gifts, is essential for our world to be shining at its full, most loving potential. We have released judgment, patted our little egos on the head, and kept them from taking charge. We find that with our expanded bandwidth, our ability to live in the bigger picture keeps growing.

Adding our sixth-dimensional consciousness, understanding how it is both part of us and how it relates to living from our 5D expression, we are then able to step into heretofore unimagined creativity. When we understand how 6D and 3D interact, we understand more deeply how we can live in the manifested world on Earth and, together, create a new reality based on deep compassion and higher consciousness. Self-serving agendas disappear because their limitations, never mind the suffering they cause, are seen for what they are and thus not chosen.

Imagine for a moment that everything you do throughout your day is from the consciousness that you are a divine being and that you create your life from this place of divinity. When you want a change, want growth, want something to serve the forces of love more actively in the universe, all you need to do is continue to energize those visions in 6D.

If you have cleared your fourth-dimensional blocks by clearing your emotional body, disconnected your DNA from its trauma expression, and learned how to identify and continually integrate the shadow parts of your psyche, more strands of your star DNA become activated, and you then know that anything that arises for you is totally in your control.

This definition of control is different from our experience of it in 3D. When we are controlling from our 3D frequency, we are attempting to control outer circumstances and other people in ways that do not honor their divinity. These ways also don't work. We are typically motivated by fear and believe that if we don't maneuver the people and situations in our outer environment, things will only get worse.

When we are instead motivated by love—love of ourselves, our loved ones, of all humanity, of all creation—we are not looking to achieve external control over others or situations in our lives. Rather we are connected to our inner (soul) guidance and simply own our ability to energize our visions in 6D in a way that they can manifest in form. We do not seek to control others or even the outer circumstances that might surround us, but instead we are committed to serving the creation of whatever supports the highest good. We are creating through our hearts (5D) and utilizing the power of our 6D expression to manifest these creations.

Self-Responsibility and Releasing Victim Consciousness

We cannot fully utilize our abilities to create a loving, conscious personal and global reality with 6D until we are willing to own that anything that occurs and has occurred in our lives is our creation. If we undergo painful challenges, it is because we chose these as an advanced soul curriculum to help us grow, and we can see how they can prepare us more fully for the ascension process.

This is very hard for me to write when I think of abused children who have no choice or ability to consciously create their situation. Essentially, most are stuck in the abuse until they become adults. I don't believe that their soul chose for them to suffer in this way, but I do believe that there was a soul choice prior to birth to have experiences that either expanded their range of what humans are capable of (including cruelty but also compassion). Or this was ultimately a way for them to go through a familiar pattern that they may have experienced over many lifetimes so that they could heal it once and for all. Our current timeline offers many possibilities for this.

Violations of any kind create deep third-chakra wounds that affect self-worth and personal empowerment. However, these wounds, once healed, allow an individual to access great self-confidence both to stand up for themselves and carry out their sacred mission, as well as providing a deep ability to stay loving no matter what.

Because of the current evolutionary movement where we are going through a dimensional ascent, the time we are in supports this type of journey. Our ability to respond from higher frequencies is no longer severely inhibited through separation consciousness and the beliefs and traumas it has induced. There are numerous healing modalities available, with new ones and ancient ones showing up each day to provide people with the support and guidance needed to heal their energy field, neutralize enough of the old trauma, and support them to operate out of higher-frequency consciousness.

It does take time, however, to clear ourselves from all this programming. In addition to having the focus and commitment to heal, we need to go through a process that most of us can only fully absorb through the passing of linear time. I like to envision this as a journey with many steps, and one of those steps that connects to 6D is to release ourselves from any victim consciousness. This means we must notice anytime we feel like we've been put upon, victimized, or not honored in the way we deserve. It means that at any point where we feel disempowered by others, we must realize we are unconsciously avoiding taking full responsibility for whatever is showing up in our lives and realize as well that we can choose to take our power back.

Disempowerment or disempowering others is the game that has long been played out on our planet. When we feel disempowered and believe that is just the way things are, we find ourselves in a place of resourcelessness. We may opt to create a dependency on others that ultimately makes us feel more powerless. Or we may take the role of being the one others become dependent on, thereby disempowering them even more. This creates a sense of safety for us as those who have this dependency are unlikely to abandon us no matter how bad our behavior, since they believe they need us. We know now this is classic codependency. Although more and more of us are stepping away from this relationship paradigm, these patterns are so strongly conditioned in our psyches that unconscious parts of ourselves, which are not on board with the new program, will still tend to play this dependency game out, just in more subtle ways.

Any time we find ourselves blaming others for our circumstances, no matter what their level of participation has or hasn't been, we are refusing to take full responsibility for our reality, and thus not only do we disempower ourselves, but we also move further away from being an active member of the co-creation team for New Earth. Only when we can take full responsibility are we able to create the reality that we truly desire. Of course, having compassion for ourselves as the imperfect humans we are is also an essential part of this process, for it is ultimately love and self-love that create the deepest transformation.

Ponder what parts of you may still be stuck in the old paradigm of victimhood, of blaming others, or of powerlessness. Ask these parts to step into your awareness. Once in your awareness, you have the power to transform them. Know that by just calling them into awareness, unearthing them from hiding in your psyche will immediately render them less potent.

One way to identify these parts of yourself is to simply notice when you feel whiny, overwhelmed, or emotionally stuck in any way. This is a sign that the aspects of you that are clinging to the old dysfunctional paradigm are afoot. Then notice if you can identify them inside you. This makes it easier to call them forth and work with transforming them. As an example, you might find these beliefs and feelings are coming from a seven-year-old inner child or a fifteen-year-old inner teenager. Or a part you might simply label "my whiner" or "my overloaded self" or "my not-worthy, not-good-enough self." Use your imagination here. There is no need to be concerned if it is accurate; rather simply sense what feels representative of what you are experiencing.

For myself, one of the more active parts that pop up for transformation holds a belief that I don't have the energy to bring more of my work forward into the world while I'm simultaneously feeling called to do just that. Its phraseology is "I'm not up to it." I can create great excuses: I'm almost 80 (whine), I don't want to work this hard (more whining), my voice doesn't matter that much (whining again). When I call these beliefs forward, I then can look at where they come from and what I need to do to transform them. "I'm not up to it" is a derivation of: I'm not energetic enough, I'm lazy (programming from my mother's words), I'll be too old to keep this going (programming from society), or it's too hard. That activates a belief that I can't do hard things. But what makes it seem hard is all those old beliefs that then became resistances, not the actual work itself.

The trick is to both dialogue with the inaccurate beliefs and to reach deep within to commit to shifting them so we are no longer *ruled* by them. Once we do this, once we have disempowered those old beliefs and patterns enough, the universe is then able to step in to help. It will present us with everything we need, whether a guide, a mentor, a new insight, or a new opportunity. But we have to do the footwork first. We need to both identify what needs to shift and make a commitment to follow the guidance that will come to us.

These beliefs are unlikely to disappear fully, and we may have to go through this process with some frequency, but they will shift enough so they no longer hold us back from being, doing, and living the life that most authentically expresses who we are and why we are here.

So, the first step is to notice whenever old parts of us resist our movement forward. The next step is to understand with compassion why these parts developed these beliefs. Then finally, to commit to work with transforming them.

For me, this book is a good example. The idea came in a few years ago. I wrote a few pages and then got stuck. Did I really want to write another book? Was it important enough that I would be willing to do all it takes to get it out into the world? (Writing a book is typically not nearly as challenging as getting it ready for publication and promoting it.) Then after a year, without losing the awareness that this book was lurking and no doubt wanting to come out, I wrote a little more and made a commitment to write on my upcoming two-week ocean retreat. But it wasn't until I was on the retreat and committed to letting the words come through by writing daily and seeing what happened that it began to move forward. Even then the resistance came back, and once again I put the book on pause for several months until I was able to renew my commitment by shifting my view about this being hard. Instead, I could invite joyfulness and vitality to join me on this journey.

If you look at my process, you'll see that there was one more step after the commitment to just do it, and this was to be able to do this joyfully. This is the step that takes this project more fully into the frequency of 5D and into the realm of creative empowerment, which is what connecting with our 6D expression brings us.

This book, before I wrote it, already existed in the sixth dimension. Your best life and your ideal way of serving our current evolution do as well. But to make it show up in 3D, we need to choose it and keep choosing it. I needed to make a full commitment to persevere, no matter what starts and stops, confusion, and self-doubts might show up. I needed to be willing to not allow any old-paradigm beliefs about myself and the world to stop me, and so it is for you as well. This is the way we both acknowledge and commit to working through our victim beliefs.

Anything you are longing for yet feel powerless to make happen is asking you to do what you need to do to be able to fully make the choice. This means identifying what you want, then asking all old beliefs and resistances that make you feel too scared or in any way unable to attract what you are longing for to make themselves known. It then asks you to keep working to the best of your ability to transform them as part of your commitment to bringing your most fulfilling life and sacred work into your reality. If it is not showing up, you need to go through these steps at a deeper level, perhaps several times, until enough of you is committed to create what you long for.

Are You Ready to Feel This Powerful?

You believe you are ready to have exactly what you want in your personal life. You also want to live from your gifts, to serve, to contribute, to use all your wonderful talents and natural abilities, some of which you may not even be aware of yet, to shift our world. Great! We need you to have personal fulfillment and be part of the team to birth this new world. But perhaps despite your conscious desire, it's not fully coming together. You may feel discouraged or simply overloaded by your daily life. You may feel that you can't risk putting time and energy into sharing gifts that you may not fully trust you have, or that you believe won't support you financially.

Or maybe you feel scared because if you really believed you could make all you wish for a reality, it feels like (1) too much responsibility, (2) you are not worthy enough, and (3) it's scary. Fears arise such as what if you are in illusion, don't have what it takes, or do it wrong? Or what if you do it right, but somehow you and/or your loved ones are harmed because of it?

Let me say with great compassion that we have been given a tall task. To take full responsibility for creating reality is daunting enough, but committing to use our full soul potential in service to our collective task of creating a 5D world on our planet is even more so. Still let me assure you, you are up to this!

You are not alone in your challenge to release, transform, and neutralize all the old conditioning, the programming that has not only followed you since your birth in this lifetime but that has been with you for several lifetimes and has become genetically part of your cellular makeup. The easier you can go on yourself while simultaneously not giving up your commitment or intent, the more you will be able to successfully navigate this journey no matter how long it might take in linear 3D time.

It is a rare individual indeed who is truly ready to step into their full power without going through a relatively long process of self-discovery, healing, and self-empowerment. To own our true inner power goes against everything we have been taught for eons.

Because of sex-role conditioning, connecting with our inner power tends to be different for men than women. Most males have been conditioned to believe they should be able to master the outer world and have defined this as being powerful. They are also taught to cover any self-doubt with bravado. However, men with this conditioning struggle to access their internal world. So many may be able to look and sound successful in creating an external life they think they should have, and they may even be able to share their abilities in a way that brings them recognition. But if they have not done their inner work, if they have not overcome this conditioning so they can connect with the sacred feminine within, then it's like building castles in the sand. There is no authentic foundation, and therefore it will not be genuinely sustainable.

For most females, self-doubt is more on the surface, more conscious, and more easily admitted. Because women have been given increased access to their inner lives, self-doubt is more obvious to them. Therefore, much linear time is spent questioning if they are up to the task of creating their reality and questioning if their gifts are real, and if so, if they can handle this much power. Women are generally more willing to work with all of this with the intent to transform their doubts and blocks and fears that hold them back, but generally they have less inner permission than their male counterparts to powerfully manifest what they are seeking to accomplish in the outer world.

With the younger generation, this sex-role conditioning has not only lessened, but gender fluidity has risen, so things may play out quite a bit differently for them. And collectively, this might be our saving grace. But all generations have their demons to fight, so my guess is they will still have to go through a challenging process to step into their full co-creative power, although it might present differently than for older generations, and hopefully transform more quickly.

At any rate, what I've observed holds people back from fully stepping into this power—besides the difficulty of mustering the courage and grit to go against conventional wisdom—are old fears, guilt, and a lack of self-love. In some ways, self-love is at the very root of all the challenges on this journey because if we lack it to any extent, we will believe we don't deserve all that good and therefore unconsciously keep it from happening. Remember, genuine self-love is not narcissistic. It is not about believing yourself to be better than others or constantly seeking love from the outside. It is understanding that loving ourselves unconditionally is about being able to both honor our gifts and lovingly accept our flaws. It means knowing we deserve this love for simply being part of creation, for simply being who we are, gifts, flaws, and all.

Being willing to accept our full power, to truly step into who we are meant to be is another step-by-step process. It is similar to the process of becoming healthy enough to take full responsibility for our reality. The first step in owning our power is to bring our fears and resistances into our conscious awareness and then make the commitment to do whatever it takes to transform what is still standing in our way, lovingly supporting ourselves while we do this.

It is not unusual for part of people's resistance to be guilt from past-life experiences. This is what contributes to the belief that if I am in full power, I might cause harm. Many folks that I work with have had experiences of being leaders or in influential positions in other lifetimes and things not working out. Often when we take a deeper look at what was really going on, it turns out that there were outer circumstances as well as other souls who contributed to the destructive things that occurred, so it was not necessarily a flaw in their leadership that created the problems. Knowing this often helps ease things in some ways. Conversely, if it turns out that it was a personal flaw, a wrong turn, a bad decision, then this in a sense is somewhat easier to deal with than the idea that we had agreed on a collective level for things to go wrong. If it was an individual misstep, taking responsibility, making amends through imaginative visualization, and then forgiving oneself neutralizes the karma and frees the person to move forward fairly easily.

There are more difficult situations, however. What comes to mind as an example are Indigenous people around the globe who were vibrating at a higher frequency than the Europeans who came and devastated their tribes and their land and replaced their spiritual awareness and unity consciousness with cruelty and suffering. This, of course, threw the natural balance of things into chaos and caused huge collective trauma. If it's something this big, and you were one of the tribal leaders who had to surrender to this unstoppable brutality, and you knew that everything that occurred had a soul agreement that you had participated in, then this involves a much more complex process to move forward with authentic self-forgiveness.

Imagine you are the tribal leader. You love your people. You are honored to be in this position. You are spirit driven rather than ego driven. You live in integrity. And yet you are not able to protect your tribe. You are not able to stop the onslaught and the brutality. And because of your highly evolved nature, you understand on some level that you had agreed to this and that you could not shift things once they were in motion. You keep reincarnating, partly to work through this guilt. If this is the case, it also suggests that you are taking more responsibility than is yours—everyone involved agreed to this whether they realized the horror it would bring or not.

At any rate, whatever your soul's backstory is, whatever the narrative around those old wounds is, the guilt needs to be healed, and self-forgiveness and other forgiveness need to happen before you are ready to accept how powerful you truly are. This is what will lead you to authentic unconditional self-love. If you have activated a high level of self-knowledge, you can count on it to help you trust that you will now use your power wisely and be able to assess more accurately what is yours to own and what is not.

It is useful to make a list of all your beliefs, fears, and resistances to taking full responsibility for both the individual and collective reality you are living in, and the beliefs, fears, and resistances to acknowledging that you are an amazingly powerful creator and can now trust yourself to create for the highest good. The "Journal Questions to Ponder" at the end of the chapter will help.

Our Ever-Expanding Bandwidth

The more we operate at higher frequencies, the more light goes to our cells to activate our cosmic DNA, and thus the more we can see and live in the big and ever-expanding picture. We have stepped far outside the narrow perceptual field our culture has conditioned us to experience and now find that we are tuned into a reality that most people still believe does not exist.

This can be an amazing gift, and it can also be quite scary and confusing. Walking into a room and knowing immediately what people around you are feeling and thinking can make you want to hide in a closet for the rest of your life. Seeing, hearing, or sensing presences that are not solid enough to manifest in the 3D world opens us up to great wisdom and consciousness, but also it can push us to the brink of sanity.

I cannot stress strongly enough that to keep our sense of equilibrium on this evolutionary journey means to consistently look within to notice what arises, to notice our ego fears and agendas, and to notice any emotional triggers. It also means we need to activate enough genuine self-love so we can still feel okay when we notice our nasty, negative thoughts without letting them have any sort of power. It asks us as well to continue to heal our old wounds enough so they are no longer operative in what we manifest in our lives and to ground ourselves in the Earth, in the energies of the natural world around us and beneath us. This is the foundational work that enables us to reach higher-dimensional consciousness without losing our balance.

As the way-showers, we don't have many models to teach us how to do this. We are the pioneers, and we are the ones developing these models for the generations to come. This, in and of itself, is a huge responsibility, especially because we are in our imperfect human form, which means we are going to stumble, perhaps screw up, and question our abilities.

We are also likely to feel frustrated about our inability to be perfect, which brings up very unhelpful judgments. The stronger our commitment to know ourselves and know our hearts without allowing judgments to interfere with our inner honesty, the more we can trust ourselves in this task. And the more effective we will be.

Since one of the central qualities of 5D is to be unconditionally loving, we need to understand what this really means. Fifth-dimensional unconditional love is soul love. The best definition I have found for this is from a book by the same name by Sanaya Roman.

Roman writes:

> Your soul offers love that does not add its own coloring to the energies about. Its love flows out transparently without being changed by the energies it touches.... Soul love is accepting. It accepts the universe as it is; it allows things to be the way they are.... It accepts the good and the bad, the high and the low. Your soul loves others regardless... as they are, no matter what their beliefs, opinions, or outlook on life.[2]

It goes on to explain this does not mean we will choose to interact with people just because we can love them with our soul. It is still important that we choose what is best for us in terms of any 3D physical connection.

Equally important as loving others, of course, is to love ourselves with soul love. Our soul's love accepts every aspect of our being.[3] Sit with this for a moment. Our soul accepts every aspect of ourselves and just simply loves us.

Are you willing to give this kind of love to yourself? You might want to go inward and really feel what it's like to fill every part of yourself with this deeply loving energy. Think of all the things you appreciate about yourself. Bathe them in this love and surround yourself with it. Now call forth everything you criticize or have shame about, including all the nasty thoughts and motivations that you might try to avoid noticing in yourself. Bathe all of these parts in this love as well. Breathe deeply. Feel this love surround you even more strongly. A new and deeper sense of well-being can now emerge. This is 5D unconditional love.

Soul love comes from the purity of our hearts. As we expand our bandwidth and expand our frequency range, we can access this more often and more easily. But that doesn't erase the fact that we are still human. We are imperfect no matter how evolved we are becoming. Perfection here is not the goal; rather the goal is to notice when we are pure of heart and to celebrate this. It is also to notice when we are not being pure of heart and to know we are still a loveable and worthy being, and then to do our very best to reconnect with our heart's purity. This becomes an oft repeated process as different situations arise in our life.

The way to do this most authentically and effectively is to develop and allow a clear-seeing witness to walk through our lives with us. This is our observer or researcher who can look at all our thoughts, feelings, actions, and interactions objectively without judgment. It is also the part who will kindly and respectfully point out to us when we are operating from a lower, less-loving frequency, whether out of old wounds, uncleared or triggered emotions, or old fears. Our witness self will show us how to recognize when this is happening, to love ourselves anyway, and then to offer us ideas about how to shift into a more loving space. (For those of you who would like more information about how to develop this, I refer you to my book *Empowering the Spirit: A Process to Activate Your Full Soul Potential*.)

The more I develop, the more aware I become of having thoughts that appall me. Thoughts of wishing others ill if my ego believes a particular area of their lives is going better than mine, for example. I call these thoughts *dark shadow* because they go against everything that my heart and soul really want and believe. I would love to pretend they don't exist, but that would put me out of integrity. They are there. I do my very best to notice them immediately, and although I do reflexively cringe when I observe them, I also know that observing and owning their existence is hugely important to keep them from having any power. And I do my best to give myself credit for having the courage to notice them and not try to sugarcoat them or make excuses. This helps me continue to love myself, nasty thoughts and all.

When we go through this type of process, we reflexively see ourselves from a very expanded bandwidth. And viewing ourselves from an expanded bandwidth makes it much easier to authentically view others in the same way.

Dark shadow is also part of our collective journey. If we try to collectively pretend we don't have *dark shadow* thoughts, beliefs, or motivations, we project this shadow onto others and can do great harm. There's rather a tricky choreography with this. To see and feel reality from this higher-dimensional expansive bandwidth without going into spiritual bypass, without going into denial, is not a simple two-step process. It is all so tempting to avoid 3D, and the murkiness of 4D as much as possible, and to just focus on our higher-dimensional awareness. But this is avoiding our ego games. I can feel love for myself and others more easily if I can avoid getting into the nitty gritty of wounds, emotions, and limiting negative thoughts and beliefs. But it won't be genuine. It will be conditional love, not soul love.

As we expand our bandwidth, our egos, which still walk through life with us, would like us to believe that if we stay in the big, big picture, all our human issues will be resolved because we can see there is a larger purpose to everything we experience. And we can convince ourselves from this vantage point that everything is dandy. But everything is not dandy just because we can observe it from a higher and expanded consciousness. We are still in our physical and emotional bodies. Bypassing our feelings and human needs is ultimately never successful because it only deals with part of ourselves.

A spiritually evolved parent whose child is diagnosed with cancer might expand enough to understand the spiritual lessons chosen with this experience. But if that parent does not allow themselves to feel the anger, the grief, and the fear in all its intensity, then they have stepped into illusion.

Without question, expanding our bandwidth is part of our current quest, but not at the expense of ignoring our feelings and old dysfunctional beliefs. In our current evolutionary ascension process, we are asked to be of both worlds while we still walk in our 3D reality. We need to identify and honor our emotions and our shadow before we can truly accept whatever challenge we participated in creating.

Our star nature, the part of us that already lives in expanded realities, is not always aware of how humans are affected by challenging experiences because this is so different from what is experienced in evolved star civilizations. To me this suggests we, in human form, are even more courageous pioneers because we are opening ourselves to their wisdom while simultaneously having to figure out how to maneuver with human bodies, psyches, and cellular programming. Our mission is unique. Just because we are up to it doesn't mean it's a walk in the park.

Why 6D Is So Important

Our 5D selves easily connect to soul love, nonjudgment, and Oneness. They give us access to unbridled creativity. But 5D itself is not the dimension we use to manifest in 3D. The fifth dimension provides us with access to creative visions, but the ability to step into our divinity to manifest these visions comes to us through our interactions with 6D.

If we use the image of Russian nesting dolls to personify our different dimensional parts, we can see that in our current biological bodies we either operate at the lower-frequency level of 3D/4D, where both of those nesting dolls are prominent in our lives, or from our 5D/6D potential, thus living from the expanded dimensionality of our 5D/6D nesting dolls. In this transitional period, we often vacillate back and forth between these pairs. Again, you just might want to observe.

Collectively we are becoming more and more familiar with 5D. Numerous spiritual teachers are spreading the word or writing books so that this awareness is no longer that unusual. The sixth dimension, on the other hand, has not yet been given the focus it needs for us to begin to create our lives more effectively and thus to step more fully into a new paradigm of life on planet Earth.

The sixth dimension is quite a magical place. In his book *The End of Time*, physicist Julian Barbour backs its existence up mathematically, and

Barbara Hand Clow in *Alchemy of Nine Dimensions* makes a scientific understanding of this more accessible. Remember it is this dimension that holds anything and everything we can begin to imagine. The form of all ideas is held in geometric configurations of light. As we energize an idea, it begins to grow in its ability to manifest in 3D. So, as I've said before, everything we might want to see on our planet already exists. But for it to show up as part of our collective reality, enough of us need to choose it.

Let's look at the concept of war again. Can we actually get rid of war? Are we ready to end it entirely? Think about this: Wars have been claimed to be things that protect our freedoms. Wars have been claimed to always end on the side of righteousness. As an example, of course I'm glad that Hitler was stopped, which happened through war. Remember, though: he was just a manifestation of our collective, unprocessed, and disowned shadow. As we evolve, we should never have to utilize war for anything. Violence begets violence. This is simply a universal law. And how tragic it is that young men and women who are participating in wars are risking their lives and mental health mostly to protect those who have control and economic power on our planet.

But until we understand our attachment to war—in other words, our belief that it serves a positive purpose—we are not going to be able to bring peace in. The basis of this belief is that there will be bad people who will do bad things and who can only be stopped by responding with violence. The current Israeli response to Hamas, or at least the narrative that the collective is being fed, is a clear example of this.

As I'm writing this, the war between Russia and Ukraine still rages as well. What deep sadness I feel for both the Ukrainian people and the Russian people. This war is senseless, harmful, and appalling. There doesn't even seem to be a narrative where anyone's well-being was at stake in the first place (rather like the war in Iraq). And the suffering that is coming from it for both Ukrainians and Russians, along with the environmental damage and horrible use of our resources, is truly heartbreaking. And that does not even begin to address the PTSD of all the civilians affected as well as all those who are in their respective militaries.

When all governments realize that we are truly interconnected, that what is good for them must be good for all or it will do no good, we can stop the insanity of war. This means, however, that we must extract ourselves from the power of special interest groups who might reap monetary profits and power, or who might seek to keep us all in chaos so we won't notice what is really going on. It also means that people must insist their governments support the well-being of all. Just because this is not the current situation on the planet, does not mean we won't be able to evolve enough to create this in our future.

Whatever thoughts and beliefs get the most hits, so to speak, or the most social media likes, are what will get energized in 6D and therefore are what will manifest in 3D. Thus we stop war when enough of us believe and energize the 6D ideal of peace prevailing. Then we can evolve our planet into a peaceful place where all are honored. This means we step fully out of victim consciousness and out of all disempowerment beliefs that say this is impossible. Current governments will spin facts or create false facts, hoping to keep us mystified, but if we refuse energetically to buy their stories, we begin to shift what manifests here. Even overtly oppressive societies, like Iran, are not going to be able to keep a self-empowered populace down. This is why it is so important to do our personal work to step into self-empowerment.

We know that thoughts are energy. The magic of 6D is that if enough of us energize specific thoughts, that's what we'll get. We began to energize the peace configuration more strongly in the 1960s and '70s. The Vietnam War created a huge backlash among the young who were getting drafted, which meant they were putting their lives on the line and were being ordered to kill others, because this is what war demands. My generation refused to buy into the idea that we had to fight to keep the world from being overrun by tyranny. The domino theory that was used as a justification for the United States to fight the war in Vietnam was ultimately debunked,[4] and those who were being called up against their will knew we had no valid justification to be there. Those young men refused to pretend otherwise and publicly showed their outrage, garnering the support of a whole generation of young people as well as many older people. This was a strong beginning, but clearly we need to put much more energy into the 6D configuration of global peace before it will manifest. When we understand 6D and how to work with it, and when enough humans on the planet commit to positive evolution, this is how the transformation will occur.

The Power of Surrender

In our current ascension process we are being asked to have a new relationship with our egos as they accompany us on this journey. Our egos can help us stay aware of our legitimate survival needs, show us where boundaries are needed, and even help ground us. But they are not to be in charge. If we allow our ego to run the show, we will end up stuck in lower frequencies and old survival beliefs. Instead, we need to keep our spirit in the driver's seat, witnessing our ego's beliefs, desires, and needs and, through practice, disconnect from its agenda while assessing any practical information that might be useful. Ultimately this will help us find the balance of living from our higher-frequency expression while in a 3D world without compromising the wisdom of our soul.

To live from the consciousness of our 5D/6D frequency means that we are guided by our heart, which is filled with higher photonic consciousness, light that holds higher intelligence. This is a feminine path, a yin path, where we create the needed shifts in both our personal lives and through our collective visions by allowing change to happen organically rather than through the masculine or yang path of actively pursuing these shifts. This does not mean we are not utilizing the energies of both our inner male and female. Certainly, there are times when action and focus are needed, but unlike our experience in the paradigm now passing away, this is not the central modus operandi because we are not seeking to make something happen. Rather we choose it and allow it to happen at the same time. We use the male part of our psyche to support the wisdom of our sacred inner feminine to give it structure.

It is the sacred feminine, though, who knows the power of surrendering to higher consciousness and guidance and who understands how to allow manifestation while simultaneously energizing the vision of how we want things to be. Again, this happens when the heart is leading; this is the feminine way.

The universe is already carrying the information and processes needed to bring our personal and collective visions into 3D form. It's all there in the sixth dimension. Our job is to align our energies in such a way to allow this to happen.

Surrender is an energetic state. It is a state of full relaxation and trust. And it is typically a hard place to allow ourselves to be because of all the old programming that tells us we need to stay on guard, and we need to push through to make things happen rather than understanding that we can hold a strong vision and allow the Divine within us to step in to energize the vision.

Surrender is a place of faith where fear doesn't enter. It is floating along the waters of life knowing that with focused intent, the river will work with you to direct the flow so you come to the exact place of your visions. There's no stress, no pushing. Just a deep sense of trust that the synchronicities, the inspiration, and the people (your global 5D/6D teammates) will show up exactly when and as needed.

Quantum physics has a similar process when it talks about the need to go into neutral to manifest desired shifts. It explains this by saying that every thought creates *carrier waves* and that physical reality can be created from these, but energetically we need to be in a state of loving neutrality to shift out of the old experience and into the new.

The sixth dimension, or the quantum field if you prefer, holds infinite-possibility carrier waves. Morphic fields form when enough possibility waves create highly energized particles. From there the waves can become powerful enough to show up on the planet in 3D material form.

The additional piece needed is for us to create an inner energetic coherence. This means that if I want to create something, I need to be enough on board internally to draw it to me. If I have ambivalence and thus am putting out mixed messages into the quantum field, even if the waves are powerful enough, they won't know where to go. It's as if I'm pushing them away at the same time that I'm trying to magnetize them.

To successfully co-create anything in our lives we need to have both this inner coherence and simultaneously speed up our vibrational field and thus raise our frequency to connect with these carrier waves. Then we need to trust that whatever shows up is for our highest good right now. Thus, this coherence comes in three ways: The first is when we are sending out the message of what we want and doing so from a high enough vibration to match the frequency of what we are seeking to manifest. The second is that we have brought enough of our opposing beliefs and desires into consciousness and have transformed our resistances enough that they no longer interfere., And the third is that we are in a state of neutrality and surrender, thus having quieted our ego and remained nonattached to the outcome.

As I've been writing this, I was offering an online course that I'd offered several times before. Only this time, I hardly had anyone sign up and felt I might have to cancel the class. The irony that I was simultaneously writing about how we create our reality didn't escape me, and this motivated me to write the journal questions that are at the end of this chapter.

I dutifully journaled on the questions, gaining clarity into some of my resistances, and when I finished, I felt that I was about to break through—only simultaneously, my left shoulder and part of my left arm began to ache. Our left side reflects what is going on in the right hemisphere of the brain and is associated with our feminine side. I realized that my feminine was not keen on teaching this course right now, even though I love this course and the interactions with my students. But I also wanted to keep a sense of spaciousness in my life because I was writing this book, and simultaneously I was enjoying down time in the afternoons to read a novel, to lie out on my porch (it was summer), and basically just to mosey through my life without that commitment.

So yes, I could and had somewhat energized the carrier waves to bring in more students, and simultaneously I was metaphorically putting my hand up to block them. Every time I thought about doing more to promote the course, I got an inner sense that I didn't want to do this. This had been unconscious before I did the journal questions, and then felt my body react. The journal questions did what I had intended: they brought up old patterns and beliefs to be yet again disempowered. But paying attention to my body presented another awareness. It was not only these old patterns and beliefs that were standing in my way, although that may have been part of it, and it was important for me to become aware of them. The stronger blockage was from the part of me that didn't want to teach a class right then but felt that I should. My point is that sometimes we don't manifest what we think we want because unconsciously we don't want it.

Breathe into this idea that you can choose any possibility you desire. Do you notice any resistance arising? Just notice and give yourself credit for noticing. Breathe again deeply into your heart chakra area, feeling your chest relax and expand, and pay attention to how that feels.

Are you needing more money right now in your life? In a state of deep relaxation, imagine an activated magnetic force field around you that draws in all the resources you need. It may be through a job offer. It may be through a raise. It may be through a path you never consciously considered. If you allow yourself to magnetize whatever is needed while in this expanded state daily, within a short period of time you will receive the guidance needed for this to show up in 3D. If it is not showing up, you are being asked to find the parts of yourself that don't feel you are worthy enough, or perhaps even hold a belief that money will corrupt you. Or maybe you have what you need and don't need more. There are endless possibilities of beliefs and patterns that create resistance. Some are universal, and some may have a unique flavor. Allow yourself to use your imagination as you seek to identify what these beliefs, patterns, or fears might be.

Calming our egos is an ongoing learning experience. The challenge to allow, surrender, and stay out of stress and panic goes against the nature of the ego. With practice, though, we become astute at noticing when our ego is jumping into the driver's seat. If we can notice from a place of loving neutrality, which is also an ongoing practice, this helps immediately. If we can go into prayer or meditation in this place of loving neutrality, we become open; we create space for the new energy to enter. Then we need to notice if we can hold this openness when the meditation or prayer is finished. Go easy on yourself. This is asking you to live in a whole different world from the one you were born into.

6D Redux

The place that British physicist Julian Barbour calls Platonia perfectly mirrors what we know about 6D. He is consciously making the parallel to Plato's world of forms. But as I said above, he goes even further since he's a physicist and backs this up mathematically.[5]

He says Platonia holds all the geometric configurations that hold the forms of everything that manifests on our planet. He also says that Platonia is permeated with mists that are created from all the ideas we hold in the now, and there are mists for every possible thought.[6]

From what I can gather, these mists correspond to morphogenetic fields. Think about this: If I think loving thoughts right now, they travel into 6D and feed and thicken the love mist. If I think angry thoughts right now, this feeds and thickens the anger mist. If enough of us think the same things at the same time (and of course, cultural beliefs help this happen), these mists become remarkably thick and therefore powerful, and then they keep replicating themselves on our planet.

Then come the shadow thoughts. I want to feed the love mist, but here comes a judgment, and then another, then another. If I tell them to go away, they will just go underground into my unconscious where they will grow more powerful. If I get stuck in them and start feeling righteous, they will also empower that unloving righteousness mist. But if I just notice them and pat them on their heads, seeing them as the pesky little judgment thoughts that they are, although they will still connect to 6D mists, they will lose their power and begin to dissolve. The result is that they will manifest less and less frequently on Earth.

Shadow feelings, like unprocessed old anger, need attention as well. If we deny the anger exists, it feeds the anger mist more powerfully than if we bring the angry feelings into our conscious awareness and allow ourselves to feel them. We can then process the anger, identify it, express it in a nonharmful way, and ultimately release it. At that point, we will no longer feed this mist. Instead, we can more effectively feed the mists that hold the vision of living a loving life and ultimately creating a loving planet.

When we view how the collective is impacted by thick mists in 6D (or Platonia if you prefer), we can see how some old, harmful beliefs are shifting. Eighty years ago, there was a strong cultural belief that women were inferior to men in intelligence and worldly competence. That belief created quite a thick mist. But by the '60s, more and more of us knew and therefore believed that intelligence and competence had nothing to do with gender. Think about what this does to the mists. The mist that formed from the idea that women were inferior became thinner, and the gender equality mist thickened. Even in hugely repressive societies, where they do their best to enforce laws that would deny women's equality, I'd venture to say that many people no longer believe that the justification behind the laws is true, so this helps thin the mists in 6D that hold the old belief.

We will look more deeply at both individual and collective change as we go further in this book.

Remember, too, that 6D is made up of infinite variations of the five Platonic solids, and those variations represent anything we can imagine. Hand Clow's explanation of how they then manifest in 3D may help you better understand the process of how 6D geometric configurations show up here. She says:

> Another way to visualize 6D is by playing with five quartz carvings of the Platonic solids. . . . Attempting to see these forms in your inner mind will help you visualize 6D. . . . Imagine the entire 3D universe constructed of these configurations. . . . Next, imagine them vibrating with frequencies while replicating things in 3D. . . .
>
> In the nine-dimensional model, the vibrating forms from 6D replicate as lifeforms of every possible variety in 3D, and also as nonliving things. The nautilus shell always grows by the Fibonacci spiral as does the sunflower, as well as many other proportions in plants and animal skeletons. The Golden Mean (phi ratio) of 1:1.618 determines the Fibonacci spiral, and the spiral is the basis of all materialization. At a subatomic level, spin generates primal movement which in turn becomes spiralic in matter. These two factors of spirals regulate how 6D geometric forms replicate in the material realm.[7]

So everything that was originally designed to show up in 3D, like the nautilus shell, started from its configuration in 6D. When we energize new thought forms in 3D to get them vibrating at a certain frequency and intensity, we activate the needed energetic spin for new variations of objects, thoughts, qualities, and beliefs to manifest in 3D. From my understanding, objects can manifest this way without first forming into mists, but qualities and ideas coalesce into these mists before showing up here. All very magical indeed.

✳ MEDITATION ✳

Rogue Cell Dialogue:
Meeting and Transforming Rogue Beliefs and Fears

Allow your eyes to soften and put all your attention on taking deep centering breaths. As you exhale, release any distractions, any concerns, any tensions. Just let this all flow out with the breath. On the inhale imagine that you are drawing in tiny golden spirals of light filled with love and consciousness and allow those tiny spirals to spread to every cell in your body. Keep focusing on your breath as you begin to feel a sense of calm and relaxation throughout your body.

Now I'd like you to imagine you are standing at the top of a beautiful mountain. It's a magnificent morning. The sky is a vibrant blue. The bright sun warms your hair and skin. The birds are singing and calling to one another. The air smells fresh and clean. As you look out over the vista before you, you take a moment and ponder your life. Ponder what works well for you and what change you long for that has not yet manifested.

As you are standing there you see there is a horizontal beam of pure light coming toward you. You watch as it gets closer and closer until it is almost in front of you, and that's when you notice that it carries an ethereal being. As this being gets closer it communicates to you that it is one of your star ancestors here to help you connect more effectively with your 6D co-creative power.

Greet your ancestor and listen while they greet you in return. This being reaches out to touch your third eye and your heart, filling you with radiating light. You notice that your heart now feels overflowing with love, love for this ancestor, love for yourself, love for all creation. Let yourself bask in these feelings for a moment.

Then your star ancestor leads you to a path that begins to go down the mountain. The sun feels even warmer. You hear the crackling of twigs under your footsteps as you follow along. Soon you come to another clearing. You see a large cave, and your ancestor leads you into it. It takes a moment for your eyes to adjust; as they do you see a ledge by one of the cave walls and you go to sit on it, absorbing the coolness of the cave.

Your star ancestor asks you to focus on what you are trying to change, what you want to manifest differently in your life. As you do this, a container appears before you. Your ancestor lets you know this container is holding some of the beliefs or fears you carry that are still getting in your way.

Take a moment and examine it. Notice its size, its material, its color. Notice how it feels when you look at it. Next your ancestor, with your permission, opens the container and out come some small entities that carry strong limiting beliefs or fears that have made it hard for you to create the changes in your life that you are longing for. Your ancestor directs you to greet these entities and lines them up in front of you. Notice how this feels.

One by one, you ask each what they represent and listen while they share the fear or belief that is standing in your way. You might want to jot it down in your journal before proceeding, and then soften your eyes and focus on your breath once again.

Spend some time dialoguing with them. Notice how the beliefs or fears they represent may still be running parts of your life. Ask them why they are still with you and what they are trying to do for you. Let them know that now you are ready to take charge and tell them what they need to change in order to get on board with you taking on the self-love and personal power to manifest what you seek. Ask too, that they no longer interfere with you feeling the comfort and confidence to use your gifts to help the upcoming planetary shift. Then, beaming them with energy from your hand, shrink them each down. As they become smaller and smaller, beam them with love and let them know that they no longer have your permission to interfere in your life. Watch what happens and notice how you feel. Then send them on their way to play together, perhaps in the cave.

You can feel that your star ancestor is pleased with your newfound power, and you notice that you are feeling both stronger and lighter.

It's time to leave the cave for now and return to the mountaintop. Your ancestor comes with you, and when you reach the place you started from, this star being gives you a hug and you feel that some of their loving, powerful energy has been transmitted to you. They let you know the cave is always there, where you can find any other beliefs or fears that are in your way and that you can always call them back to accompany you there. Slowly you leave them and bring yourself back to your room, pondering what you have just experienced. You wiggle your fingers and toes to get back into your body, noticing any sounds around you. And finally when you are ready, go ahead and open your eyes. You might want to journal on what you have just experienced. The messages you received will support your journey as you continue with this book.

Note: Find this meditation on my YouTube channel, Wisdom Within Us, in the "Meditations to Raise Your Frequency" playlist.

Journal Question to Ponder

1. What emotional wounds or traumas are still affecting you in your life?
2. In what areas of your life, if any, do you feel disempowered? What beliefs are you carrying that help to create this?
3. Where do you still feel victimized in your life?
4. Is there anything you are holding yourself back from doing, despite your soul's urging, out of a belief that you are not up to it or that it will be too hard?
5. What can you do to help yourself transform these beliefs?
6. What fears or beliefs do you have about stepping into full power?
7. Are you willing to recognize your leadership abilities? What would be different in your life if you stepped fully into this leadership? Do you have any awareness of other lifetimes that may make this more difficult for you? If so, journal on what happened. Then contemplate if you can forgive all the players involved including yourself.
8. What do you notice about your ability to love yourself unconditionally? You might want to conjure up something you believe to be your worst quality. Imagine yourself acting this out and bathe yourself in love. Write about if you were able to do this and if so, how it felt.

3

The Creation of Our Personal Reality

As creators, we have conjured up amazing experiences for ourselves during each of our lifetimes; some of them wonderful and some quite awful. Much of what we have created for the last several millenniums has come from our unconscious, and our unconscious has generally been packed with traumatic events that have lived unprocessed in our emotional bodies. We have disconnected from our creative power, from our divinity and typically have found ourselves in situations where we believed we were simply the victim of circumstances.

From this narrow bandwidth we've had no understanding of what our soul is seeking to learn or how to shift out of the suffering we have found ourselves in. And although on occasion we may have managed "a reward lifetime" while reincarnating, we were unaware of how we created it in the first place.

This is all changing now. We are lighting up more of our star DNA, our cosmic DNA, and exponentially increasing our ability to live in ever-expanding awareness. We are unearthing the wounds, traumas, and beliefs that kept us from knowing who we really are. We are learning how to heal and disempower those wounds, triggers, and limiting beliefs and now are ready to own that we are creators and, therefore, to take conscious responsibility for our creations.

Take a moment and ponder your life. How does it look to you? How does it feel? Are you happy, satisfied, peaceful? Are you unfulfilled, stressed, anxious? Do you have enough resources that your bills are paid and you have the freedom to live a lifestyle that works for you, or are you often in financial struggle? Is your energy vibrant or drained or both?

What about your relationships? Do you have the love and support in your life you've been seeking? Do you feel isolated, lonely, or misunderstood? When you are with loved ones and friends, do you feel inspired, openhearted, joyful, or are there relationships that energetically drag you down? When things are not working well in relationships, are you able to own your part and still be loving toward yourself? Do you tend to own more than what is your part or, conversely, tend to deny that you played any role in a dynamic that has turned sour?

Do you have a sense of purpose in your life? A sense of why your soul might have chosen to incarnate at this point in linear time to be part of this major shift of consciousness, this collective ascension journey? Do you find that your work and day-to-day activities feel meaningful, satisfying, and fulfilling? Or do you more often feel you are just trying to survive, to get by?

What about your health? Are you in good health or suffering from chronic pain or other types of disease? Do you take good care of your body, appreciating what it can do for you and giving it the nourishment and rest it needs? Or do you tend to ignore what is needed for it to operate at its highest potential?

Whatever your answers to these questions, there are no right or wrong creations. When we're living in the big picture, understanding our multidimensional nature, we know that all of what is going on with us in 3D is simply an experience. All experiences can support our growth and deepen our compassion for ourselves and all others. Conversely, all experiences can be used to inhibit our growth and close ourselves off from our inner divinity. The more we can operate from a higher frequency, the more we are able to consciously choose the experiences that are most helpful to our growth and soul resonance.

To fully take charge of our experiences, it is important to remember that our conscious motivation might be quite different from our unconscious motivation, and each of the categories above can contain multiple layers of intent and motives that may well be contradictory. When we understand how this works, we have more tools to stay in charge of the personal reality we are living in.

As an example, I found I would often run into computer glitches when I would advertise online classes and workshops, making it hard for students to register. The glitches stopped around the time I received a book contract for my last book in 2019. I felt I had broken through and finally cleared old fears and beliefs from my field and that now I would stop creating this kind of limitation.

That was naïve of me. As a psychotherapist, I know better. We don't grow and transform linearly. Recently, I was yet again consciously working with these old beliefs because I found myself ambivalent about writing this book. Once I recommitted, I again thought I was finished with these patterns. Then I ran into a computer glitch on a registration form for another upcoming course. The message was clear: there was more work to be done. I had worked with old beliefs and fears but now realized how my ambivalence about the book hadn't gotten to the deepest issue, which was old other lifetime fears of being too public. Unconsciously, I created this registration issue to get my attention!

I had a choice of ignoring the issue that might have caused the computer glitch (it was minor). I could have just seen this as me being a victim of cyber issues. If I had, the universe, reflecting the part of me committed to growing through my issues, would no doubt have given me a more obvious message. Ultimately, I'm the one creating this limitation, these glitches, and because I'm committed to growth and transformation, I will attract things that let me know there's more work to be done. Once I own that I'm constructing a reality different from what I consciously desire, I can work with it and create something else.

Here's the important part though. We are humans! Just because I know something is true does not mean that I can immediately transform things. We are all in process. The key is to realize that I am a creator here. Creating limitations does not mean I'm bad, unworthy, or in some way less than, or defective. It simply means that I have chosen a harder curriculum. And, although my conscious intent is both to grow through this quickly and unearth and transform anything else in my unconscious with opposing intent, this does not mean I will succeed right away. There may be more rogue beliefs and fears to unearth.

If you have created things in your life that are not what you are truly seeking, go easy on yourself! Simultaneously make a commitment to work with the old patterns and beliefs that interfere with you creating what you consciously desire.

Here's how 6D plays into this. The part of me that intends to get my work to a larger and larger audience, to step into a larger public role already exists in the quantum field. The part of me that still is holding on to old fears that this is dangerous also has an energetic creation in the sixth dimension. Whichever configuration that I energize most is the one that will show up most in 3D. Unconscious intent typically holds more power simply because it is unconscious. Currently, I've been unconsciously energizing the more limited choice. Now that I've become aware that once again I had a hidden motivation to limit myself to feel safer, I can work on de-energizing this configuration, and instead energize the one my soul truly desires. If I find more obstacles as I go along, it just means the curriculum I've chosen is more demanding than I realized and will take more time for me to master.

When I went within to work with the part of me that is still holding onto the terror and trauma from being public and getting targeted in other lifetimes, I could feel the intensity of the fear. To calm this part down, I had to call upon my guides and higher-dimensional parts of myself for comfort and reassurance that I was safe. This helped a lot but did not totally calm the fear until I thought about the idea that since all timelines occur simultaneously, what I needed to do was pull the traumatized part of myself out of the dangerous timeline and into a different timeline where I was safe. Miraculously, that worked. The fear disappeared, although sadness and anger arose, so the healing is not complete. But clearly I had made progress.

When we seek to uncover hidden motivations for anything we are trying to manifest, it is important to remember that several contradictory beliefs, desires, and intents can be a part of this. So not only was I unconsciously blocking what I wanted because of my old fears, I was also creating this block to learn things that I could share with others to help them break through as well. Thus, a self-defeating hidden motivation ("I'll do anything to be safe including undermining my ability to fully carry out my soul mission") was living simultaneously with my hidden motivation to work on transforming it. This provided me with more tools to share with others and ultimately allowed me to be more helpful.

Know then that whenever you find yourself unable to manifest what you consciously wish for, there are likely to be many levels of internal motivation, both conscious and unconscious, that hold your contradictory intent. If you are feeling stuck about not having what you are seeking show up in your life, keep checking inward and asking old beliefs, patterns, and fears to come to the surface. Visiting your cave from the meditation in chapter 2 can help.

How Our Personal Reality Intersects with Others' Journeys

Although I can create my personal reality, I cannot create someone else's reality, no matter how close I may be to them, no matter how much I love them. One of my adult children has been through some hugely challenging years. I have felt a lot of concern and anxiety at times because of this. Watching loved ones going through hard and perhaps debilitating journeys and knowing we cannot fix this is challenging, to say the least.

Despite how tough this has all been for me, I know all experiences can serve my growth and evolution. I also understand that this is an important learning edge in my own journey. Can I allow myself to connect with a sense of ease and joy while this is happening? It is not helpful to anyone if I suffer along with my adult child, yet to feel joyful while she is suffering seems wrong, despite knowing that getting stuck in fear and anxiety for her doesn't help her break through. She has her journey and I have had to learn to honor this.

This experience has pushed me to face hard truths about myself. I have had to work somewhat continuously to clear out guilt that I cannot help her create an easier journey for herself. I have had to keep working with the awareness that all experience is simply that, and my job is to release my attachment to believing that her journey should be a particular way. I have had to learn and keep learning how to love someone unconditionally while disconnecting energetically from any outcome. The only part of my personal reality that I can create is my own journey, which includes learning how to lovingly release all others to their own. It also means that I need to keep opening myself up to trust and faith: if it is meant for her to break through and heal, she will. I can support her in her process, but the rest is fully up to her.

The other learning process for me is to keep honoring my sadness, fear, and anger around the fact that I am powerless here. Honoring those emotions is what is needed to clear my emotional body and not contribute to any murkiness in 4D.

Because we have been so trained to merge love and codependency, this kind of lesson has become universal. How do we love and support others while totally honoring their creative power? How do we deal with the guilt, based on the old-paradigm belief that we should be able to change reality for others so that it will not overshadow the energy of clear love? How do we love ourselves enough to allow feelings of joyfulness and ease without ceasing to care about the well-being of those we love and of all beings?

The answer I've found is to stay conscious that joy and ease feed a positive collective energy and therefore make it possible for more and more humans to experience lives filled with this. We are all connected after all. When enough humans live a joyful, fulfilling life with wide open hearts, the collective reality of the planet will shift.

Holding Your Egoic 3D Self in Your Heart

Part of preparing to enter Earth's new reality, preparing to become full creators, is the practice of loving our 3D egoic selves—the parts of us driven by ego needs and beliefs. In our perfectionistic society, we have been conditioned to believe that our flaws are something to be ashamed of. And for many on this ascension journey, there is a lot of frustration and self-denigration when they find that they cannot consistently hold a higher frequency. It is impossible to be perfect and impossible for all but perhaps the few most enlightened beings among us, to be authentically in higher frequencies all the time, yet we have been programmed to believe this is something we should be able to achieve. The irony, of course, is that this programming is exactly what makes this journey so challenging.

Notice your feelings about this challenge. When we are vibrating and thus experiencing life at our 5D/6D frequency, it feels wonderful. We begin to believe we will consistently feel this way, and then we don't. This brings up frustration first because suddenly it appears we have lost access to feeling this good. Then, with our perfectionist conditioning, we often go into the self-judgment that lowers our vibration even more, and that makes things harder and even more frustrating. The challenge is to honor the fact that, at this point in our development, we will go through these vibrational shifts, and that is just part of the process. This is the way to not get stuck in the lower frequencies.

The old phrase "we cannot push the river" comes to mind. We were born into and have been living in a third-dimensional reality that, because of separation consciousness, has been out of balance for several thousands of years. Our physical incarnations are relatively short, and yet those of us seeking to be in higher frequencies and thus live a more enlightened life typically carry the belief that once we understand something, we should be able to make it so. It doesn't work that way. If we don't release ourselves from believing these "shoulds," we will ultimately wear ourselves out and make this journey much harder than necessary.

Our egoic selves will still hold the old conditioning believing that to be good, we should be perfect. If we stay conscious, we can release our attachment to these "shoulds" by noticing them and giving them less and less power as we go along. This helps us feel freer and have more energy, and so we will be able to stay in higher frequencies for longer.

Creating a loving relationship with our egos helps us to not go into spiritual bypass. People often go into bypass when they are unconsciously afraid of their darkness or their dark experiences (trauma) and thus keep denying this part of themselves, or they may simply be disconnected from their emotional and physical bodies so that they are unaware that only part of themselves is participating in their spiritual growth. This creates a light polarization, where you only connect with that which you define as spiritual and avoid anything that you might consider "dark" whether those are feelings, beliefs, or thoughts. This might feel good in the moment, but it is ultimately unsustainable. You cannot be embodied and light polarized at the same time. Your ego will not disappear. Your shadow will not disappear; they only go underground where they can do more damage.

This is not to judge those who are on that path right now as it is what they have chosen both consciously and unconsciously as part of their ascension curriculum. There are spiritual teachers of good heart who are feeding this. To the outsider, it might look like this is an advanced path, just like it might look to someone struggling financially that people who live in expensive houses, drive expensive cars, and wear expensive clothing must somehow have unlocked keys to happiness. But that is illusionary.

We are going to have ego issues. We all have dark shadow parts. As long as we do no harm, there is nothing wrong with this. The more we learn to love our 3D humanness, the closer we can become to living authentically as 5D humans.

Dear friends of mine had a recommitment ceremony some years ago, and one of their adult children who had gone through her own struggles spoke about how good parents weren't the ones who adored you when you were doing everything right, but the ones who adored you just as much when you weren't. This is unconditional love and a good metaphor for the relationship we are being asked to cultivate for ourselves. To love ourselves unconditionally, to love ourselves as much when we are failing as when we are succeeding will ease and, ironically, speed up our journey. This type of love is the vibration of 5D compassion, and it is what every being on our planet deserves.

Notice your internal responses when you observe yourself not being good. How do you relate to yourself when you have unkind thoughts for instance? Are you able to see them without judgment or with minimal judgment and without thinking that they are correct? Can you be loving and neutral to yourself when going through painful experiences? Just observe and remember that we are all in this together. We are all interconnected, and if we seek to lift ourselves and humanity to the higher-dimensional frequencies we are meant to live from, we need to accept the darkness as well as the light. Give that 3D egoic self of yours a lot of hugs. It is just bumbling through with the rest of our 3D egoic selves on the planet.

Getting to Know Your Ka

According to Nicki Scully and Linda Star Wolf in their book *Shamanic Mysteries of Egypt*,

> Ka is the expanded awareness that begins to infuse the physicality of the human.... [It] vibrates at a slightly higher frequency than matter but its frequency is close enough that it can connect with matter and permeate it. Ka lifts matter itself to a higher frequency, and with that expansion, more information and greater consciousness is available to the human once the ka is connected.[1]

They go on to say that as we are activating more of our DNA, this allows the ka more access to us at a cellular level, which connects us to the collective soul and awakens our memory of a huge body of wisdom that lives inside us all.[2]

From the multidimensional perspective of the 9D Vertical Axis, our ka exists in 6D as an idealized energetic blueprint of our soul. It holds our highest potential and as we learn to connect with it more fully, we bring it into our cells, filling them with more light and expanding our perceptual bandwidth. Pre-birth memories, especially about the gifts and mission our soul holds in this incarnation, become clearer. And we have a stronger connection to our star ancestors and their wisdom.

The more we have activated our 5D frequency, the easier it becomes to fully embody our ka because this frequency is much closer to our ka body than our 3D frequency is. The more our ka permeates our cells, the more vitality we have, and the more powerfully we can express our authentic selves. If you can imagine yourself, if you can feel yourself at full radiance, you are seeing and feeling how it is when your ka is fully *in*.

In these early stages of our ascension journey, the amount of ka we infuse varies from day to day, even, perhaps, from moment to moment. Learning to observe how connected we are with our ka without judgment is an important practice. To help you with this, I've included a ka meditation at the end of the chapter.

As we strengthen our connection and therefore expand the amount of time that we are living with our ka in, we are connecting with the sixth-dimensional part of us, our 6D nesting doll; a nesting doll that radiates higher-dimensional light. It is through this process we step into consciously creating our reality both personally and collectively. This is also how we become fully empowered to carry out our pre-birth contracts about sharing our gifts with the world.

I recently watched the documentary *Hallelujah* about Leonard Cohen, the legendary singer/songwriter poet. I think that his life and his life struggles are such an interesting example of being fully clear about one's mission and simultaneously unclear about how to step into its full manifestation. It wasn't until he was in his seventies, and after all his money had been stolen by his agent, forcing him to go back on tour with his music, that he received the recognition he always deserved. During that tour, every concert in all the multiple countries he performed in sold out to huge crowds. If you listen to his song called the "Tower of Song," it's clear that he had come to the point where he no longer had a choice but to carry out his mission. When he performs his songs, his ka is fully in, fully participatory. Not just the lyrics but the sounds themselves hold a higher-dimensional frequency. Yet that did not erase his personality or 3D struggles. This is an example of the process we are all embarking on. His depiction in his work of his combining his flawed humanness, his concern for the well-being of humanity, and his ongoing spiritual quest inspires and supports us all in seeking this for ourselves.

Because of his age and later a cancer diagnosis, Leonard was clearly compelled to compile music that he had started when he was younger but hadn't brought to completion. Two albums finally came together and were released the year he died. His popularity has continued to expand after his death because of the spiritual frequency of his music.[3] As the collective becomes more conscious, music or art forms that reflect this high frequency are being more appreciated.

For those of us on a conscious journey, understanding that we are still going to have to grapple with our humanness is essential. Knowing, too, that if we are open to raising our frequency as much as possible and allowing our ka to permeate our cells, the energy to carry out our pre-birth agreements becomes stronger, as does our ability to recognize what they are.

When our ka is in, we are joyful. We feel guided and protected. Because we are incorporating our 5D consciousness as well, our hearts are open, and our creativity is thriving. Pay attention. As way-showers, we are journeying to embody this higher-frequency energy of who we truly are.

Stepping into Leadership

I venture to say that 75 percent of us, or perhaps more, who have now incarnated to help with this planetary transition carry trauma from other lifetimes related to leadership. Once we have activated enough ka, though, we no longer have much of a choice to avoid our role because the energy to actualize our full selves has become so strong. It seems to be that there comes a point where if we still resist stepping into the role we accepted before birth, we will likely become depressed, anxious, or even so ill that we end up leaving our physical bodies, perhaps to start again in a new incarnation.

These old cellular fears of stepping into who we are meant to be are another reason the ascension journey is so challenging now. So many of us know we are here to lead the way, whether publicly or behind the scenes, but the old fears we carry fight against this. We may know consciously that we are not going to get burned at the stake or dragged into the dungeon and executed, yet not all our cells believe this. Even when we are not destined to be in the spotlight, simply going against the norms of our families and our larger society can trigger a trauma response that slows us down or sometimes stops us dead in our tracks.

Simultaneously, there are more new and effective techniques being developed that help us deactivate these trauma responses. But we need to recognize that the trauma is impacting us before we can effectively seek the help we need.

When we go into self-doubt about our gifts, when we find ourselves hiding in an old comfort zone that interferes with our growth, when we overstress in our day-to-day life so that we have no energy to break free—all of this may well be our way of avoiding the missions our soul has taken on. A lack of clarity or confusion about what you are supposed to be doing may also be a sign that you are avoiding playing the part that your soul has agreed to.

Before I wrote *Activating Your 5D Frequency*, I kept sensing there was something else I was supposed to do in this lifetime that would propel me and my teachings more into the public eye. I had already written two books, but they were self-published, and promotion was definitely not a skill of mine, so although they had some readership, it was relatively low. I was in my early seventies, in fine health and generally enjoying my life, but there was a sense of sadness, of something not completed, and I was not sure that it would get completed in this lifetime. I had pondered writing another book on occasion but mostly felt it was not going to happen. Then without my expecting it, there was a breakthrough, and the book unfolded almost magically. Getting the contract with Inner Traditions, which was what I needed for my work to become more visible, and the opportunities that came from the publication of this book attracted students from all over the world.

I believe that book came through me because I had worked long and hard with my fears and past-life trauma. This was part of the mission I agreed to before my current incarnation. However, if I chose not to write it, it's not that I would have been building negative karma because I hadn't fulfilled a pre-birth agreement. We always have free will. But there would continue to be a sense of incompleteness, of knowing that I had not actualized my potential. I would not have allowed enough ka to come in for me to step through my fears, doubts, and hesitations and fully do what I have showed up in this lifetime to do. This might ultimately have created some depression and perhaps even shortened my life.

If there are parts of this that ring true for you as well, this is your soul tapping you on the shoulder and letting you know it's time for you to own your gifts and to share them. It's time for you to break through any concerns about being too weird, about being too visible with your unconventional views and allow yourself to utilize the energy of your ka to take the necessary risks to be who you've come here to be.

There are many permeations of leadership. Not all leaders are standing at the front of the line directing others. Leadership is being willing to show your uniqueness, being willing to be a beacon of light to anyone who might choose to connect with this. Leadership happens ultimately when we overcome any fears of being fully authentic and allow our true soul to shine through. You might want to take some time to ponder both your fears of leadership as well as what gifts you have that are not being fully shared with the world.

Accessing Our Past

At this point in our evolution, the models we have for what life is like in a 5D/6D society tend to show up in two ways: what we remember, and what we are shown from our star ancestors who now have become our guides. Our expanded bandwidth provides us access to images of other lifetimes on this planet when fifth-dimensional societies were flourishing. We may well have memories of our lives in them whether these memories include a lot of specifics or are merely a vague sense. Lemuria, Atlantis, and prehistoric Egypt are the best-known of these societies and probably the largest and longest lasting.

From the time I first heard of Lemuria several decades ago, I always had a sense of it being watery and feminine, but my memories have not included specifics, even though I sense this is where my soul first landed when I came to this planet. As linear time has passed, I've had more of an emotional sense of this continent and how it felt to live there. I remember that we were rather ephemeral, more in our light bodies. And I remember the love and kindness where all life forms were honored as well as the ease and flow of daily life. I believe this stemmed from our ability to simply create whatever we needed, which means we were naturally connected to the sixth dimension.

Lauren O. Thyme in her book *The Lemurian Way* has very specific information that came both from her guides and from her recollections. Much of what I have read so far in it resonates for me and helps expand my memories. What I also know is that memory is rarely precise. And it doesn't have to be fully accurate to be illuminating. To educate us, to help us reconnect, the recollection needs to hold an energy aligned with our experience. This means it holds a frequency that we can feel into and translate in our own way, so it becomes more accessible both for ourselves and for us to share. But as with all translations, some are better than others. Those of us tapping into these memories are likely to hold varying images, all of which may still be aligned with the Lemurian energy.

Thyme's section on grids, energy stations, and light temples[4] was new information for me and immediately felt accurate. She writes about how the Lemurians used sacred geometry to lay out their society for built-in harmony. They also used the ley lines of our planet to both enhance their energy and to use the vortices as higher-dimensional portals.[5] There's an inner sensation I get when I read something that feels true, and reading her description activated this sensation.

Notice if you have access to similar inner guidance. Keep paying attention to your responses when you read or hear stories that have been eradicated from our accepted history. You may get an immediate intuitive confirmation that this connects for you or, conversely, that something is off here. Or a third possibility where you don't know yet, but are open. These signals come from our heart being in alignment with our mind. This is the same skill we need now as we navigate through what is real and what is not real as our outer reality continues to shift.

Another sense I've had about Lemuria is that when it fell, its descendants scattered around the globe and gathered in different Indigenous tribes, tribes that carried higher consciousness but created little external structure. It is also said that some Lemurians went underground, specifically in the Mt. Shasta area, and are thriving there. I have no sense of this but suspect that I will as I continue on my evolutionary path. I just don't have enough inner clarity for this to resonate as accurate information yet.

Awareness about Atlantis came quite differently for me. When I first heard about the legend, I did not feel much of a connection to it. Then around twenty-five years ago, I did a session with a client who talked about her past life there. As I guided her in a meditation, I started to get some very clear visual images. I don't remember the details of how this all unfolded, but together she and I identified that she was still holding some trauma from this lifetime, and it was interfering with her well-being in her current life. The visual images I had when I did the guided meditation with her are still clear to this day. I saw how technologically advanced Atlantis was and that at the time of her soul's experience, the male principal was dominating, causing the society to be extremely out of balance. She was a scientist and had fallen out of grace with those who were in power in her field. The details of what happened to her are vague now other than it was unkind and traumatic, and I see her being isolated in a room, but the visual images of the buildings, the vibrant colors and the advanced technology are still clear in my mind.

It is believed that Atlantis went through three falls; the first two were where the society was almost destroyed permanently, and the last one when it was. The final destruction was around twelve thousand years ago when there was a huge earthquake and tsunami, and the continent went underwater. I've heard varying accounts of what happened. One is that it was simply a natural disaster. Another was that it was an alien attack that created the Earth's changes. Yet another was that it was from an inside group that went against the group called the Law of One, who lived by the fifth-dimensional awareness of Oneness, and who were in power at the time. I sense that what I saw in the past-life session was from the second time that the Atlantean society deteriorated, not the final time, because I believe that by the third time, the society had already declined more physically and there would have not been the same vibrancy to the structures.

Once I did that session, I felt a much stronger connection to Atlantis and do believe that I had at least a few lifetimes there. My soul spent more time in Lemuria and feels a stronger energetic connection to it, but currently I have some strong visual images that I believe to be memories of what Atlantis looked like in its golden age, which is thought to have been between 50,000 and 30,000 BCE. I'll be writing more about this when I talk about sacred geometry and architecture. As I've said before, Atlantis held more of the masculine energy while Lemuria held the feminine. This is a little tricky to understand because when both societies were at their best, there was a sacred balance between the masculine and feminine. It is as if Lemuria was more in a feminine body but had balanced the inner masculine, and Atlantis was more in a masculine body but had balanced the inner feminine.

What is most important to understand is that both societies were much more evolved than we are yet. Whatever memories we can garner of living there can help guide us as we take more responsibility for creating not just our personal lives, but a new collective reality as well.

Connecting with our star ancestors can provide other important models and guidance for us. Those of us who identify ourselves as starseeds sense that we have lived in one or perhaps many of these advanced higher-frequency star civilizations. The best-known ones to us at this point include the Pleiades, Sirius, Arcturus, Orion, Andromeda, and Lyra, but more are being uncovered as we go through this collective journey. Many of us, too, are hybrids, meaning we carry the genetic codes from more than one of these civilizations, as there was and is a great exchange of talents and education between these societies.

Often there is a great sense of finding our real home when we connect with these star civilization energies, a sense of finding our true families. In higher-dimensional realities, time is quite different than it is here. Past, present, and future exist simultaneously, so our soul's past experiences and future experiences are also going on there now.

As I connect more with these star nations and the souls who identify with them, I notice that I can sense some of a person's star origins. For me, this is like when I traveled as a student in Europe for three months in the late 1960s, and after a while I developed a sense, when meeting other young travelers, of what their country of origin was even before we spoke. The differences were subtle, but identifiable. I find the same with star ancestry. For example, Sirians have a kind of intellectual quality, the Pleiadians create a strong heart connection, and the Arcturians have the ability to bring a scientific and often highly technological aspect to things.

Eva Marquez does a lovely job giving more specific information in her book *Activate Your Cosmic DNA* based on her experience guiding clients to uncover their origins. In a reading I had with Eva, I was able to visit various planets that surround the stars of the Pleiades, and that in turn connected me even more strongly to my experiences there.

The temple on Alcyone, which is part of the Pleiades, was the most significant for me because part of it was a university where I teach students from several different star nations. The ancient temples in Egypt, especially Karnak, reflect what these star civilization temples are like in terms of layout. It seems clear to me that temples such as Karnak used temples from Atlantis as a prototype, and the one on Alcyone was a prototype for the Atlanteans.

According to Hand Clow, who channeled the spirit of Alcyone in *The Pleiadian Agenda*, and who has shared with me that she, too, knows that she is teaching in the university there on Alcyone: "Earth is Alcyone's laboratory and Alcyone is Earth's library."[6] She goes on to explain that as our library, Alcyone holds the records of a new sacred culture, and Earth, as a laboratory, plays a major role in seeding new biology to be part of this. We are developing this sacred biology through our ascension process and ultimately seeding this to spread throughout the galaxy. This is possible in our now because we are returning to a celestial alignment that occurred in our solar system 225 to 250 million years ago, and Earth holds nine dimensions in its field. It is on Earth that love can be experienced in the physical.[7] And it is this higher-frequency love that transforms our bodies to becoming the new human by combining our twelve-strand DNA with the depth of experience we have gained in going through the dimensional descent. We are now ascending with this wisdom and level of compassion vibrating in our cells.

I share all this to stimulate your memories and your wisdom. The more of us who access and share our experiences, the stronger the energies of these advanced civilizations now become on our planet. Knowing who we really are, understanding both how vast we are, and how we can retrieve this information that actually lives on in our souls broadens us in the conscious creation of our individual lives and expands our vision of where we are going collectively.

Frequency Matching for Manifestation

All thoughts, qualities, and creations have a frequency. This relates to how slowly or quickly the energy involved is vibrating, but with infinite variations because every thought, vision, and creation will vary slightly to hold its individualized expression. When we want to manifest something in our lives, intuitively raising our frequency to match that which we desire is part of doing this successfully. The challenge of course is to sense the frequency of what we want accurately enough, and then to raise our own vibration, rogue cells and all.

Remember anything we can imagine already exists in the sixth dimension. This means that its energy already has a specific frequency. On one hand, if we go into an emotionally neutral state, being clear about what we want and simultaneously being receptive, open, and nonattached to the outcome, we can then raise our own frequency to the energy of what we desire and bring it in, even make it happen instantly. But the complexities of our emotional bodies make this more difficult.

It is certainly likely that there will be technologies developed where we could dial in what we are seeking and a hertz number (a unit for measuring frequency) would show up. Then we could use another device that would shift our own frequency to that number. However, this would lose the essence or the spirit of the thing we were attracting. So, although there could be a physical match, one might not realize the energies they were drawing in.

As an example, I'm seeking more money to ease my life in this material realm. Money can have all sorts of frequencies. Is this money drawn in from love? Is it drawn in from desperation? Does it hold some energy of exploitation? Or does it reflect the abundance of the universe? In each of these cases (and I'm sure there are many more variations), the frequencies vary subtly from one another, and that might not be measurable on the physical. Can a machine match the frequency of love that our heart emits, for instance? It might be able to match the Hz, but the energy a machine generates and the energy our heart generates cannot be the same.

Here's another way to understand this. If I use frequency from music to heal something, it is not only the hertz of the music that matters, but the energy of the musicians, too, that will determine if it is a good match for me, and therefore if it will create the healing it is meant to. So, although the solfeggio frequencies can hold healing energy, if they are created by musicians who themselves are not in alignment with healing energy or simply not in alignment with the energies your particular body needs, it won't be effective.

Then there are our rogue cells, those parts of us that have a different and generally unconscious agenda that could generate the energy of resistance. If I'm seeking to create more money in my life and have consciously defined this as having the energy of abundance, love, and ease, but I'm carrying wounding that has the energy of a belief that I don't deserve this abundance and ease, then there may not be a strong enough frequency match to draw this to me. Seeking healing is another good example of this. If part of me has some attachment to staying sick, perhaps because my life feels overwhelming or I have a negative relationship with my physical body, this can stand in the way as well.

Fear of our power can also be a factor. If I can create my perfect life simply by working with my frequency, this defies all cultural conditioning and illuminates that I really am a divine human. Although that all sounds great, once I own this power, there is no going back without contracting my bandwidth and putting myself back into a narrow box, which at that point is unrealistic since I will have already stepped so far out of my comfort zone and out of my conditioned belief of what life on our planet is. This awareness in and of itself will bring up old fears to be worked with and neutralized before I can allow myself to reach this advanced state.

Judgments about ease are also a factor here. Do I have a right to have my life be so easy? Will people resent me? Of course, the more ease we activate in our lives, the more energy we have to inspire others to realize that this is available to them as well.

So, there are often many personal impediments to work through in order to consciously manifest our desires, especially if we are trying to manifest something quickly. Nonetheless, this potential is always available to us. We just need to get out of our own way.

When I think about some of my own experiences with frequency matching, a few examples come to mind. The first was many years ago when my husband and I learned through feng shui that the screen door that was sticking on the front door of our house was blocking prosperity. My husband installed a new screen door, and we did a little ceremony, and then waited for more money to flow in. The first thing that happened was we had an unusual expense. Nothing awful, but clearly the opposite of what we intended. Then a friend asked us if she could borrow some money for something important. Reluctantly we agreed. Somehow through the process we must have unconsciously gone into neutral and released our attachment to having more money, when suddenly quite a lot showed up from an unexpected source. This was before I understood energy and vibration in the way that I do today, but we did sense that we had energetically shifted something by just accepting the initial money drain without giving up hope and intent. I believe that the drain was the universe's way of helping us release our resistances so that prosperity had a clear path, and we could then match the frequency to bring it in.

Fire walking is a very concrete example of frequency matching. The way you can walk over hot coals without burning yourself is to raise your vibration high enough to match the energy in the heat. Our community had a festival that included fire walking. The woman who facilitated the walk had us chanting and meditating together before approaching the burning coals. We were given clear instructions not to walk unless we fully knew that we were ready and would not hurt ourselves. Most of the people I was with were already confident they could do this. I was not.

Although I view myself as emotionally and mentally brave, I'm not particularly physically brave, and so while I participated in the preparation, I didn't expect myself to walk. Once before the hot coals, however, watching others as they danced across, I realized I could do it. I walked, didn't burn myself, and then walked a second time to make sure that I could remember I had really done it. I believe the reason I was able to do this was because I had no expectations of myself, so my ego did not get in the way. My frequency could then rise naturally, no doubt syncing with the frequency of the group. If I had walked to fit in or to show that I was as evolved as others, I probably would not have been able to raise my frequency high enough and might well have gotten singed.

As we raise our frequency for manifestation, it's also important to feel into what we are seeking to manifest. Essentially, we want to engage our physical as well as our emotional, mental, and spiritual bodies as much as possible. When we envision what we are seeking, this comes from our mental body. The clearer the vision, the more powerful. To include our emotional body, we then feel into both the emotions that arise when we imagine this vision has already manifested and how our physical body will react. On the physical, this could be a deep sense of relaxation, of lightness, of doing an ecstatic dance. On the emotional, this is joy or contentment. And finally, connecting with our souls' response. That may be more subtle for most of us, but when our visions and desires are in alignment with our soul essence, there is a strong sensation of well-being that arises. We are more connected to our ka, and therefore more connected to who we truly are.

Putting It All Together

As is clear from the above, creating our personal reality is a complex process. We are being asked to explore multiple layers of our psyche and extract the beliefs and fears that have held us back, while simultaneously connecting to and envisioning stepping fully into our multidimensionality and soul potential and staying as loving and nonjudgmental as possible while we do all this. That's a lot!

Owning up to the awareness that we are creators and that our inborn power is remarkable helps free us to release the old, limited conditioning and step out of the narrow boxes we've created from our cultural programming. There is a sense of lightness that occurs whenever we can do this, understanding that at first, this is likely to be just a momentary experience. But little by little these sensations will stay with us longer and occur more frequently.

Remember, too, that even as we release the old and connect more strongly with our ka, we are still in a transitional stage. Our vibrations, and therefore how we feel, will be in flux as we go back and forth between our 3D/4D frequency and our 5D/6D frequency. It is simply part of the process for our egos to grab ahold of us over and over again. Just know that each time this happens, its grip on us weakens a bit more. Our expanded bandwidth allows us to increase our navigational abilities on this journey and see more clearly, no matter which frequency we may be holding onto at a particular moment.

We can now acknowledge that our souls have chosen all of this for us. We know we have willingly agreed and committed ourselves to lead the way for humanity's current and profound transitional journey, and any of our fears and resistances arise only to clarify what we all need to shift within ourselves.

Most importantly, we know that as we love ourselves unconditionally, we create a safe and loving container to accompany us on our journey. This is how we strengthen our ability to not only connect with our personal transformative energy, but to learn how to consciously plug it into the collective as well.

✳ MEDITATION ✳
Meeting Your Ka

Allow your eyes to soften and put all of your attention on taking deep centering breaths. As you exhale release any distractions, any concerns, any tensions. Just let that all flow out with the breath. On the inhale imagine that you are drawing in tiny golden spirals of light filled with love and consciousness and allow those tiny spirals to spread to every cell in your body. Keep focusing on your breath as you begin to feel a sense of calm and relaxation spread throughout your body.

Now imagine that you are in some beautiful place in nature. It could be by the ocean, in the mountains, the desert, in a meadow. It can be somewhere you've been or somewhere you create in your imagination. The sky is a vibrant blue, and the bright sun warms your hair and skin. Let your eyes drink in the physical beauty, the shapes, the colors. Listen to any sounds: the birds singing, cawing, and calling to one another; perhaps the sound of the water; or of tree leaves moving in the breeze. Spend a moment to walk around this beautiful spot in nature, touching things with the palms of your hands, feeling the energy. Notice any fragrances.

Then find a comfortable spot where you can sit down while keeping your spine straight and tall. You might want to call in the directions, to feel the energies through the front of your body, through the back, through the left, and then the right. Pull in energies from above and from below and take a moment to sink into the stillness within.

Now slowly allow your consciousness to rise. Feel or see it move through the canopy of the fourth dimension. Feel the love of the fifth dimension begin to permeate all of your cells. And now allow it to move into the sixth dimension where you begin to intuit or see geometric energy patterns all around you. Some of you will feel this; others of you might get very vivid visual images.

As you see and sense these energy patterns, call to you the special energy pattern that is you. Call in your ka body, your perfected energy form. Maybe it is very faint at first, geometric but wispy—but as you put your attention on it, it becomes more vivid. Feel it radiating out powerful and beautiful energy. Let this ka of yours appear in whatever form it wishes to make itself known. Then thank it and welcome it.

Now imagine that you can begin to pull this form down into your body through your crown chakra. Allow this to happen, then sit with it and notice how this feels.

You might want to experiment with noticing the frequency of your four bodies—your physical vibration, your emotional vibration, your mental vibration, and your spiritual vibration. Notice the sense of inner alignment growing within you. Notice any sense of strength and clarity. Allow yourself to stay with this feeling.

If you can experience your ka, if you can feel it filling your cells and expanding your sense of personal power, surround yourself with a color. Each time you see this color in the coming days and weeks, it will help strengthen your connection to your very special soul body.

Now slowly wiggle your fingers and toes to get back into your body, noticing any sounds around you. And finally when you are ready, go ahead and open your eyes.

Note: Find this meditation on my YouTube channel, Wisdom Within Us, in the "Meditations to Raise Your Frequency" playlist.

Journal Questions to Ponder

1. When I think of what I want to manifest in my life, how would my life be different if I manifested it?
2. Is there anything about this that I wouldn't like?
3. What old beliefs and fears am I carrying that are interfering with this manifestation?
4. What judgments am I carrying about myself that are interfering with this manifestation?
5. How have these judgments, beliefs, and fears served to protect me in my past?
6. How do they serve now to hurt and/or stifle me?
7. What are the lessons my soul wishes me to learn from this experience?
8. How would I support my soul's full expression by learning this?

4

We Really Can Change the World

Social growth, like emotional growth, is never a linear process. Back in the 1960s, when I came of age and was part of the social movements of the times, I carried the belief that not only could we change the world but that we were changing the world. Of course, I was young and naïve in many ways and certainly had underestimated the true nature of those in power. Still, seeds were planted, and the world did change, just not enough.

In the 1960s and 1970s, traditional cultural beliefs were beginning to be widely questioned. It began with the Civil Rights Movement in the early '60s, a movement I became active in during high school when I learned of the injustices our country had done and was still doing to African Americans. I was not alone in beginning to wake up to the awareness that much of what we were taught about our world came from a very contracted bandwidth and was often untrue. Kennedy was president and inspiring idealism and service to the higher good. His assassination increased my commitment to working toward the creation of a better world and impacted many others of my generation.

Then came the Vietnam War, which gave rise to the anti-war movement, and from there, the early days of the women's and LGBTQ movements. Collectively we were learning that the American ideals of equality had been severely limited to only certain groups of people. The songs of musicians like Bob Dylan; the Beatles; Crosby, Stills and Nash; Joni Mitchell; Joan Baez; and many others became a source of our education, and large numbers of us began to question the status quo. Even back then we held a vision of the old world falling away, replaced by a world of peace and love. We were also concerned about the changes going on in the climate and how we treat our planet, as well as how we were treating all people around the globe. We began to envision what now we would call New Earth, where all were treated fairly, and all life was honored.

The slogan "make love, not war" reflected this consciousness. Love was a central theme of the hippie movement, and since now we understand that it is the primary energy of stepping into our 5D consciousness, we can see that those days were the beginning of the evolutionary process we are currently in. Interest was also increasing in Eastern philosophy and religions, astrology, and tarot. These interests broke through more of the limitations of the traditional Western perceptual bandwidth. And of course, the use of psychedelics added to these perceptual shifts.

The counter-cultural movement of the '60s and '70s was made up mostly of young, privileged middle-class white people, although the energy was inclusive and welcoming. The views of the movement, never mind our hair and dress, caused a lot of backlash, especially from the older generation who saw our protests of the Vietnam war and our unconventional look as un-American. Even the idea that people were questioning the government's reasons for the Vietnam War was considered heresy by some. Thus, the polarization in the United States began to come to the surface. Sixty years later, after going underground for some of this time, this polarization has grown even more extreme.

When people become motivated by fear and victim consciousness, they will go to great lengths to keep what is familiar. And they are easy to stir up. When people feel left out or treated unfairly, no matter what their demographic, they tend to respond with fear and anger. If they have been raised with the cultural belief that their particular group is somehow more deserving than others, this becomes more intense. And if external change begins to shake the very foundations of how one thinks the world should be, and people no longer know what is and isn't true, then it becomes easy to look outside of oneself for a leader who makes people believe that change can be avoided, and the world as they believe it should be can be controlled by imposing restrictions that give the illusion that the old and familiar can be preserved.

The current split in the spiritual community where one group is certain that they have superior spiritual awareness of what is really going on is made worse through what I believe is targeted internet propaganda that exposes some collective lies while simultaneously creating others. And they instruct the followers only to access information that supports these views. This intensifies the polarization.

When we understand how we create reality from 6D, we realize that to create anything, enough of us need a similar vision to see it manifest. The current polarization and fractionalizing make it hard to hold a unified vision that can manifest quickly enough to avoid the harsh realities occurring ever more frequently on the planet. Is this part of the process? Certainly, there must be some sort of collective agreement, but my feeling is that this agreement is based on the old belief that change is difficult and suffering inevitable.

So, although I feel sad and frustrated that, yet again, we are doing it the hard way, I know in my heart that we still will do it. Large numbers of us will continue to awaken. We will change the world, take our power back, and together enter a golden age for humanity.

Underneath all the disagreements, all the fears, all the lies, all the confusion about what is or isn't true, I believe that most humans on the planet seek the same thing. Most would choose peace over war, love over hate, kindness over cruelty, fairness over injustice. These are areas where we can all come together. However, if people believe their safety is being threatened, and their so-called way of life at risk, those values can be quickly thrown aside and replaced by old stereotypical beliefs of distrust, bigotry, and hatred.

Since the rise of patriarchy, which was a product of the dimensional descent, cultural beliefs arose that disconnected us from our hearts and our inner wisdom. We threw ourselves out of harmony, out of balance and began to believe that in the natural order of things, men were superior to women, some people and groups were of more value than others, and that if we perceived someone as an enemy or a threat, it was fine to be cruel to them and their children. We stopped understanding that we are all interconnected, that we are part of each other and of all creation. This lower-vibrational consciousness was activated in our genes and still lives there.

We saw in recent Western history how easy it was for Hitler to rile up the average German, as well as many other Europeans whose countries he invaded. He got people who were generally kind to turn against their Jewish neighbor or friend. This has continued with other groups in smaller wars since then. Authoritarianism makes people feel safer if they are part of the in-group, the group that is being identified as better or superior in some way.

To create collective change that reflects our higher-consciousness potential, we need to stay conscious of those fear genes. They are part of our trauma expression, although they rarely, if ever, get identified as such. They lead us to stop taking responsibility for our creations and incite us to believe whichever leader we choose to follow. Jesus's teachings that encourage you to love your enemy get easily thrown out the window. Or perhaps more accurately, they easily get spun so that love of the enemy can mean forcing them to take on whatever the primary cultural values are as defined by those in power. The cruelty, for example, of how Native American children were treated, separated at a young age from their families and sent to live in supposed good Christian households where they were often emotionally, physically, and sexually abused, treated as less than, and punished for talking their language or honoring their culture in any way is a sadly clear example of this type of consciousness.

So here we are in 2024 with the world literally and figuratively on fire, and many of us who chose to be here now to help shift humanity into a higher-dimensional frequency are feeling overwhelmed. How will we carry out what we are here to do? How are we to proceed?

The Nature and Challenge of Change

One of the great ironies currently in play is that changing our world into a loving, vibrant, peaceful place could happen easily. No one truly benefits from the way things are, even the so-called elite, even those nasty aliens who, according to Patricia Cory in her book *The New Sirian Revelations*, have been controlling things here for quite a while. Just because you control things does not mean you are happy and thriving.

What makes this change so difficult is that we don't really believe it can be any other way. Suffering has been the norm on this planet for so long that it has become woven both into our worldview and into our DNA. We have been trained to give away our power, to look outside ourselves for solutions. We have been programmed to be sheep-like and easily controlled by the power elite while believing we are free, and thus we hold ourselves hostage to these norms. To fully release this old conditioning may be daunting, but that's no reason for us not to do it. And as we activate more of our star DNA, we have more inner resources on hand for this challenge.

Remember everything is energy. What we see manifesting in our world is simply energy vibrating at a slower rate, creating an illusion of solidity. Quantum physics shows that when you get to the tiniest particle of matter, it doesn't stay a particle. It stays in motion, going from a particle to a wave and then back again. The mess we see now on planet Earth is not solid. It can shift once enough of us make a clear, conscious decision. Don't forget, our loving, vibrant, peaceful planet already exists in its energy form in 6D, waiting there for us to choose it over the old beliefs and fears that are there as well.

Remember, too, it is the old beliefs and fears creating the current resistance to positive change that makes things feel so difficult. The fact that these beliefs and fears are a product of millenniums of trauma makes them even more powerful because they often remain unconscious, or at least, the awareness that they are from trauma stays unconscious. Even those of us aware of them are still working on shifting out of this powerful old programming that says life is hard, suffering normal, war and pestilence inevitable. All of this contributes to the belief that we are powerless to create change.

Think about what these beliefs create in 6D. Envision if you will that infinite variations of our world exist there, running the whole continuum from utopian to horrific. These visions are all vibrating in 6D, and the ones we energize the most create the morphic field for what shows up here. We need to collectively decide which of those worlds will manifest on our planet.

If we look at what we've currently chosen, we see that perhaps around 50 percent of the people on Earth have a decent outer life. Yet within that, large numbers struggle with depression, anxiety, and illness that simply create another form of suffering. Simultaneously with the climate crisis becoming more and more intense, and the war that's currently escalating in the Middle East, our sense of outer security keeps diminishing. Add in the lack of consensus reality, and you have a third dimension in great chaos.

Like the Chinese word for chaos suggests, we are in a time of both danger and opportunity. For the old to fall away, our 3D self apparently needs the outer world to be shaken up enough to get us to let go of it. This shake-up can lead both to stronger resistance and to opening more of us to expanded ways of viewing things. Our perceptional expansion allows us to open to more possibilities and a much wider range of what we consider to be real. So, amid this mass confusion, we are also being pushed to expand our bandwidth. The more of us who continue to expand, who can look within and connect to our inner wisdom, who can reclaim our multidimensional nature and take our power back, and the more of us who rely on the wisdom and love from our heart, the sooner we can choose the variation of this planet where all can thrive.

For those of us who are participating consciously, who know that our souls have chosen to serve a higher-dimensional agenda, our task is complex. We need to both hold and empower this vision of a loving, harmonious world while taking a deep and honest look at the ingrained limited beliefs we, too, are holding. Once we identify them, we then need strategies to transform them. As we shift these beliefs, we model to others that this can be done.

Our dormant DNA, those ten mysterious strands, hold the awareness of our enlightened potential where we can activate enough power to pick this New-Earth timeline. Our trauma DNA wants us to hold on to the old, to the familiar. We can choose which part of our DNA expresses itself, which part lights up, but because we still are healing our old wounds, and still hold dysfunctional beliefs in our unconscious, the journey in its complexity can become convoluted. So, the first order of business is to acknowledge the contradictions within us and to be gentle with ourselves. Then to breathe deeply and consciously expand our container to comfortably hold these contradictions. As we do this, we are developing a new, more evolved relationship with ourselves that empowers us to activate the transformative energy needed. Then we become able, little by little, to shut down the trauma DNA and incrementally give more of our star DNA its expression. (The meditation at the end of chapter 7 will help you with this.)

Even though I carry a strong belief that we will create a loving, just, thriving planet, and know that my soul mission is to help with this the best I can, I also can find within me a part that just wants to give up. This part feels tired and overloaded with the intensity of energies bombarding all of us. This part of myself is still operating out of the old-paradigm consciousness that life is a struggle, which is what is creating the fatigue in the first place. If I try to pretend this part doesn't exist, I can push it underground, but that will only strengthen it. If, instead, I meet this part with great compassion and keep working to strengthen my connection to Source, which is where all the energy I need to carry out my mission comes from, I begin to feel revitalized. And, as I've said in many ways, this is not a one-time process but rather something I need to repeat with some frequency as I continue to shift out of old limiting beliefs.

Numerous other collective beliefs operate to make things more challenging. There are the old standards like we're not good enough, worthy enough, loveable enough. Then we have the belief we should be perfect, and therefore if we have a misstep or a delay, it can trigger a whole set of internal responses that reinforces the old standards. All of this serves to wear us out, hold us back, feed our self-doubt, and create the illusion of struggle and powerlessness.

Change can be exciting. Change can be invigorating. Change can bring out our very best qualities. Or not. This is all up to us.

Collective Shadows

Much like owning and integrating our personal shadow, which is essential for our own growth and well-being, we need to go through a similar process with our collective shadow or it will deter us from our current evolutionary path and ultimately bring us down. All cultures have their gifts and their demons. The larger and more influential a culture, the more important dealing with its shadow becomes. If we want to create a beautiful, healthy, loving planet, we need to look at the collective darkness and transform it so it will not do harm and impede our way.

Germany has had to go through a painful emotional and psychological journey to heal from the horrors of the Nazi era and from the Holocaust. But they have been doing so. They do not try to pretend or hide what really happened.[1] As they own their painful history, they increase their understanding of how these things can happen and therefore increase the likelihood this will not happen again.

South Africans used the traditional Indigenous African process of "Truth and Reconciliation" to heal from the horrors of apartheid. Nelson Mandela and Desmond Tutu spearheaded the creation of a commission by this name, and sixty-five other countries have established something similar to heal darkness in their past.[2]

Testimony in "South Africa's Truth and Reconciliation Commission was established to adjudicate the brutal, racist tactics used by the country's apartheid government.... Testimony of thousands of victims of apartheid was broadcast on television and radio, entering the homes of hundreds of thousands of viewers worldwide. It was recorded to help ensure that the crimes of apartheid would not be forgotten, and should never be repeated."[3]

The United States, sadly, has done just the opposite, and there's a current movement to intensify this. It is a good example of how a nation reflects the same experience as individuals: the brighter the light, the larger the shadow.

The United States was founded on the ideals of equality and democratic process. We have a ground-breaking constitution and an amazing system of checks and balances to keep our government on track. On the other hand, we are still reeling and trying to avoid confronting the horrors our government has perpetrated throughout our nation's history. This includes slavery, Jim Crow, the Trail of Tears, Indian boarding schools, and the internment of Japanese Americans during WWII. Racism has been woven into the foundation of this country, and while in the last sixty or so years we have put laws and policies into effect to help remedy this, the reality is it just went underground to fester and more subtly wound people of color. Racism along with antisemitism and fears and hatred of other vulnerable minorities such as those in the LGBTQ community have come above ground once again, which although painful to observe, hopefully will allow for a more authentic healing, but sadly not before its disowned shadow does more harm.

There's a global shadow that also has not been addressed. It was part of the average German following Hitler and is part of the current popularity of authoritarian leaders across the globe. That shadow is our collective willingness to obey authority. People who otherwise are generally decent and kind will do awful things to others simply because a person in authority tells them they must.

An experiment called the Milgram Experiment was done at Yale University in the 1960s. Its purpose was to study obedience and how far people would go to obey someone in authority. Participants were put in front of machines with dials that they were told could create electric shocks for a person they could see and hear behind a glass barrier. They believed the person was selected randomly from a group of volunteers when, in fact, the person behind the glass barrier was an actor. When a so-called wrong answer came from the fake subject in the glass booth, a person in authority instructed the unknowing participant at the machine to deliver what they believed to be dangerous shocks to this subject. They began with a low, slightly uncomfortable amount, and then as the subject kept giving the wrong answers, they were ordered to keep increasing the intensity of the shock despite seeing the person in the booth appearing to be in great panic and pain. Sixty-five percent of the participants ended up giving the maximum shock that was clearly explained to them could be very dangerous to the subject's health.[4]

Although there were ethical questions about the deception used on the participants, what happened is important for us to understand. When we believe that someone else is wiser and more powerful than we are, we are vulnerable as a species to being coerced into doing some awful things to others. What happened to the German people during the Nazi era is the most widely known example in recent history. But this is happening all over the world now, whether it is the treatment of immigrants at the borders, prisoners, or anyone who people in authority tell us deserves to be treated cruelly. If the narrative includes the idea that these undeserving people could harm us in some way, this obedience and cruelty become even more likely. We need to realize that we all have this capacity, and if we don't look at it and admit that as humans we all hold this potential, it can far more easily rear its ugly head.

For us to move out of the suffering of the last several thousand years on this planet and truly transform it through our higher-dimensional consciousness, we need to be mature enough to acknowledge these collective shadows as well as to become aware of all the lies we've been told, no matter how scary or painful this might be. We then can hold all in compassion, own our inner power, and through this, transform this dark energy. All avoidance only strengthens the mists that hold the dark part of our collective consciousness in 6D and interferes with our evolutionary process and ability to create a higher-consciousness planet for all of humanity.

Envisioning and Reclaiming Ecological Balance

The current imbalance in 3D is becoming more and more obvious as intense weather, famines, and debilitating illnesses increase. The effects of our disconnection from the natural world, our lack of consciousness of how all things are interconnected, and our lower-frequency idea that we are here to conquer nature all have brought us to the brink of self-destruction.

The Earth's health is essential to our well-being. Because of our disconnection, most humans no longer understand this and have lost the awareness that all creation holds consciousness. Our use of petroleum is a clear example. This oil is part of the blood of Mother Earth. Extracting the amount we do takes a vital nutrient and lubricant out of her. She is not going to allow this without responding. And her response is becoming more and more intense in the attempt to give us the message. However, as the symptoms of the imbalances become more catastrophic and thus harder to ignore, this simultaneously creates a reverse movement as more of us wake up.

Much like our collective shadow, we need to acknowledge the damage we have caused supporting our modern lifestyle. Ultimately, we need to no longer use harmful ways to meet our needs. We have access to higher-dimensional information to create what we need to maintain a comfortable, albeit nonexcessive, lifestyle for all. There is no need to sicken the Earth for our energy use, to use toxic chemicals to grow our food, or to torture animals in factory farms to provide our sustenance. These are all examples of how we create this imbalance and make life in 3D more stressful and painful.

Because we are moving into our fifth-dimensional frequency in this ascension journey, love quite literally needs to be at the heart of all we create. It is this love coupled with the 5D quality of unity consciousness that will help us rebalance. In the energy of higher-vibrational love, we hold compassion for all humans, all creatures, all plant life, even ETs with a negative agenda, and of course we hold great compassion for our Earth. And it is from this love we commit to do no harm.

This is the energy that will change mass consciousness so we can begin to transform life in our world. Simply bringing this energy in is part of what needs to happen so that all here can thrive and so universal thriving becomes the norm.

Even things we might not realize we want to flourish becomes part of this. Consider the poison ivy plant. Like all creation, it is a living, conscious entity. Yet do we really want it to thrive? This is a plant humans want to avoid, and because of this, we may think we want it to disappear. Still like all creation, it is a part of our ecosystem and so must serve a positive purpose. A quick Google search revealed:

> When ripe, the white fruits [of the poison ivy plant] are a favorite food of many migrant and game birds, as well as white-tailed deer. The seeds are adapted for sprouting after digestion softens the seed coat. Poison ivy sap has been used to make indelible ink. Field experiments have shown that poison ivy is tolerant of being inundated by wastewater and could potentially be used to treat sewage.[5]

When we are in loving energetic alignment with ourselves, when we are living from our 5D frequency, we become energetically aligned and telepathically tuned in to all sentient life. We naturally avoid what may cause harm to ourselves yet provides something positive for other lifeforms. All creation has consciousness, so, for example, when we are in balance, so-called invasive plants create their own boundaries to not interfere with other plants that need to thrive close by.

We have lost much awareness of the magic that being in balance brings us. And we have lost much awareness of how out of balance we have become. Rebalancing occurs as more of us pay attention to what is happening on our planet from our expanded bandwidth. From this awareness, our focus shifts to finding solutions, shifting the collective will, so that together we create a new reality from loving higher-frequency consciousness.

Creating Higher-Dimensional Reality on Our Planet

The more we understand how we create manifested reality from 6D, the more we understand that infinite possibilities exist there waiting for us to make our collective choice. The clearer and more united we are in envisioning what we want to create, the sooner and more universally it will occur.

For the last several decades, many groups have attempted to do this. Global peace meditations are a good illustration. They are scheduled enough in advance so that large numbers of people can participate, and they are usually designed to happen at the same time around the planet. This does send a clear intent into 6D.

So why don't we have peace yet? I believe there are several reasons. Partly, we have not dealt enough with those rogue cells that carry the belief that peace is not truly possible. As I've said before, they are the product of millenniums of trauma, and they are embedded in our ego responses to life. They unconsciously interfere as we simultaneously visualize and meditate for peace. Remember, though, that they lose their power when we bring them into our conscious awareness.

There are also people energizing an opposing creation because they carry the belief that war solves issues. Then there are those who profit from war and beings who benefit from keeping our planetary frequency low and therefore seek to keep us in chaos and pain. Finally, there is not a strong enough unified vision of what a peaceful planet would look like, feel like, even sound and smell like.

In my heart, I know that most humans on the planet are good people. They want to be kind and fair. They want to be loved and loving. They want to feel appreciated, and they want to feel safe. This is what a higher-dimensional planet offers to all of us. Those who profit from war, chaos, and others' suffering are only a small minority, yet clearly there is a process we need to go through for this new type of world to show up.

In my book *Activating Your 5D Frequency*, I give many examples of a loving, just, peaceful, and thriving planet to help people envision it. And chapter 9 gives some of this as well. Those images are the endgame. Although I believe they are essential, and we need to keep focused on them, and while I address the psychological journey to get there, I don't provide physical details of how the shift will occur. This is because it is a journey of faith. It happens as pockets of people all over the globe commit to energizing these visions and owning their inner power, which activates more of their star DNA. This is occurring now. I believe how things unfold will be organic. The path will light up for us as we collectively follow our hearts. This is rather like following the yellow brick road that leads us to Oz. Except, unlike the wizard in the story, we can be authentic wizards. We simply need to acknowledge this.

More and more souls are showing up on the planet who are intuitively holding higher wisdom. Although they are going through many human challenges, as they mature I believe they will be stepping up and carrying more unified images that will support the coming changes.

We also are being called to hold an expanded container in a way that minimizes the disrupting power of opposing views. This is how we disempower the polarization. It is in this container, because it allows all views, that the strength of the heart can lead us to the creation of New Earth. When the heart leads, we will all seek to create a planet that holds a loving higher-frequency vision and agenda. We may well be able to bypass the current areas of nonagreement simply by following the energy of unconditional love.

Activating Our Starseed Memories

Deep in our cells we are carrying all the information needed to create New Earth. It is encoded in our DNA, and as we raise our frequency, we retrieve more and more of this knowledge. We remember what it is like to live collectively from a higher-dimensional frequency where compassion, harmony, fairness, and peace have become implicit. We remember being that lighter, brighter version of ourselves, and as we do, we connect more frequently with this part of us.

There are two primary ways to activate our star DNA. One is an internal process of navigating our way through 4D by acknowledging and healing our traumas and learning to honor our feelings so we keep our emotional bodies clear. This includes the ongoing practice of acknowledging and integrating our shadow. Keeping the 4D canopy clear gives us more authentic access to the higher-dimensional information we carry in our cells.

The other is that the photon belt, in its twenty-six-thousand-year cycle, is now closest to the Earth, and we are being bombarded by the information and consciousness contained in its light through the solar flares currently hitting the planet. Barbara Hand Clow, in her book *The Pleiadian Agenda*, talks about this at length, and I highly recommend it if you want more information. Other teachers and healers all over the globe are absorbing this information and offering *activations* to help others. Some *activations* will happen through guided meditations like the ones at the end of these chapters; others through energy clearing and exchanges that also can provide the light needed to open parts of those dormant strands.

I do want to add a bit of caution in terms of energy exchange. Just because something sounds good and is wrapped in a pretty package does not mean the energy is of the light. This is where it is so important to stay grounded and to have a strong sense of who we are, as well as to have healed much of our trauma and transformed old beliefs of powerlessness. We need to trust our own guidance. If an energy worker has not done enough of their own work, they may be transmitting some energy that reflects their wounds. Most will be doing this unconsciously with no intent to do harm, although there may be those who are simply on a power trip. Just stay conscious. Stay aware. Pay attention to what messages your body is sending you. If something feels off, trust this.

And if something feels right, trust this as well. We are all getting flashes of memory. Some of it is stimulated through books and podcasts. Some through experiencing the energy of the stars in the night sky. Some through the bounty of the Earth, whether from working in harmony with nature or tuning into the wisdom of the rocks and crystals, the animals, birds, or any part of the natural world that is accompanying us in our lives.

Allow your imagination to open. Allow your skeptical mind to relax. Keep giving yourself the message to *remember*. Maybe it will happen on sacred sites or simply in the sacredness of your own being. It can come in dreams, through creative expression, through sound, through dance. It can come in numerous ways. You will know it because it has an energy of peace, of open-heartedness, of a deep sense of connection to all of life.

Then allow your images to expand. Perhaps you can see and experience the feeling of a pristine village filled with joyful, flourishing life. You might get a sense of colors, of structures, of how daily needs and experiences are organized. You might have a particular area of interest, anything from ecology to wellness techniques, to food production and distribution, energy production . . . the list is endless. But my point is that your memories may move you to recollect ideas that we need now on our planet. So put out an intent to consciously explore areas you are interested in, areas that you are drawn to, and just notice any flashes of insight that come your way.

It is also possible that you will not get clear images, but you will get a sense of things, a feeling. Let yourself sink into the sensation of this and see what happens.

As our star DNA becomes more activated, some of the memories that come through may not be positive. Both Lemuria and Atlantis experienced becoming out of balance, which ultimately led to their destruction. Some of the currently evolved star civilizations also went through periods of lower frequency. If you tap into this, stay as grounded as you can in the present, knowing that you are currently safe while allowing any unprocessed feelings from those experiences to arise. If you stay open to working them through, then more is likely to be revealed.

There is another way to expand our starseed awareness that I am just beginning to tune into as I am writing this. According to Lauren O. Thyme, the Lemurians used gold light that held universal love and consciousness for their well-being. I have just begun to get a sense of the unique feeling this golden light provides. It seems to have more weight, more substance than light in general, even though it is higher-dimensional, so it has a different quality to what we might think of as weight and substance than what we experience in 3D. The closest I can come to explaining it is the feel of a high-quality down comforter. As I open more to working with this, I sense it will show me new directions, new ways to use this gold light in order to illuminate which road to follow. Perhaps it shows up as golden nuggets on that yellow (gold) brick road.

Consider what Thyme says about being a human: "Within that Gold Light canopy . . . humans are multidimensional light stations, continuously transmitting and generating impulses through the field of energy."[6] You might want to take a moment to feel within yourself as a multidimensional light station and see what arises.

Author and channeler Caroline Oceana Ryan also brings us a lot of important information about the frequency of gold, which can give us a deeper understanding of the gold light that Thyme speaks of. In a channeling, Ryan was told the following:

> Gold was used in many ancient pyramids to assist transmissions of energies and of messages sent between persons and groups, not only around the Earth but also into space and between galaxies.
>
> It was also revered for its ability to hold information and to

facilitate shifts in vibrational frequencies, including in portals and stargates.

Gold's divine purpose is to remind humanity and the Earth Herself of the vibrations of the higher realms, and to demonstrate [Divine] transformational capability. . . . Gold in its etheric form desires to cleanse and to heal, to assist and to uplift all who call upon its essence.[7]

Approaching the Golden Age

What an exhilarating time we are in. It is a rare opportunity to be conscious and to live with awareness as our planet and humanity go through this deep transition. We are moving toward a new golden age predicted by numerous Indigenous and ancient cultures across the globe. However, as we do, collective resistance is intensifying.

All changes in the third dimension go through the process of death and rebirth. Some deaths are easy, almost sweet as we say goodbye to one way of experiencing ourselves and our reality. Other deaths can be drawn out and painful when the part of us that fears and resists change takes us over. Still, other death experiences can invoke anger that change has to happen at all. If I were creating a poster for this movie called *The Earth Show*, it would have images packed with drama, trauma, and adventure, and loaded with special effects. The reviews might include that after the quests were completed, there was ultimately a happy ending. Or perhaps a happy new beginning would be more accurate. However, if I created this movie just on my own, I'd much rather skip the drama and trauma, but this does not appear to be what's on our planetary menu right now.

You might think you want to ride this change by grabbing some popcorn and sitting back to watch the show, and no doubt there are higher-dimensional beings from other places who are doing just that. But all of us here have, on some level, chosen to be part of the cast. We wrote most of the script together before incarnating and the production began. (Apparently, I got outvoted in terms of the drama/trauma aspects.) We saw there were several different versions, and we weren't sure which would play out. Given the current split in what we call consensus reality, it seems likely that at least a few of those versions are playing simultaneously, making it all the more intriguing, perhaps, despite the confusion.

After writing this, I picked up Barbara Hand Clow's *The Pleiadian Agenda* and looked at the preface. I read this book decades ago and had very little recollection of its specifics. I was surprised to see the title of the preface is "Reality Splitting."[8] Perhaps I had saved this information in my subconscious, but all conscious recollection had left. And here I am now in 2024 writing about this very thing. Although I don't focus on other-dimensional control programs impacting our Earth, which the book speaks of, the essence of the message is the same: we are in charge of our reality. There are natural universal cycles we can work with, and the one we are currently entering supports our becoming ever more aware that we have this power. We can recreate a spiritually conscious, loving world.

Having chosen to come in at this time with a mission to support this change, we aren't likely to just sit back and watch the movie, but rather to be active players in the gestation of the new. How intense the death of the old becomes and how easy or difficult the birth of the new is up to us. We have all the cosmic encouragement we need to do this with grace. We have numerous techniques and strategies to access our creative powers, to continue to open and follow our hearts, to stay grounded and emotionally and mentally clear. The more we use this ability, the easier and more successful this planetary transition becomes.

✵ MEDITATION ✵
Planetary Healing: Planting Portals of Light

Hold a crystal in your hand while doing this meditation. A Lemurian seed crystal is ideal, but any crystal that is special to you will work.

Allow your eyes to soften and put all your attention on taking deep centering breaths. As you exhale release any distractions, any concerns, any tensions. Just let that all flow out with the breath. On the inhale imagine that you are drawing in tiny golden spirals of light filled with love and consciousness and allow those tiny spirals to spread to every cell in your body. Keep focusing on your breath as you begin to feel a sense of calm and relaxation travel throughout your body.

Imagine now that you are walking in a beautiful meadow. The sky is a brilliant blue. The sun is warming your hair and skin. You listen to the birds cawing and singing and calling to one another. Wildflowers in brilliant hues surround you as you feast your eyes on the visual beauty everywhere. You breathe in the fragrance of the fresh air wafting in the breeze.

A beautiful structure appears before you. You walk over to it slowly and realize that this is a sacred temple, and it is yours. It is a structure that is perfectly aligned with your energy. Notice its shape and color. Walk closer, and when you come to the entryway, stop and feel its texture. When it feels right, enter this sacred temple. It may be dark at first, but there are candles for you to light with the matches placed near the entrance. Go ahead and light the candles, and spend some time looking over this space, noticing all the objects, and gently touching things to absorb the high-frequency energy within them.

Now notice there is a stairway off to your right. Walk up the stairway slowly, and as you do you realize it leads to an upper deck. As you reach the deck you see that the sun has set, and the night sky is now above you.

Find a comfortable place to lie down and gaze at the sky.

There's a bright sliver of a moon above you, and all the brightest stars and planets stand in full relief against the dark backdrop of the heavens.

Lying there you realize that all around our planet, light workers have been creating a starlit grid to pull down to our planet the frequency and wisdom of our star ancestors. The more you relax, the more you see this light grid forming everywhere around you. Pull some of the filaments of light into you, then spend a few moments feeling into this light, breathing it into your heart.

Know that focusing on it helps us to deepen our own soul recollections. Pay attention to anything that might arise in your awareness.

You now realize that numerous others around the globe are holding etheric hands together, with each doing their part to shine this grid of light more brightly around the Earth. It has been activated with love and consciousness and holds the ancient wisdom of those who came to our planet to seed its evolution. See yourself joining this group while still lying on this deck, and feel the light intensify. Bask in the warmth and power of drawing in this collective light.

And now let your awareness go into Mother Earth, to the dimension just below the Earth's crust that holds the gems and crystals and metals all programmed with the star wisdom of those who have seeded our planet. They have been left there for millenniums waiting for the time when the ancient knowledge buried there can be drawn up into our bones.

Consciously draw this energy into your bone marrow and into the crystalline structure within your cells to intensify this connection, to more strongly activate the inner light grid below the surface of Mother Earth.

See now that there are portals of light that reach from within the Earth and rise up into the atmosphere that surrounds us. . . . Notice that these portals of light merge with the light grids being pulled down from the heavens.

Know these portals, these columns of light, are being planted everywhere around the globe to emit the frequencies that will lead us all into the coming golden age that will lead us into the creation of New Earth.

Notice if you can feel the energy of your star ancestors in every cell of your body. Then vibrate this energy out to the light portals knowing they are transmitting this loving, healing high-consciousness frequency everywhere on our planet.

Be aware that the crystal you are holding in your hand has journeyed with you to your sacred temple and amplifies the energy of the light grid and of the planted portals of light. Bring yourself slowly back, rising from your mat on the deck, walking slowly down the stairs and through the temple. Walk into the meadow, and then, still holding the crystal, slowly bring yourself back to your room. You may want to wiggle your fingers and toes to get back into your body, noticing any sounds around you in your room. And finally, when you are ready, go ahead and open your eyes.

Take some time to journal on your experience.

Note: Find this meditation on my YouTube channel, Wisdom Within Us, in the "Meditations to Raise Your Frequency" playlist.

Journal Questions to Ponder

1. When I envision a peaceful, loving, spiritually aware planet, what does it look like? What does it feel like? Can I imagine living in such a place where all beings have what they need for a comfortable life, and all are thriving?
2. What beliefs do I hold about why we have not manifested this yet?
3. What have I been taught from my family, education, religious background, and the culture in general about human nature?
4. What have I been taught about how safe the world is and why I should or should not trust others?
5. What dysfunctional beliefs have I already shifted about why the world is hard and why so many suffer? What methods did I use?
6. What parts of me still believe this? (Once you have written down your answer to this last question, you might want to revisit the meditation at the end of chapter 2 to help you call forth these parts of your psyche and re-educate them.)
7. What scares me about living in our current world?
8. What tends to scare me about change?

PART TWO

Reclaiming and Living in Expanded Sacred Connection

5

Sacred Geometry and Other Light Languages

As we are reclaiming ancient wisdom and tools that link us to our higher-dimensional abilities, we become more able to connect to our star ancestors and other higher-dimensional guides. They offer us a direct way to access these abilities by downloading us with information and helping us remember the wisdom that has lain dormant in our cells. They currently can get closer to us because of the photonic light codes blasting our planet that help us energetically align with them. Their guidance connects us more strongly with our fifth- and sixth-dimensional frequencies and provides support for us to carry out our sacred mission.

Remember the fifth dimension connects us with our creativity and our higher-dimensional visions, the sixth dimension holds the manifesting magic for us in sacred geometric patterns. We can see these patterns because they show up in numerous objects in 3D, all variations created from the five Platonic solids (see fig. 2.3). The energy and qualities held in these patterns travel via our thought forms between the third and sixth dimensions. These thought forms also get transmitted through higher-frequency sound. Even though sacred sound is a primary quality of 7D, it creates unique energy patterns in 6D that directly connect with our creative and manifesting abilities.

Sight, Sound, and Sentience

As we evolve, there will continue to be new and ancient ways uncovered to increase our access to the meaning held in individual frequencies; however, what we have most available to us now is through sacred geometry and verbal forms of light language that vibrate primarily through our visual and auditory senses. When we add the feelings that these invoke in us, ultimately, as we use them as our inner compass, we increase our fifth- and sixth-dimensional abilities even more.

There are still Indigenous cultures around the globe who have kept much of their connection to their 5D/6D frequencies. Learning more about them lets us know more about the gifts we will be able to reclaim as more of our star DNA lights up.

According to Credo Mutwa, an African *sangoma* (shaman) who himself was part Bushman:

> The Bushmen people of Africa have eyesight so keen they can see the mountains of the moon, and hearing so sharp they can detect the sound that heavenly bodies make in their movement around the Sun.[1]

He goes on to note that we possess twelve senses, most of which have been deadened by patriarchal cultures that have disconnected themselves from the natural world. These senses include the ability to influence not only animals but inanimate objects as well.[2]

Mutwa, who just recently passed, had a mission to share the sacred wisdom of his people with the world, and by doing this, he broke from their traditional rules and left himself vulnerable to their anger. For centuries it had not been safe to share tribal information and wisdom with outsiders. But he was aware that the time we are in now is different, and he had the courage to follow his own path.

Native American leader Sun Bear, an Ojibwe medicine man who was directed by his guides in the 1960s to share the native wisdom of his people with humans of all ethnicities,[3] dealt, too, with resistance that was similar, although not as intense, as Mutwa's. Because these men were willing to break the old rules and share tribal wisdom, they helped all who were open to validate our human potential and activate the fifth- and sixth-dimensional abilities needed to usher in this new golden age.

The Indigenous cultures who were able to keep those DNA strands open didn't need to know the details of sacred geometry or light language to access divine wisdom. They could use dance and drumming and no doubt many other forms of intuitive connection we may not know about. This is more Lemurian and more shamanic, although according to Thyme, the Lemurians did use sacred geometry for the placement of the structures in their communities as well as for the design of their energy stations and light temples.[4]

Atlanteans, being much more technologically oriented, used the specifics of sacred geometry more frequently and more visibly. At its evolutionary height, they mastered sacred architecture and created amazingly complex structures with higher-dimensional information radiating from these designs. Although I have no personal recollection, I feel that they incorporated light language into their culture as well, but at a higher development than we have access to right now.

Since everything in creation is energy, and all energy has vibratory patterning, to extract higher-dimensional wisdom from the energetic configurations of any higher-frequency sound, or what we call light language, we simply need to match its resonance with our own energy. According to J. J. Hurtak, in his book *The Book of Knowledge: The Keys of Enoch*, the auditory transmissions of light language that we currently know about, come most specifically through using a combination of sounds from five ancient languages.[5] He says these five ancient languages, Egyptian, Chinese, Tibetan, Sanskrit, and Hebrew, when combined, unlock higher-dimensional communication.

Enoch carefully instructed me to use these languages . . . Egyptian and Chinese to unify all the biochemical languages working horizontally in the human body. . . . Sanskrit and Tibetan fire letters to unify all the biochemical languages working vertically in the human body . . . Hebrew fire letters, sacred energy sounds, and thought forms of Light to connect with the intelligences of the Pleiades and Orion, unifying all crystalline languages of the third eye so as to open the template of the mind for the Eternal Light.[6]

I believe these five languages had their root in Atlantis and spread to various areas around the globe when Atlantis was permanently destroyed. In traveling through the sacred sites of Egypt, it became clear to me that the earliest hieroglyphs, which are visually the simplest, hold the highest-dimensional resonance. It also became clear to me that Judaism was an outgrowth of Egyptian spirituality but at a point in linear time when patriarchy was beginning to take hold. Hebrew letters probably developed from later Egyptian hieroglyphs that had become more complex as the civilization became more distant from its original 5D/6D roots, but the symbols in the letters still carried some of the resonance that connects us with Divine Mind. We can use wisdom from the vibrations of sacred geometry and sacred sound consciously now to aid us in opening our dormant DNA strands.

Connecting with Sacred Geometry

Sacred geometric configurations come from the sixth dimension. Their vibration exists in higher dimensions, but the energy form they take emanates from 6D. The five ancient languages above likely got their symbols, hieroglyphs, and letters directly from these geometric configurations.

You might want to go back to chapter 2 and look at the chart with the five Platonic Solids (fig. 2.3). According to Robert Gilbert, as taught in his Gaia series, *Sacred Geometry: Spiritual Science*, each of these contains packed thought forms of the Divine. (In other words, they are a direct link for us to cosmic wisdom.) He goes on to say they are manifestations of a cosmic language that higher-dimensional beings use to communicate with one another and with which we can learn to transmit and receive from as well.[7]

As simple as the Platonic solids might look, these sacred shapes are the building blocks of everything that manifests in the 3D world. Add the sphere that contains each of them, and all of what we experience as materiality emerges from these configurations and their correspondence with the phi ratio (Golden Mean) and the Fibonacci spiral, which provide the mathematical consistency of how these patterns move through space.

Although I don't claim to understand the mathematics here, what I do understand is that the resonance of numeric configurations also connects us to higher-dimensional wisdom and that the phi ratio and Fibonacci spiral connect us to infinity, because the numbers themselves can grow infinitely larger and infinitely smaller, which is another way of accessing the wisdom of the Divine. The Golden Mean or phi ratio and the correspondence of the Fibonacci spiral are all contained within the shapes of the Platonic solids.

My experience so far is to allow myself to feel into this all intuitively. I do not have any direct translation for what these forms evoke, but the more I connect with sacred geometry and all the configurations that arise from it, the more my body and my heart begin to respond. I can feel an opening and an activation and do believe this is directly lighting up some of my dormant star DNA. This is not something that our left brains know how to process linearly yet, but as I learn more about the mechanics of sacred geometry, the greater my sense of awe. Everything that we perceive in the universe comes from these five shapes and the mathematical correspondences within them.

This includes us. Our ka body, the energetic blueprint of our unique soul, is made up of the energetic configurations of these shapes. They are in our physical bodies as well and can be found throughout the natural world if you understand what you're looking for.

Each of the five Platonic solids corresponds to an element: The cube, also called the hexahedron, is Earth; the tetrahedron is fire; the icosahedron is water; the octahedron, air; and the dodecahedron, the most sacred of all, is aether or spirit.

The dodecahedron is so powerful that the ancients kept it secret from most of the populace. It was only to be used by initiates of certain mystery schools. It is said to connect to our life force and higher knowledge. "The Dodecahedron opens us to the potency of all the elements that material reality is made of, helping us raise not only our vibration but also the vibration of the space we reside in."[8]

If you pay attention, you will see these shapes all around you. Besides being everywhere in nature, they are also used in advertising, and consciously or unconsciously can be used to create fragmentation in an energy field including our collective energy field.

The more we are grounded and in a state of personal empowerment, the less impact this negative use will have on us. It may create some annoying static, but it will not throw us off our game so to speak. Control programs imposed from the outside only work if we are disconnected from our core essence.

When used in their integrity, these shapes and the frequencies they emit create a field of harmony and grace. They expand us and activate our higher consciousness. This is why ancient 5D civilizations not only laid out their communities in sacred geometric alignment, they built their structures to emit these energies as well.

As I was writing the last sentence, I realized that when I went to type the word *sacred*, I had instead typed *scared*. The alphabetic closeness in English of these words is interesting. When our reality is fragmented, it throws us into fear. Fear, unchecked, is a powerful emotion that can cause great harm both to the individual feeling it and their response to that feeling, which affects others around them. A scared populace is easily manipulated by anyone who claims to have the authority to save them, to make them safer. This is how Hitler worked, and this is how all authoritarian leaders come to power.

Because of the way that males have been generally conditioned in our society, many are unconsciously trained to get angry or to project anger when they experience fear instead of acknowledging being scared. They are trained to believe that being afraid is being weak. Thus, a scared populace will include men who express their fear through anger and violence. I don't mean to exclude women here, or others with different gender identification, but given the culture, this response is most common with men.

When a society is out of balance, it will either go to the extreme of male energy (yang) or female energy (yin). Patriarchy is, by definition, an imbalance of too much yang, too much masculine energy, not balanced with the feminine. Intuition, compassion, unity consciousness, and spiritual connection, which come through the feminine, become less accessible, and as I've said before, this creates a lot of insecurity, especially in men, and this insecurity then gets played out on the Earth stage as dominance and control. Goddess energy and therefore the sacred feminine went underground under patriarchy, and without this energy, the sacred masculine energies were not supported and therefore could not show up in our world; instead both male and female polarities show up in their immature forms. Nazism is an extreme form of this patriarchal imbalance, as are any tyrannical authoritarian systems. Violence becomes the primary means of control, although in our more technological societies, disinformation is used as a more subtle but equally powerful force, as well as the manipulation of sacred symbols. As we reclaim balance in our evolutionary journey, we are reclaiming our connection to both the sacred masculine and sacred feminine. This balance activates a level of empowerment that no longer leaves us open to control.

Imbalance caused by an extreme amount of female energy unsupported by healthy male energy creates chaos and paralysis. The healthy feminine holds the visions, but those visions cannot show up in creation without the structure of the healthy masculine.

The four elements represented by four of the Platonic solids divide equally into male and female energy, so in sacred geometry, the cube and the icosahedron are feminine, and tetrahedron and octahedron are masculine. The fifth element, represented by the dodecahedron is both, and thus would generate its own power.

To create a harmonious, loving world, we need to reclaim the balance between the sacred masculine and the sacred feminine. Then, I suspect, the power of the dodecahedron would only be used for positive ends.

Balancing the Dualities Within Us

Because of the reciprocal relationship between 3D and 6D, if my inner male and inner female are out of balance, this creates energy configurations in 6D that, in turn, can amplify the imbalance in 3D. If this imbalance is true for large numbers of people, which it currently is, the collective imbalance intensifies. Conversely, as more of us regain the inner balance of these two polar energies, the harmonious energetic configuration in 6D is strengthened, so more harmony shows up in 3D. All that to say creating New Earth is an inside job, and balancing our inner polar energies is part of this. The more of us who engage in this process, the sooner this will manifest in our physical world.

Our internal imbalance can show up in our lives in various ways. Too much unhealthy feminine energy will get us swirling in our emotions. We will have little access to any objective perspective. Distortions will occur that will show up most prominently in relationships, and we will be stuck in victim consciousness. In its extreme, it leads to insanity.

If we have too much unhealthy male energy, we will be unable to connect with our essence, we'll feel disconnected from ourselves, other people, and all of creation. This disconnection leads to seeking power and control of all those around us. In turn, this can lead to cruelty and violence to help us feel externally powerful and therefore safe.

Even healthy feminine energy, if not balanced by healthy male energy, interferes with our well-being. We may be wise and tuned in to universal truths, but without the support of the healthy masculine, we will be unable to use this effectively in the world. We may have great visions, but they will not manifest in the physical. It is the healthy masculine that provides us with the ability to act and to create as well as providing us with boundaries and protection.

Healthy masculine energy not balanced with healthy feminine energy is the classic workaholic dynamic. We will get things done, lots of things, but we will have little, if any, emotional and spiritual connection.

Shakti Gawain in her book *Living in the Light* gives a wonderful example of a healthy relationship between the inner male and female. She says:

> To fully integrate the inner male and female, you need to put the female in the guiding position.... She is ... the door to your higher intelligence.
>
> The nature of the feminine is wisdom, love and clear vision.... The male nature is all out risk-taking action in service to the feminine, much like the chivalrous knight and his lady.
>
> Through his surrender to her and his action on her behalf, our male energy builds a personality structure within us that protects and honors the sensitive energy of our intuitive female.[9]

This is not about gender. No matter what your gender, transforming unhealthy male and female energy within to reclaim the inner balance of both these polarities is important for our personal well-being, as well as for the health of the collective.

The yin/yang symbol gives us a beautiful visual representation of this balance. It expresses the wisdom of polarity when it's in harmony. Light and dark are also implicit here in this symbol. The Middle Way philosophy of Buddhism guides humanity to reclaim balance. It is the healthy response to our current polarization, and in practice asks us to expand our energetic container to hold all views and all ways in neutrality. This does not mean we condone doing any kind of harm, but we simply understand that the light without the shadow is only part of creation. The shadow does harm when it is unintegrated with the light, and the light in its own way does harm when it is unintegrated with the shadow because it is disconnected from the natural cycle. This causes people to bypass their darker thoughts and emotions that, left untended, get projected onto others or create illness for themselves.

When we are heart-centered and therefore activating our 5D frequency, stepping into loving neutrality, which I write more about in chapter 8, can be done with ease. We naturally honor how we are all interconnected. We release the energy of judgment and can feel compassion for all, no matter what their views, even no matter what their behavior. Again, this is never about condoning harm of any kind. It is about understanding from the depths of our being that we are all one, and when part of us is acting out, it reflects the imbalance in collective consciousness.

Once enough of us attain a balanced inner state, we will ultimately get rid of doing harm to one another or to any part of creation. As always, keep in mind that we are in transition, and we will find ourselves running judgments and opinions. All that is needed to neutralize any energy that could do external or internal harm is for us to observe it within ourselves, send it love, and allow our compassion to expand.

Other Forms of Light Language

My friend Eva Marquez teaches a wonderful course on light language and how it connects to our chakras. She details this system in her latest book: *Embodying Our Cosmic DNA*. Eva has been speaking light language for a few decades, beginning with just allowing the energy of it to come forth without concern of how it might translate, but the more she works with it, the more she understands the content of it as well.

In some ways, I'm a newbie to light language, but in other ways not. I was at a Halloween party in the 1970s dressed as a priestess and accompanied by my two best friends at the time who were also dressed as priestesses. We told everyone we were from the blue star planet . . .

and the man I was dating face-painted blue stars on each of our third eyes. I decided it would be fun to not speak English and found myself spouting a lyrical language and having very interesting "conversations" with fellow partyers. (We were all part of an alternative community in Springfield, Illinois.) There were a few people who were able to respond in a similar language, one of whom is my current husband of forty-plus years. He and I had a great conversation speaking this way.

Around ten years ago, when I first heard about people speaking light languages, I went back in my memory to that night. Although I had very little context for it, I knew intuitively this was what I was speaking. By this time both my husband and I knew that our souls originated on the Pleiades. The spiritual community we currently lived in was also doing a lot of rituals incorporating the blue star. (Although the blue star was not exclusively connected to the Pleiades, just to the Great Star Nations in general.) The synchronicities of that party so many years later began to take on a whole new life.

Fast forward to now, and I can still speak the lyrical sounds of that language. I understand that the content of the sounds of light language is not the essence of the communication. Rather the energy produced by the sound is. These sounds open a portal to higher consciousness where we can communicate with higher-consciousness beings. The frequency of these sounds opens us to feeling them; we absorb and connect with their energy as we create the sounds of this cosmic language.

For linear thinkers who rely on the logic of the left brain, this is a difficult concept to understand and accept. We are asked here to suspend disbelief and allow the intelligence of our heart to lead us. Auditory light language opens the heart and communicates from the energy of love. It brings comfort and harmony and opens us to realities that can't at this point be processed through our left (logical) brains.

From the perspective of the nine-dimensional axis, we are utilizing the vibration of the sacred sound of the seventh dimension to create energetic geometric configurations in 6D. I've mentioned Emoto's water crystal experiments before, which provides a clear example of how this works. Cymatics shows us a similar outcome when it uses sound to create patterns with sand on an electromagnetic plate.

"In the beginning was the word" is the phrase that contains the ancient wisdom that all of 3D creation was originally produced by resonance. You might want to go over the information about the 9D vertical axis in chapter 2 to help you connect with how the dimensions work together.

Fragmentation vs. Harmonization

When one walks into a room filled with fear, tension, and animosity before even knowing consciously what is going on, we will feel it and no doubt want to turn right around and head in the other direction. When we enter a room filled with love and calmness, we sense this as well and, of course, want to stay. Energy is palpable and the more we have activated our 5D frequency, the more tuned in we are.

Chaotic energy is swirling around in the collective now, which in turn can create chaotic energy within us. Chaotic energy is swirling within us as well, created from our fears and resistance to stepping into this next level of our evolution, while simultaneously seeking the creation of a loving, harmonious, and just world. Individual chaos is strengthening the outer chaos. Learning to recognize this energy and having strategies to not allow it to have power over us is an essential practice as we actively participate in our evolution. Remember that no matter if there is conscious orchestration to create this chaos, we are all interconnected, and therefore we all participate in creating this mess and all the suffering that comes with it. This is why planetary transformation is ultimately an inside job.

The current fragmentation of consensus reality makes this even more challenging, but as I've stated before, we are all up to this challenge. More and more of humanity is waking up, activating our dormant DNA strands, and learning to hold more of the energy of higher-frequency love.

Part of the positive intent of sacred geometric patterns is to emit the energy of harmony and balance. The mathematical alignments contained within them connect us to universal order and universal wisdom. It is in the sixth dimension that these frequencies take shape. And it is from here we create what manifests in our 3D world.

If we use these images to manipulate and fragment what we are manifesting here, we are disrupting energy patterns that could manifest harmony and grace throughout our world. If enough of us hold a conscious intent to not get sucked into their misuse and instead meditate on these sacred images themselves, allowing their energy to permeate our cells, we feed the collective with love and unity consciousness, which in turn supports a shift in both our personal and collective world.

Lightening Up

The large quantities of light codes now coming onto our planet are contained in photons that are filled with cosmic information being transmitted from the central suns of our galaxy. Somewhere I read that the star Cygnus, which is seen as a black hole at the center of the Cygnus galaxy,[10] is the primary or great central sun in an intricate structure of central suns, which is like a galactic neural system. Although I can no longer find the source that talked about Cygnus in this way, I'm including this information in this book because intuitively it feels accurate to me. Cygnus sends its solar messages to the Sirius central sun, which sends them to Alcyone, which is our central sun and the brightest star in the Pleiades. Alcyone communicates directly with our sun, Sol. According to Hand Clow, those in the Sirius star system are the keepers of 6D, while Pleiadians are keepers of 5D, and those of us on Earth are keepers of 3D, so this gives you an idea of how the cosmos holds and transmits its information down the vertical axis through the central suns.

The universe is a remarkably ordered and interconnected system where all parts are created to be in communication with each other.

The more we reconnect with unity consciousness, the more we own our innate Oneness with all that is, the clearer this becomes for us.

Cygnus holds the point of a singularity, which is a concept from physics. Scientists concluded Cygnus was holding a singularity because of it being so compact and yet emanating amazing power. They have found that the only thing this small that can emit this level of power is a singularity.[11] All creation as we know it emerges from a singularity.[12] According to Robert Gilbert in his *Sacred Geometry* series on Gaia, it is a portal for the divine mind—a container for all that is, and it also exists within us. Although it is beyond the scope of this book to explain the details of this, just realize that the singularity within us is a fractal of the singularity of Cygnus, which may well be a fractal of an even grander central sun. Because we are holographic and live in a holographic universe, we always hold the cosmos in a microcosmic state inside. So, the important point here is to know that there are portals inside us that hold the consciousness of all that is.

The light codes that our sun has received from the galactic system of central suns are also being absorbed into the heart of the Earth, and so she, too, is emitting them to us. I believe there is a point of singularity at her core as well, which is at the center of the first dimension. Credo Mutwa talks about a huge golden pyramid in the crystal iron core of the planet. I see the point of singularity at the center of this pyramid.

Recently I learned from Caroline Oceana Ryan of golden pyramids that are in the center of our sun, and thus I assume, as well, in all the central suns. This information resonates so strongly for me that I feel it needs to be included here.

Below Ryan speaks of this information that she received in meditation journeys for a webinar she offers. Be aware, though, that in addition to being aligned with the golden pyramids in our sun, the Great Pyramids in Giza are also in alignment with the stars in Orion's belt. This does not negate Ryan's information but rather suggests to me that those stars may well have informed the placement of the golden pyramids in our sun.

> In the open center of our Sun Sol . . . we found there the three Golden Pyramids on which the three Great Pyramids of Giza are based.
>
> These pyramids are full of the Divine Golden Light particles—the Gold Frequencies in action. . . .
>
> This Light form is shifting the sacred geometric nature of our human DNA codes, upgrading them so we can return to the 12-strand DNA of higher consciousness.[13]

These pyramids that I sense must also hold points of singularity within them are all communicating with each other. The golden pyramid at the core of the Earth can then transmit this energy to us as well, so we are not only receiving light codes from the neuro-network of all the central suns but also from the heart of our planet.

Physiologically these light codes provide us with the opportunity to hold more higher-dimensional light in our cells, to become quite literally enlightened, which is the underlying process going on for us in our ascension journey. The more we absorb this light, the more of our dormant DNA strands become activated.

Our body, like the universe, is a miraculous system, and our mind allows us to consciously work with this system. The further along we journey in our ascension process, the more skilled we become at doing this.

Richard Rudd in *Gene Keys* explains how it is light that ultimately transforms our DNA.

> Research into DNA has demonstrated that one of its more unusual electromagnetic properties is its ability to attract photons (elementary light particles), causing them to spiral around the double helix. It is this ability of DNA to weave light around itself that reveals its true hidden role in your body—to act as a superconductor whose sole purpose is to increase the frequency passing in and out of your body.[14]

The meditation entitled "Activating Your 5D Light Codes" (found on my YouTube channel, Wisdom Within Us) helps you consciously experience absorbing these light codes.

While right now human life in and of itself is filled with challenges, some of the emotional overwhelm that people currently feel is also connected to the bombardment of these light codes that are coming from the photons hitting our planet. Even though the codes hold wonderful energy, the intensity and the collective lack of information about what is going on, in addition to the climate crisis, wars, famine, and systems of oppression, threaten to and in many cases create even more chaos and imbalance. To stay in a peaceful state while this is occurring, we need to understand what's happening and have ways to ground ourselves and keep connected to our inner core.

We need to commit to staying as peaceful as possible and to absorb these light codes without throwing ourselves off-balance. I'll give more suggestions in the next section, but for now just realize that we can stay in charge of this process, to slow it down and speed it up as needed.

Lightening up also means keeping our sense of humor. It means reminding ourselves of the great cosmic joke of being in a human body on a planet still somewhat stuck in 3D while simultaneously doing our best to raise our frequency and the collective frequency. It means appreciating the slapstick of bumbling through daily life. It means keeping a loving, higher, and even somewhat amused perspective of it all while watching the Earth Show with all its current insanity. I find, too, that my guides have a hilarious sense of humor and on occasion will create comic scenes that lighten me up, lest I get too serious or attached to some silly inner story. Perhaps yours will do that as well.

Strategies for an Easier Journey

You might want to take a moment now to just breathe in the awareness that you are absorbing cosmic light simply by being in your body and on our planet at this point in Earth's cycle. You may notice that your cells are vibrating more quickly than you are used to. If you can surrender to this feeling, it becomes more and more pleasant, like a cosmic massage. Your heart becomes more open, and your bandwidth of perception expands. When you find yourself resisting this, you are likely to feel anxious and stressed. This can be experienced as being overwhelmed and overloaded, and you may find yourself immobilized or conversely reactive and angry.

Using the breath to move into a deeper state of relaxation as well as observing where you are holding tension can help you move into the energy of surrender. It's really a surrendering of the ego, which of course does not want you to do this. When you find areas of tension, do your best to breathe into these areas. If that doesn't create enough release, then journal or use other ways to look at what the tension represents, paying attention ultimately to what the fear is that underlies it. A note of realism yet again; remember this is an ongoing process. Every time we expand energetically, our ego gets scared and often we will tighten up rather than lighten up. That's okay. Each moment of surrender brings us closer to being able to hold higher-dimensional energy for longer periods of time.

The reactivation of our star DNA is contributing to the collective chaos for several reasons. To start with, as I said above, many are not aware of this process and don't have any strategies to effectively maneuver through this. And then, most humans have been disconnected from their bodies and are therefore ungrounded and thus easily thrown more out of balance. Those of you reading this are already ahead of the curve because you have an understanding of what is happening. Give yourself credit for this, and remember we are in the advanced curriculum at Earth school, so go easy on yourself. You don't need to ace every course, just do your best.

Meditating on sacred geometric images, such as Metatron's Cube or even one of the Platonic solids, helps calm the nervous system. The meditation at the end of this chapter will give you this experience. Listening to forms of light language can as well. Eva Marquez has some great examples of this on her YouTube station of the same name. I would recommend this one filled with healing energy, "Healing Transmission with the Language of Light" (found on Eva's YouTube channel, Eva Marquez). These are all gifts from our sixth-dimensional consciousness.

There is an upside to this collective chaos. If we let it, it can shake us out of old beliefs, especially beliefs that there is only one way to see things. The more we allow ourselves to release any rigid belief and instead observe our lives and life on this planet with curiosity, the more we can live in times of great change without getting stuck in the fear it can produce.

✳ MEDITATION ✳

Messages from Metatron's Cube

Fig. 5.1. Metatron's Cube

Note: This meditation is best done from the one on my YouTube channel (see page 146) where you can listen while looking at the cube.

Spend three to five minutes staring at the image of Metatron's Cube. You might want to set a soft timer. Notice if you can see the five Platonic solids within the cube. Notice how the image morphs as different shapes come into the forefront of your vision.

Now take several deep centering breaths and allow your eyes to soften. As you exhale release any distractions, any concerns, any tensions. Just let that all flow out with the breath. On the inhale imagine that you are drawing in tiny golden spirals of light filled with love and consciousness and allow those tiny spirals to spread to every cell in your body. Keep focusing on your breath as you begin to feel a sense of calm and relaxation spread throughout your body.

Envision yourself sitting in a comfortable chair in a sunlit room with white walls. On the wall in front of you hangs the image of Metatron's Cube. With your eyes slightly open, focus on the cube. You begin to feel its energy permeate all your cells. Notice any sensations that arise.

Breathe deeply a few more times, sinking into the comfort of the chair and the beauty of the room. Perhaps there are fresh flowers in a vase on a table near you. Breathe in their fragrance. Hear soft uplifting music playing in the background.

Now breathe the energy of Metatron's Cube into your heart. Let it sit there for a while and allow yourself to feel its angelic vibration. Then slowly allow that vibration to rise inside your body until it comes to your third eye. As you feel the energy in this chakra, ask Metatron to send you a message. It might come in the form of a vision or an auditory phrase or simply a feeling. Spend a moment or two just paying attention. Then as you are ready, slowly bring your awareness back into the room you are reading this in.

Breathe deeply, bringing yourself into a more focused state, and after taking some time to ponder the message, journal on it and what you believe it means for you.

Note: Find this meditation on my YouTube channel, Wisdom Within Us, in the "Meditations to Raise Your Frequency" playlist.

Journal Questions to Ponder

1. Are you aware of your spirit guides? At what point did you become aware that there are guides available to help you on your journey? What kind of relationship do you have with these guides? If you are not aware of them, are you open to them showing up in your life? Why or why not?

2. Do you have any memories or images of what the ancient societies of Atlantis and Lemuria might have been like? If so, write about them.
3. Is there still a need for you to heal your inner male and inner female, both separately and with how they relate to each other? If so, what kind of healing do you envision?
4. How do you handle the chaotic energy of the outside world? How do you handle any internal chaos?
5. What role does humor play in your life? If you find yourself getting too serious, do you have strategies to lighten up? Write a bit about them.
6. What changes have you been through in recent years that suggest you are absorbing more light codes and opening some of your previously dormant DNA strands?

6

Sacred Architecture, Sacred Sites, and the Frequency of Our Structures

Most, if not all, of you reading this are familiar with feng shui. Its purpose is to bring harmony to the energy in our homes so the chi, which is life force energy, flows through our living space in a way that supports our well-being. We want it to travel at its highest frequency to bring us good fortune in relationships, prosperity, health, and so on. Although, of course, this does not replace doing our inner healing and inner rebalancing, energetic alignment in our personal space opens energy portals that may otherwise be more difficult to access.

When you walk into a home that has the chi moving harmoniously, it feels open, spacious, light, loving, and ideally inspiring. Imagine then what it would be like to live in a community, a village, or a town where all the structures are designed and aligned to emit these higher-frequency harmonious energies. Everywhere you go, you get a sense of love, support, and creativity. Breathe into this idea for a moment and notice what feelings this evokes.

As we evolve, as we fashion our world from our fifth- and sixth-dimensional frequencies, we will create this. While our old world is dying and the old paradigm of suffering and discord begins to recede, something new and wonderful is waiting to be born. We will collectively be creating an updated version of the ancient sacred architecture we brought originally from the Great Star Nations. And because we have learned much through the pain of our dimensional descent, we may well find, as we reclaim our true abilities, that our updated version vibrates at frequencies never before experienced on this planet.

Ancestral Architecture

The laws underpinning sacred geometry were used on Earth by the Lemurians, then later by the Atlanteans and the very ancient Egyptians. They were used in Stonehenge as well as many sacred sites in Mexico and Asia,[1] and no doubt many other places around the planet. Hand Clow says, "From the ancient Egyptians to the Classical Greeks, geometry was part of the search for truth, a way to order the Universe." She had a vision at the Acropolis that anchored this awareness into her consciousness.[2] Even biblically there is an awareness that the Kingdom of Heaven can be recreated on the Earth through the creation of the heavenly city, which is a city designed from the laws of sacred geometry.[3]

When we align energetically with the harmonious geometric patterns that reside in 6D, we can draw them down into 3D manifestation. Part of the way we can do this collectively is to create structures using the mathematical precision of this geometry to hold these higher frequencies. Although the examples of these structures that we currently see around the world are denser than what existed in Lemuria and Atlantis, they are still emitting higher-dimensional frequencies that connect us to their energetic blueprint in 6D and ultimately to the energy of the Divine.

While my brain rebels as I read the details of the number sequences and ratios involved in all this, what remains is a deep understanding that there are universal numbers and numerical patterns. They come from the source of divine intelligence and can be used to create a physical environment that elicits harmony and well-being. When used consciously to construct physical space in terms of proportion, area, and alignment within and between each part of the structure, and when the structure itself is created in alignment with the land it is sitting on, these numbers connect us to universal energies and thus to divine intelligence itself. From a simpler perspective, they help us pull down celestial wisdom and anchor it so that when we are in the presence of these structures, we can absorb this intelligence and bring it into our cells. Thus, the numerical correspondences are activators of higher-dimensional consciousness. The structures based on these correspondences become a microcosm—a tiny replica of the higher-dimensional macrocosm, the fully expanded bandwidth of creation.

We know through Plato's writings that he was directly influenced by the ancient Egyptians and understood Atlantis to be a literal place whose wisdom was transmitted to the Egyptians through Thoth (as told in the Emerald Tablets). Thus, he provides us with a relatively recent, Western-world example of how higher-dimensional star civilizations brought their understanding of cosmic universals to our planet, and how using the cosmic universality of proportion and numbers creates harmony. The East also used sacred mathematics and symmetry for the construction of their temples and holy places.[4] Even with a slightly different mathematical system, there are enough universal correspondences to support this cosmic language.

Much of this wisdom has been lost over at least the last two thousand years or so in the West. Although the Renaissance popped it back into our Western timeline for a while, much of this ancient understanding of universal harmony and beauty based on sacred mathematics has been largely ignored in terms of how we create our environment. Many of the great European cathedrals were based on the old tradition, but most of our other structures seem haphazard or even disharmonious, which reflects the state of mass culture.

As we move through this current evolutionary leap, these ancient harmonies will ultimately become commonplace. And the more we can envision this, the more it will begin to show up in the material world.

Imagine for a moment how it would feel to live in a home that is not only harmonious in terms of its inner space but constructed on the land using sacred mathematics that naturally connects it to higher celestial influences. You might get a picture of this in your mind's eye or a feeling about it in your body. Breathe into it. Then imagine walking outside and down your road where everything emits this frequency. Let that sink into your cells for a moment.

Think now of being in the central area of a city or village where all the structures have been designed this way. The energy is uplifting wherever you turn and wherever you look. You can begin to feel this enter all your cells. Perhaps it brings a smile to your face and a softening in your heart.

I don't think this ultimately needs to be done in a left-brain way where everything is measured. We are intuitively drawn to beauty and harmony. If we have done our inner work, if we are living more and more from our 5D/6D frequency, much of the sacred design will occur effortlessly. This uplifting feeling will continually activate our hearts, so we move through our village or city holding love and gratitude for all. Bringing heaven to Earth is ultimately about bringing the wisdom and consciousness of advanced star nations where many of us have resided, and experienced this connection to divine consciousness. Reconnecting with this now can help us heal and hold these healed frequencies here.

I went to a high school that, according to local legend, was originally a prison. The teachers and administrators in my recollection held a pretty positive energy for the most part (this was in the early 1960s, and the public high schools in my city were divided up in such a way that the one I attended was a college prep school, so students were relatively serious about learning from the start and disciplinary issues were minimal). Still, its shape and structure lacked harmony, symmetry, and inspiration. Imagine if instead of being rectangular with long hallways, it was shaped in a way that pulled in loving, higher-consciousness energy. Perhaps it would have a round structure with an open courtyard in the center, and class areas coming out from there like spokes on a wheel, with their design in total alignment with higher frequencies. Students, teachers, and administrators alike would all have been inspired to be creative thinkers, to create art and beauty all around us, to create an environment where the energies encouraged and supported everyone to be their best selves.

As we transition out of the denseness of 3D and begin to manifest higher frequencies through the structures we create, we help more and more people awaken. Imagine if all schools were designed or redesigned with this understanding. Imagine if this was true for all hospitals, all public buildings, and even prisons where this is no doubt needed the most, if we truly want to rehabilitate people. (Note: there would be no need for prisons in a 5D/6D society once the transition is complete.) As more and more people awaken, what we create collectively will change to reflect this consciousness.

Environments and People

Who we are is reflected in our environment, and the environments we create reflect who we are. If we are feeling chaotic, we are likely to create a chaotic outer experience. If our environment, especially our home, is chaotic, it reflects some disharmony inside us.

As our frequency rises, as we hold the vibration of the fifth and sixth dimensions, we will find that we have no tolerance for outer chaos. Clutter and messiness throw us off our game. This is not a judgment. It's an awareness of how energy moves. We don't have to be perfectly organized, only attuned to the understanding that all physical forms and their relationship to each other emit frequencies. Clutter and disarray confuse the energy around us. Instead of opening channels of ease and harmony, energy gets stuck and obstructed. Clearing the clutter and straightening the disarray opens these channels.

How we use color is also an important piece of creating a positive environment. There are calming colors, and there are activating colors. There are colors that open our hearts. I recently saw a sunrise over the ocean that was so stunning it took my breath away. The physical beauty and intensity of the colors bathed the waters and the land surrounding them with such beauty as to crack one's heart wide open.

Take a moment and survey your environment. How does it feel to you? Do you get a sense of upliftment or is there some heaviness? Is there a symmetry and order to the objects that surround you? If so, notice how this feels for you on a cellular level. If not, take a moment to ponder what might need to shift to create an uplifting feeling.

Then notice where your living space is located. What do you see when you look out your windows? We all deserve to live in natural beauty. Those in rural areas are surrounded by it. The suburbs tend to have less but still will have yards and trees and hopefully sky views. But perhaps you live in a congested area in a city. You look out your window, and there's only the view of another building or a rundown street. Buy a small house plant and place it on or close to the windowsill. Hang representations of stars or spirals or flowers in front of the window. Hang Tibetan prayer flags. Bring in shells and rocks that speak to you. There are always simple ways available to shift the energy around us, and I strongly encourage you to do this.

Imagine if all structures on our planet aligned with the natural laws of harmony. Imagine if everywhere you looked emitted an uplifting energy. Imagine the effects it would have on everyone living on Earth. Imagine a future timeline where this already exists.

We all have a right to live in harmony, and as the energies of the evolutionary process strengthen on our planet, we will find ourselves creating this sense of harmony everywhere. Of course, this is a slow transition in 3D. We have high-rises, we have high-density populations needing a lot of housing in small areas. But there are always solutions. If collectively we understand how environments affect us and together commit to creating this wherever we find ourselves, this supports a profound planetary transition.

Our use of chemicals and toxins in general also needs to be addressed. So much of our food is grown with chemicals. Chemicals are used to beautify our yards, to keep insects out of our homes. They are used in everyday home products, even simple things like laundry detergents where so many have been convinced to use fragrances in addition to the chemicals that may be added to the soap. It is no wonder we have such a high amount of cancer diagnoses. Our bodies are not designed for this. Think, too, about what all these chemicals and toxins do to our collective energy field.

Planet Earth is our home, yet we have continued to disrespect her, and quite literally trash her by believing we continually need new and more products. Then we dump the old things without an awareness of what this does to our world. Capitalism is fueled by planned obsolescence and convincing people through advertising that they will be happier if they have the latest fashion, the latest tech upgrade, the latest appliance. As more of us become conscious of the collective ramifications of this, we begin to look at purchases with more consciousness and refuse to fall prey to the ads that promise happiness and well-being when this can only truly be delivered by our inner work and spiritual connection.

As we tune into our environment with more awareness, we will also see that the noise level created by machinery needs to be addressed as well. Nature produces a multitude of sounds: birds singing and cawing, waves crashing on the shore, dogs barking, wind, and rain. But these are sounds of the natural world, and although some of them may be disturbing, they are not designed to negatively impact our frequency. Modern world sounds are different, and even though we believe they serve a positive function, like sirens for example, the beeping of vehicles backing up, weedwhackers, leaf blowers, lawn mowers, construction noises, horns honking, alarms beeping, helicopters, jets, planes, even our appliances—all these mechanical sounds jangle our nerves and can thus threaten to disconnect us from a sense of inner peace. As we evolve, I believe we will find new and quieter ways to carry out things that may be important for our safety, and we will only use that which is in balance with the natural world.

Necessity of Beauty

When we are surrounded by beauty, we have a reflexive response. It feels peaceful and relaxing. We feel surrounded by an energy of well-being. What the ancients knew, and what artists like Leonardo da Vinci knew, is that there is an objective, mathematically measurable structure to beauty, whether it is in the waves of the ocean, the petals of a flower, or the human face and body.

Aristotle and many of the Greek philosophers understood this as well. In his *Metaphysics*, Aristotle said, "The chief forms of beauty are order and symmetry and definiteness, which the mathematical sciences demonstrate in a special degree."[5] He was referring to the golden mean or phi ratio, the foundational mathematical sequence in sacred geometry. It provides us with a set of proportions found in nature, and when applied to all manner of visual culture, it thus can be seen as a beauty formula.

These values were how the ancient Greeks built their world: from the mathematical proportion of their architecture to the way they composed the twisting bodies of discus throwers in sculpture. This kind of objective beauty, drawn with rulers and set squares, inspired artists of the Renaissance hundreds of years later in their buildings and paintings. Leonardo da Vinci, from his *Vitruvian Man* to his painting of *The Last Supper*, consistently used this ratio in all his art.

Although we may believe that our experience, and therefore assumption, of what is beautiful is connected just to our sense of sight, it runs much deeper than this. It is connected to how it makes us feel. There is a natural symmetry, a natural order that aligns with our soul. When we look at beauty, which is a visual representation of cosmic harmony, our hearts respond. We experience a lightness of being, even perhaps ecstasy, because it creates an energetic activation within us. It is the line from the Keats poem, *Ode on a Grecian Urn*: "Beauty is truth, and truth, beauty—That is all Ye know on Earth, and all ye need to know."[6] This type of beauty is universal. It is not based on culture, and it likely activates some of our star DNA.

Beauty is not just experienced through the art and architecture we can see. It can be experienced through all of the arts: through the harmonies of uplifting music, through poetry, through literature, and through the sounds of the natural world. Birdsong, the rhythm of the ocean, the lion's roar—these all provide us with this opportunity. We do, however, need to stay open to fully experience this. If we have been dulled to beauty, if we have been conditioned to shut down the senses within us that naturally respond to it, we will not notice and will not understand.

Much modern art intentionally evokes disturbing feelings to represent how far we have wandered from living in harmony. It is not beauty. It will not open our hearts or activate higher frequencies, but it does provide an important message to our intellects, and there is something intrinsic in its creativity that can help us open and expand our bandwidth, should we choose. However, I would not recommend hanging any disturbing art in one's home.

Modern jazz, which many people cannot relate to because it refuses to be linear, can have a fascinating energetic effect. It can take a familiar tune and expand it to an intense discordant sound that, if we allow ourselves to surrender to it, actually expands us and becomes harmonious, and then when it pops in the original tune, something within us will have been changed. So, while these art forms go beyond the overt symmetry of classical beauty, their unique creative expression can provide new pathways to open higher frequencies within us.

Sacred architecture, too, based on the proportions of sacred geometry, is designed to open our inner experience of higher-dimensional frequencies. It may end up looking quite a bit different from the magnificent structures that the ancients produced, but the inner effect will support us in new ways for living in a loving, spiritually based world.

To live without the inner experience that the external expression of beauty provides us is to live a life of constriction and dis-ease. As we refuse to participate in the restrictions of our dysfunctional culture, our creative energy expands and with it, our ability to stay more in our 5D/6D frequency.

Ancient Sacred Sites

There are numerous sacred sites around the globe, and more are being uncovered every day. Many of these sites still hold the frequency of advanced star civilizations. As we go through our own evolutionary process on our ascension journey, we become more and more able to read these frequencies and unlock the ancient wisdom that will help us transform life on our planet.

Visiting these sites and absorbing their energy can be deeply transformative. My personal experiences both in Egypt and on the Isle of Lewis in Scotland, where the famous Callanish Stone Circle is, as well as several not-as-well-known standing stones, were profound and spontaneously connected me with higher-dimensional realities.

The Giza complex near Cairo is well-known for the Great Pyramid, one of three large pyramids standing together, and for the Sphinx, which welcomes one into the complex. When I visited the three pyramids, I noticed they were placed in an odd relationship with one another. They are not in a line or spaced in what would seem to be a logical way. It was later I learned of the theory that they were aligned with the stars in Orion's belt, which finally made sense of what I noticed. Orion is another one of the Great Star Nations that is connecting with us now and helping to guide us through this transition. From Caroline Oceana Ryan's information (which I've written about in chapter 5), the pyramids also align with the three golden pyramids in the center of our sun.

Mainstream history says the Great Pyramids and Sphinx are around forty-five hundred years old. However, according to the Egyptologist who was part of the shamanic journey I took there in 2005, the Sphinx and the pyramids are at least 10,000–12,000 years old. The scientific erosion suggests it was built before Egypt was a desert ten thousand years ago.[7] Although the pyramids do not show signs of water erosion, it appears that they had an outer shell of white polished limestone that has disintegrated, so what we see now is the stone underneath the polished limestone exterior. None of this has been carbon-dated because at this point, the materials they are built of can't be.

Although we don't have 3D proof here, what resonates as true for me is that both the Sphinx and the pyramids were built shortly after Atlantis fell. This could also correspond to the biblical flood. According to the Emerald Tablets, Thoth went to Egypt during the destruction and brought the advanced Atlantean knowledge with him.[8]

Our Egyptologist also explained why the pyramids could not have been built from the prevailing low-tech theories that included using ramps, ropes, and pulleys. He said they were built using antigravitational rods to lift and set the stones. After hearing this, while visiting a temple far south of Giza, I noticed a hieroglyph of two men facing each other and holding rods under a huge stone that was hovering over the rods.

The assumption that these amazing pyramids were built as tombs never made sense to me. Although there may have been ceremonies upon leaders' deaths in the King's or Queen's chambers to reconnect the spirits of the deceased with their star families, which again would have been long before the practice of mummification, there is great mystery that surrounds these amazing structures. The more recent hypothesis that they were power plants makes slightly more sense, but I feel they were far more than this. There's also a theory that there's a landing pad for alien ships on top of the Great Pyramid. This gives it a direct connection to the Great Star Nations. I sense that higher-vibrational beings were able to get into what is called the King's and Queen's chambers energetically and radiated out higher-consciousness frequencies throughout the land like radio transmitters, but without audible sound. This helped the society maintain balance for its populace.

I realized as I was journeying through Egypt, which was before I learned about the 9D vertical axis and thus this form of our multidimensionality, that well before our mainstream history, the very ancient Egyptians were highly advanced beings who lived in what I now call a 5D/6D society. As the culture continued, there was an ongoing de-evolution that occurred until it ultimately fell apart altogether. Still these structures exist, as do many of the very ancient temples that still stand throughout the country, and they all give us some access to an advanced civilization that thrived for a while on our planet.

I also realize now that the ancient temples throughout Egypt were modeled after the temples from various star civilizations, especially the great temple on Alcyone in the Pleiades that Eva Marquez speaks about in her book *Activate Your Cosmic DNA*.[9] I have visited this temple in meditation and its grandeur is, well, otherworldly. It also houses areas of great healing and areas of great learning where teachers and students from many advanced star nations come to teach and learn, providing a grand university for our universe.

Although the Egyptian temples have been desecrated by invaders, especially Christians who defaced the images of the Goddesses, and of course have also deteriorated from the passing of time, they are still magnificent. When they were first built, their walls were coated in paints made of gemstones, all of which have faded by now, but the grand columns and porticos remain. One of the newest temples, the Temple of Hathor in the Dendera complex contains a zodiac, which our Egyptologist pointed out originally came from a much older temple because the position of the planets on it is based on a much earlier time. If I remember correctly, it came from around eleven thousand years ago.

My husband and I returned from our journey transformed by the energy of these ancient and powerful structures. There is no question that they are still emanating higher-frequency vibrations and, because we did a ceremony in them, their effect was intensified. We, on our planet, are very blessed to have access to these ancient emanations of higher consciousness.

Although being there in person certainly is the most direct and powerful way to absorb these frequencies, they will still come through even by meditating with photographs. If you are drawn to ancient sites that hold these higher vibrations, invite the frequencies into your life. The effect may be subtle at first, but it ultimately will contribute to expanding your perceptual bandwidth, which in turn helps you connect more deeply with the ancient wisdom you hold within you. Connecting with this wisdom is how we best navigate through the current shifting of our consensual reality.

My experience in Scotland with the standing stones was much less extensive than my experience in Egypt, but in many ways equally impactful. I arrived a few days before an astrology workshop I signed up for was taking place, and I went off with a few other students in their rental car to a single and less famous standing stone than the ones in the Callanish circle. It was rainy and cold, and when we arrived at the stone, I stood before it, and within seconds I realized that, despite how it looked and the material it was made of, it was not solid. I felt like I could walk into it, and I realized that it was a portal for other-dimensional beings from star nations to show up on our planet. This was such an immediate and intuitive awareness that it overwhelmed me. I returned to the car rather than continuing to stand in the rain and just allowed myself to feel into what had happened. After that, I managed to contract a cold that deadened my senses for the rest of the trip. It would be easy to blame it on the wind, rain, and chill of April in Northern Scotland, but I knew it was because I would not be able to absorb anything more after my experience with that stone. This was also before I knew about *Outlander*, yet in looking back, it seemed a place where walking through to another dimension would be perfectly possible.

These are just a few examples of clues I have experienced personally that have been left for us around the planet to tell us the real story of our origins and the nature of reality. The narrowly conditioned bandwidth that most scientists still operate from keeps much of our population uneducated about this story and therefore disconnected from their true potential.

Modern Sacred Sites

As people around the world are awakening and reconnecting with their star heritage and thus their higher-dimensional frequencies, new sacred sites are springing up everywhere. The energies of these sites connect to the light grid that currently surrounds the Earth and that the meditation in chapter 4 can help you experience. If viewed from outer space, the energies emitted from these new sites would likely look like an elaborate light show. They have been designed, whether consciously or unconsciously, to hold more of the photons that are being blasted onto the earth right now. These frequencies are then pulsed into the atmosphere. Where there is darkness, they shine into it, allowing us first more awareness as the darkness reveals itself, and then their energy begins to transform it.

There are two types of sacred sites being created right now, the first are being built by larger spiritual and educational communities, or in parks and other public lands. The others are by individuals on their residential land. The former tends to be visible and more grand, and perhaps some of them will remain for posterity, the latter smaller and more personalized.

The community I live in was created by Linda Star Wolf and her late husband Brad Collins. Shortly after my husband and I returned from Egypt and were guided to buy land here, Star Wolf's beloved teacher, Seneca Elder Grandma Twyla Niche, transitioned. The night she passed, she came to Star Wolf with instructions to create a Blue Star Medicine Wheel in an area on top of the mountain with a magnificent view. The Wheel was created, and around the same time, Star Wolf received a download from the Goddess Isis that she was to build elemental temples all around the land.

It became clear that the Blue Star Medicine Wheel and the land it was on held the energy of what would become the Spirit Temple. Next, the newly purchased land of Dove Mountain, adjacent to the original community that would ultimately house Star Wolf's institute, the

Venus Rising Association for Transformation, was selected for the four elemental temples. Figs. 6.1 and 6.2 are photos of two of the elemental temples.

The Earth Temple, shown in fig. 6.1, was created ceremonially with thirty-seven ancestral stones, each stone weighing 1000–2000 pounds. Wind Daughter, the Medicine Chief of the Panther Lodge and adopted daughter of Sun Bear, oversaw the placement of the rocks. A rock representing the Great Star Nations was added to the traditional medicine circle stones. She then led the ceremony to activate the temple, which many of us attended. Sacred ceremonies such as vision quests, rites of passage, weddings, and shamanic journeying with the ancestors and animal totems have since taken place here, and you can imagine the spiritual energy this temple emits.

Fig. 6.1. Earth Temple Medicine Wheel at Venus Rising Association of Transformation

The Fire Temple has on both sides of its entrance a dramatic wrought iron filigree structure where fire can be ignited from propane tanks. It has been used for numerous fire walks. A powerful community ceremony took place to activate it, with lots of drumming and chanting to call in this sacred element. As it turned out we ended up calling in more fire than we intended as a few weeks later, the community almost burned down due to a brush fire getting out of control. Luckily the ultimate damage was minimal, but we certainly got the message about being careful playing with fire, and why elemental balance is so important.

The Air Temple, shown in fig. 6.2, was built a few years later and is a large open-air structure with sides that can be rolled down in bad weather. This is where Venus Rising students gather for teachings, Shamanic Breathwork, and intensive personal work. To me, it represents a much smaller-scale version of part of the university in the temple

Fig. 6.2. The Air Temple of Venus Rising Association at Transformation
Courtesy of Venus Rising

on Alcyone, and its energy likely connects directly with this university.

The Water Temple is the newest elemental temple and provides a lovely movement of energy with its cascading fountains flowing down the hillside. Much emotional healing occurs on this sacred land, and the Water Temple supports this outcome energetically, encouraging students to heal and release the old wounding and reclaim a healed emotional body. A grand statue of the Goddess Isis stands on the top of the hill overlooking the cascading water.

In addition to the elemental temples, there is an Instar Medicine Wheel, which was envisioned by Anna Cariad-Barrett when she was writing a book with Star Wolf called *Sacred Medicine of Bee, Butterfly, Earthworm and Spider: Shamanic Teachers of the Instar Medicine Wheel*. According to Cariad-Barrett, the Instar Wheel represents "the transformational journey we undertake on the path of sacred purpose ... [and] offers us a sacred medicine which is larger than the sum of its parts and that can bless and inform our sacred purpose and soul expression as 'human beings doing' on Planet Earth."[10]

It is a journey that Anna recognized was connected to the Great Star Nations, and she wanted the Instar Wheel to be a star tetrahedron, which is also a Merkaba, a three-dimensional geometric shape, to represent this journey. My husband Dennis worked with her and others to create the design, and Star Wolf's son Casey Piscitelli built it (see fig. 6.4 on page 167). This happened in 2012, so we were able to do a powerful ceremony on its platform during the 12/12/12 and 12/21/12 portals to connect with our star ancestors (spiritual portals open on dates with repeating numbers, such as December 12, 2012). Again, these rituals and ceremonies energize these sacred sites even more.

A stunning statue of the Goddess Sekhmet, who was also part of Star Wolf's original vision of destroying the old, dysfunctional world, has also found her place on Dove Mountain. While being created, the artist consciously infused this statue with Sekhmet's energy, and when standing near her, this transformative energy is palpable (fig. 6.3).

Fig. 6.3. Statue of Sekhmet at Venus Rising Association for Transformation
Courtesy of Venus Rising

Although many students come to visit Venus Rising's sacred sites, many other sacred sites are being created in more public spaces. I was excited to find out that *apachetas*, which are sacred stone structures from the Pachakuti Mesa tradition of Peru, are being built around the world.

The practice of building apachetas started and has primarily taken place in South America, but it has now expanded. "Created to use time-honored rituals, an apacheta serves as an altar or energy vortex, a portal through which we can profoundly connect with Pachamama [the Spirit of Planet Earth], who upholds our vibrations of prayers and ceremonies within the vast blessings of nature."[11]

Stephanie Red Feather, who has been initiated into the Pachakuti Mesa tradition explained this more in-depth to me. She also told me about an apacheta she helped build near Kansas City, Missouri, at the Hollis Renewal Center.

According to Red Feather, the apacheta is a sacred pile of stones like stone cairns, meant to mark the place where ley lines on the Earth intersect or mark other power centers and energetically significant points on the planet. They are used like any outdoor altar where you can pray, give offerings, have ceremonies, and connect with Earth spirits, ancestors, guides, and your star family.

Over time as the tradition has evolved, apachetas no longer need to be placed on ley lines or power centers; you can build one wherever you are led to, and through intention, connect it with the energetic grid of the planet. They can be personal, built on land where you live, or communal, like the one at the Hollis Renewal Center.

Red Feather estimates that the number of communal apachetas created from a community building activity in a public place may now number in the dozens or even hundreds around the United States alone. To stay within the tradition, the United States has been divided into regions with groups of people who are keepers of the Pachakuti Mesa tradition in each region. They oversee the building and management of the apachetas in these public places, and their permission needs to be granted before they can be built.

For the apacheta at the Hollis Renewal Center, once permission was granted, an invitation went out to people locally who were interested in this tradition. Participants brought stones, crystals, shells, sacred waters, ashes from sacred fires, dirt from sacred locations, flowers and sage, corn meal, tobacco, and the like as offerings to this sacred structure. Noisemakers were used to activate the apacheta, and caretakers were assigned to care for and feed it once it was activated, to keep the sacred energy alive. Although apachetas can be as small as six inches around, at Hollis, it is three feet across and about three feet high. The base is always made from twelve foundation stones of around the same size placed in a particular order, with all of them touching. These represent the twelve sacred *apus* or the twelve sacred mountains (and mountain spirits) of the Andes. All apachetas are built on this round foundation.

These simple but powerful structures are showing up all over as another way to increase the high-frequency energy around the globe. Since all physical reality is created from vibrational patterns of energy, the energy these structures emit is helping us create a loving, high-consciousness reality for planet Earth. They energize the potentiality of this energetic blueprint form in 6D so it can manifest more and more in our 3D world.

Fig. 6.4. Instar Medicine Wheel Star Tetrahedron at Venus Rising Association of Transformation

Fig. 6.5. Sunflower Installation at Southwind Park facing North.
Courtesy of Bob Croteau

Writing this section has brought me some lovely surprises. I hadn't known about the extent of the apachetas being built around the world until I talked with Red Feather. I had reached out to her to ask about her personal one, and then to my delight, I found out that these are making a large contribution to the creation of modern sacred sites around the globe. Another surprise came when my husband reminded me that Bob Croteau, an old friend of ours, had built a structure for a public park in Springfield, Illinois, that he thought might fit into this part of the book. I contacted Bob and again found out that this installation was far more interesting and sacred than I realized.

According to Bob, the Rotary Sundial installation as it is called, which is a solar sunflower calendar has many aspects (figs. 6.5 and 6.6). It

Sacred Architecture, Sites, and the Frequency of Our Structures ✳ 169

Fig. 6.6. Sunflower Installation at Southwind Park facing South.
Courtesy of Bob Croteau

was built on eighty acres of land that a family donated to the Springfield Park District with conditions that the park be built from scratch, that it be fully handicapped-accessible, and showcase renewable energy. Since Bob worked for the city and was known for his expertise in alternative energy, he was approached by the park district for this project.

His installation was designed to provide lighting for the park through solar power. In addition, he also created it as a solar calendar. He had already designed a sunflower calendar as part of his master's project at the University of Illinois but had not come up with land or funding to build it. Now he had the land, and the Rotary Clubs of Springfield became interested and provided funding. Much like the ancient calendars, such as the Adam's Calendar in South Africa, which is estimated to be somewhere between seventy-five thousand and one hundred thousand years old, Bob's calendar marks the solar geometry of where it is placed. Solar geometry measures the angle of the sun to the Earth at a given location.

The centerpiece is a twenty-five-foot tall, eighteen-foot-wide metal sculpture of a sunflower with four solar panels in the center. Their individual cells represent the seeds, which send solar energy to the park's electrical grid. Amber LED lights ring the perimeter shining outward on the petals at night. The installation includes a sculpted bee on the top (see fig. 6.6) whose tail casts a shadow at solar noon. The shadow falls on a line of granite markers straight to the north with the shortest shadow occurring at the summer solstice and the longest at fifty feet long, marking the winter solstice. At winter solstice, you can see it moving about an inch per minute, giving one the feeling and sense of motion of the Earth's actual movement.

The calendar line transects a thirty-foot circle with six sunrise- and sunset-viewing benches of the solstices and equinoxes. Farther out from these benches at fifty feet from the center are boulders that extend the alignments. The boulders are from the Illinoian Glacial Stage of around 150,000 years ago, thus bringing a sense of ancient time into the installation.

There is also a sundial component to it on the south end. A fourteen-by-twenty-two-foot ellipse is set using two rows of bathroom sink cutouts made from recycled granite countertops, marking the hours of the day for both Standard and Daylight Savings Times.

It is a human interactive sundial because there is a five-foot-long granite foot piece marked with the months of the year. One can align their toes on the marked month and become the gnomon (the part of a sundial that casts a shadow). As one's shadow falls across the hourly stones, it marks the time of day.

At the far other end of the 100-foot installation, there is a four-foot granite circle compass to give folks a sense of direction. In Bob's words: "The purpose of this space is to get a sense of the solar geometry, of our movement through space, and our place in the universe in the hope that we will take better care of this spaceship Earth."

From its inception and long before it showed up in form, Bob connected with the spiritual energies underlying this creation. A granite marker at the end of the installation states a quote that came to Bob in his visualizations: "The arms of this Compass reach out around the Earth gently holding the thin fragile layer of life clinging to it. Let us do the same."

These modern sacred sites are no doubt springing up everywhere, and in many cases, they are not identified as such, but a sensitive person can feel the energy they are emitting. The sacred purpose of these sites does not make the news. Just know they are there, supporting our evolutionary transition.

Creating Your Own

Similar to the larger sacred sites springing up around the planet, more and more individuals are creating sacred sites in their yards, on their land, and in their homes. These, too, feed the star grid and the crystalline Earth grid, as the meditation at the end of chapter 4 will help you understand, bringing us ever closer to creating a loving, peaceful, just, and harmonious planet filled with people living from their 5D/6D frequency.

Altars, Reiki grids, personal pyramids, as well as apachetas and the like, all serve to both ground higher spiritual energies and emit these higher frequencies for healing, protection, and connection. They often arise from different traditions and generally come with specific instructions to aid in aligning with the wisdom of the Earth and the stars. They transmit higher-frequency information and help us connect with other dimensions, other-dimensional beings, and higher-dimensional parts of ourselves.

During the Pleiadian alignment of November 2022, Eva Marquez offered the world a ceremony in one of her vlogs with the intent that those who connect with the cosmic wisdom of the Great Star Nations help humanity's evolution by planting a crystalline grid on their land. The vlog shows us, as well, how to program these grids with the frequencies of higher-dimensional wisdom to bring them more fully into the Earth. She explains, too, that those choosing to create this grid were acting as an energetic bridge from the cosmos to the Earth and that this grid would combine with others around the planet to connect with members of what Eva calls "the Ground Crew."[12]

She came up with a lovely but simple ritual that energetically ran the wisdom coming from one's soul star family through the heart and down into the Earth, and then reversed it to be pulled back through the heart and up to one's star family while holding the energy of Oneness. Once the crystals were activated in this way, they would be ceremonially buried and would keep informing and connecting with other ground crew members from this point on. She also pointed out that these activated crystals, once buried, would collect more Earth wisdom data to transmit back up to our guides so they could better aid us in our evolutionary journey. The end notes for this chapter include the information to find this vlog if you feel called to ceremonially plant these crystals.

This is just one of the many examples of how we are building a foundation all over our planet to support our transition from 3D/4D to 5D/6D. Think about this energetically. While personal sites might be small, they are put in place with intention, love, and higher-frequency vibrations. The frequency they emit combines with all the other higher frequencies we are grounding and planting around the Earth. Much like a laser show, all these energies emit light that connects with all the higher-dimensional light being emitted around the planet. This combined light creates patterns that form new energetic configurations in 6D. The more these patterns are strengthened, the more we will see their qualities show up in our 3D world.

If you have not yet created sacred sites inside and/or around the outside of your home, now may be the time to do this. You can use instructions from different traditions or allow your creations to unfold in new ways as well if you are guided to do so. Remember creativity is one of the central characteristics of 5D, so using one's own guidance and inspiration keeps the vitality of personal altars alive. What counts is your intention to draw higher frequencies down to Earth that then can rise from her heart to be run through your own heart and its wisdom.

This is one of the many ways we prepare to step more fully into the co-creative role that our sixth-dimensional frequency aligns us with. We use our 5D creativity to envision and ultimately construct a material form that then connects to, informs, and strengthens its energy configuration in 6D.

Connecting the Dots

As we evolve, as our perceptual field expands, we understand at an ever-deepening level that everything in physical manifestation emits frequency. If these manifestations have been intentionally or organically aligned with the sacred geometric patterns that emerge from Divine Mind, the energy of our world begins to lift. We understand at the cellular level that everything is a fractal, a piece of the Divine. Sometimes this fractal will be distorted, but it is part of the Divine nevertheless. We now can increase our ability to attune to this pure source energy that will shift our planet.

We are developing our ability to better discern what is distorted and what is not. Through this discernment, which comes from clearing out the old programming, wounds, and illusions that have kept us from accurately reading the wisdom of our heart/mind, we can consciously energize and strengthen the energetic configurations in 6D so they harmoniously manifest more and more on our planet.

We can use the gifts left for us from the advanced star civilizations that once were here on Earth, combining them with universal wisdom that comes through sacred geometry and our own creative constructions upon which we will create New Earth. Higher-frequency information comes from all directions. We just need to open our hearts and minds to allow it more fully in.

✳ MEDITATION ✳
Visiting Advanced Civilizations

Allow your eyes to soften and put all of your attention on taking deep centering breaths. As you exhale release any distractions, any concerns, any tensions. Just let that all flow out with the breath. On the inhale imagine that you are drawing in tiny golden spirals of light filled with love and consciousness and allow those tiny spirals to spread to every cell in your body. Keep focusing on your breath as you begin to feel a sense of calm and relaxation throughout your body.

Now I would like you to imagine yourself in a beautiful spot in nature, perhaps by the ocean or the mountains or in a beautiful meadow. Drink in the visual beauty around you, noticing all the colors and shapes. Listen to all the sounds: Do you hear the birds calling? Are there waves crashing or lapping onto the shore? How about the rustling of tree leaves? Feel the sun warming your hair, warming your skin. Enjoy the gentle breeze. Notice any fragrances in the air.

Then pause and look out over the scene before you. You'll notice a bright horizontal beam of light coming toward you. You sense the loving and affirming energy that it holds. As it gets closer and closer, you realize that it is carrying a small vehicle, perhaps one shaped like a star tetrahedron or Merkaba. The vehicle lands in front of you. Its door opens, and you step inside. You find there is a place for you to sit and feel secure as the vehicle begins to move, carrying you gently through time and space.

When at last you land and step out of this vehicle, the sight before you takes your breath away. You are overlooking what appears to be a magical city. Its structures, which look as if they are made of shimmering light, are colors you may not have seen before, and they are emitting a beautiful, peaceful energy that begins to connect with all of your cells. As you walk closer, you begin to feel yourself grow lighter and lighter. You sense there are others all around you, and when you get closer, they, too, are shimmering and emitting this energy. Smile at those you meet, and see that when they smile back at you, you feel warmth and comfort moving throughout your body.

You come to a park filled with stunning plants and flowers that are shimmering as well. Sit on one of the benches and just allow yourself to bask in this energy. As you are sitting there, a guide shows up and sits next to you. You may wish to dialogue with this guide, asking about where you are and why you are there. They may have some important wisdom for you to take back to your current 3D life.

Perhaps they will lead you around so you can see the beings who live here go about their daily lives. Maybe there is a special place that your guide wants you to see. Allow yourself to absorb as much as you can about this place you are visiting.

When you feel ready, your guide walks you back to the park and to the vehicle that transported you here. As you get in, you realize that something deep within you has shifted from this experience.

The vehicle takes you back to the place you began this journey. After landing gently, breathe deeply and feel into and ponder the experience you just had. Now slowly allow yourself to come back into the room you are in, wiggling your fingers and toes to help you more fully get back into your body.

Journal on what happened for you in this visit.

Note: Find this meditation on my YouTube channel, Wisdom Within Us, in the "Meditations to Raise Your Frequency" playlist.

Journal Questions to Ponder

1. Does your home give you a sense of inner harmony and well-being? If not, what do you need to do to create this for yourself?
2. How do your buying habits support or harm our environment? What else can you do to minimize your impact on our landfills?
3. Are you using toxic products in your home? How can you eliminate or minimize their use?
4. What sacred sites around the world are you drawn to? If you have visited them through your travels or in meditation, what kind of transformation have they activated in you?
5. Have you created your personal sacred sites both inside and outside your home? If so, are you tuned into the frequencies they emit? If you have not created these, write about what you can envision creating.

7

Time, Timelines, and Timelessness

Time in and of itself, is a fascinating concept. We say a lot of strange things about it. Things like: time is speeding up, I need to stretch time, there's not enough time, and where did the time go? Still, if time even exists, which physicist Julian Barbour questions in his book, *The End of Time*, our experience of it seems based solely on our perceptions. As our perceptual field expands, our inner experience of this phenomenon we call time expands as well.

From our 3D perspective on planet Earth, time is tied to observable linear sequences and cycles: the body is born, the body grows, the body dies; the sun rises, the sun sets; daylight lengthens, and daylight shortens. This does not change as our consciousness expands. What does shift, however, is the realization that once we move beyond the third dimension, all time occurs simultaneously. That's enough to make our left brains go a little crazy. Our right brain, though, is totally at home with this notion.

Because the right hemisphere of our brain is connected to the fourth dimension, it experiences past, present, and future simultaneously, and this is the hemisphere where our emotional experiences are held. This is why trauma that occurred years before, or even lifetimes before in linear time, still affects us until we process it through.

To emotionally process through the trauma, we need to be able to identify, express, and release the feelings related to it in a non-harmful way. Then we need to bring the emotions of the experience into the linear experience of time in our left brain, where we can now understand on an emotional level that these events have ended, rather than feeling that they are still going on. Time doesn't change as you can see, but our perception of it does, and this can greatly affect our lives.

Because the right hemisphere of our brain functions in the fourth dimension, it affects us in various ways. When it is in balance, when it is in alignment, the fourth dimension holds many gifts. However, when it is out of balance, which it still is for most humans on the planet, we become susceptible to the lower astral worlds, the lower frequency aspect of 4D, which holds all the archetypes both positive and negative, where we are easily manipulated through fear, unprocessed trauma, and repressed anger. Fourth-dimensional consciousness is intrinsic to this hemisphere of our brain, which is why I say that in our evolutionary process, we are shifting out of being 3D/4D humans and becoming 5D/6D humans.

Once we clear our emotional field and thus get ourselves back in balance, our 4D frequency increases, allowing us to go into a higher aspect of this dimension. This clears the 4D canopy that I talked about earlier and opens the higher-dimensional portals. In turn, this helps us light up more of our DNA strands and shift out of living from the beliefs of our brain, a 3D/4D experience, into living from our heart and our soul, 5D/6D consciousness.

In this higher consciousness, while in our human body, we still experience the gamut of emotions, but our primary emotion is love in all its forms. It is from this frequency and perceptual field that we can use the gifts of 6D to continually create a high-consciousness, loving reality. 5D is physical like 3D but it is a higher frequency dimension where physical manifestation is less dense—a lighter, brighter version of what we call physical. It is from this fifth-dimensional expression we can most effectively incorporate our 6D potential, which holds a higher frequency version of the emotional and spiritual aspects of our consciousness.

When we operate from our 5D/6D frequency, we experience time quite differently. On the one hand, we step more fully into the now, into the present—which holds the richness of all potentiality—and we also step into the awareness that there are multiple timelines, all of which operate in different realities. Much like streaming channels, we will typically choose to watch one show at a time while in human form. To be in the now means we are both watching the show and being in the show simultaneously. Do the past and future disappear at this point? The sun still appears to rise and set as the Earth rotates. Nature still births itself, ages, and dies. We may not care if it is four o'clock or ten, but in our 5D/6D frequency, while still in human form, we are living in the cycle of things, and thus are still a part of the natural world. I suspect that when one expands beyond the sixth dimension, it is possible to watch several channels and be in several channels simultaneously, but this is far beyond the scope of my brain and this book—and I believe, far beyond our current evolutionary imperative for now.

It is important, though, to understand concurrent timelines because we have the potential and are developing the ability to consciously choose which timeline to live in. To do this in a fully conscious way, we have to disempower our old belief system that tells us this is impossible, that we are not powerful enough, deserving enough, smart enough, or brave enough. And equally essential, we need to be ready to take full responsibility for our lives and the reality we create.

Linear Time, Timelines, and Tapping into Other Lives

When we have memories of other lives and other lifetimes, we are tapping into different timelines that have become part of our soul experience. When we look at this from a higher-dimensional perspective, understanding all time is simultaneous, we realize those lifetimes still exist, they are just not on the channel we're dialed into, but they can still affect us. This is a bit tricky because it could be on a future versus a past timeline, but given some consensus about some of what has happened historically in what we call the past, I'm going to assume that we have an intuitive sense from the perspective of the 3D timeline our current incarnated soul is living on about whether we are remembering what has already passed on this timeline, or tapping into what has not yet shown up.

To make this even more complex, our soul itself is on several different timelines and in several different places at one time. For example, I know that my soul is currently in some form on the Pleiades and also in the pre-birth or spirit realms that Michael Newton uncovered in his hypnosis practice and wrote about in several books including *Destiny of Souls* and *Journey of Souls*. I share this only to point out that our potential perceptual bandwidth is so much larger than anything we've been taught and, likely, anything we've allowed ourselves to imagine.

We have two primary ways in which remembering or tapping into past-life experiences is relevant to our current life. One gives us the ability to access gifts and talents we've developed in other lifetimes. The other gives us the opportunity to release guilt and trauma responses by giving us access to becoming conscious of them, and therefore able to heal other lifetime wounds and shadow issues.

What we have labeled natural gifts have more than likely been qualities that our soul has had in many other lifetimes. Locating these lifetimes can strengthen our abilities or at least our confidence in these areas.

A few years ago, I attended a past-life workshop led by Shama Viola from Damanhûr. The method Shama uses to help us remember another lifetime is to have oracles read the details of a relevant past life for each participant before we begin. Most of those details are not shared with the participant until the end of the workshop. As the workshop proceeds, a few hints are given here and there from the oracle reading to the participant to uncover their own memories. I was working with a lifetime that I had no conscious recollection about before (and I do have a lot of memories of other lifetimes that my soul has experienced). It turns out that I was a *curandero* in Peru known both for my physical, emotional, and spiritual healing abilities, and I had been trained from an early age in the collection and use of herbs. Although I have always understood that I had a natural gift in terms of emotional and spiritual healing and have had no need to have this validated through other life connections, and while I have also always had a strong sense of what the physical body needs, I have never been drawn to collecting or studying herbs. Still, although I have no training in physical healing, I've always been able to follow my intuition and successfully find alternatives to the symptom-based focus of Western medicine. Gaining awareness of this Peruvian lifetime validated what I already knew about myself but hadn't fully owned.

Another example is that I know (again without clear memory) that I've been an astrologer in other lifetimes. From early childhood I was fascinated by the stars and loved the several times my father took me to our local planetarium. When someone would ask me when I was around seven what I wanted to be when I grew up (a question that was standard procedure in the early 1950s), I would say, "an actress with a hobby in astronomy." I didn't know about astrology then, and professional choices were culturally limited for females, so at that age, I didn't realize I could just skip the actress part and become an astronomer. I also didn't know that my real interest was not in the science of the stars and planets, but rather how they affect us psychologically and spiritually. Although I do not consider myself a professional astrologer, I have studied astrology and used it in my practice for years. Still, when going over someone's chart, I will occasionally have a flash of insight that goes far beyond what I have learned in this lifetime, and I can feel it is information coming through from another timeline that my soul has experienced.

I've also had many memories of being a writer and spiritual teacher.

As a child, as soon as I learned to write, I started writing stories. I also started winning essay contests, often just scribbling out the essay at the last minute before it was due, and then finding I'd won first place. I think it's safe to say that anything you were drawn to or recognized for when you were young has already been with you for many lifetimes. You may have squelched these interests and gifts because they were not considered acceptable in your family, school, or religious institution or because they didn't work out well for you on another timeline, but they are still there waiting for you to reclaim them, now more powerfully than ever. I've written about this in my book *Empowering the Spirit: A Process to Activate Your Soul Potential*. You may want to refer to the book for more in-depth information.

Another reason to tap into past lives is that it allows us to look at our shadow experiences. We may well have been perpetrators of abuse, misused our power, or in other ways caused harm, and this gives us the opportunity to free ourselves from the karma our soul has been carrying. We can use this awareness to hold great compassion for those we harmed and for ourselves, which then allows us to process through and release its energy from causing us pain and mucking up our emotional field in 4D.

Finding trauma where we were harmed in other lifetimes, and that still triggers us and keeps us in fear and disempowerment, is another gift available as we look over the 3D timelines our soul has experienced. As a therapist, I encourage clients first to look at their current lifetime when they have trauma triggers as, generally, there are current lifetime traumas that need to be addressed first. Those traumas, however, often mirror traumas our soul has experienced in other lives, and which are at the root of our wounding. We may find them through noticing that we have overreactions to events taking place or to challenges we are facing. And although the overreactions may be triggering current life trauma, usually from our childhood, there is a different quality to it when it also occurs in another lifetime. One way to notice this is to pay attention to the intensity of your reaction. You may get a sense that it doesn't match a response you are having. For example, you might have an anxiety reaction to being in a new location but for no apparent reason.

Part of what we experience prior to each incarnation is an option to be born into life situations to help us release wounds that we've been carrying from lifetime to lifetime. Often, this option includes us going through some similar wounding but then developing the awareness and finding the methods to heal ourselves once and for all. Sometimes the core wound might be simply: I'll never be loved and honored or there's something wrong with me and I never deserve to be free of this feeling. We can carry these beliefs in a soul configuration that follows us through many incarnations. Going into these past timelines and helping this part of us heal, both through processing the feelings that arose and then through transforming the belief systems that followed, can finally shift the energetic patterning that keeps us stuck in old pain.

Another very important aspect of facing and working with shadow experiences, which I've seen time and time again and have experienced firsthand, is people holding themselves back from stepping fully into their soul mission because of painful past-life experiences. It's the proverbial fear of being burned at the stake yet again. So many starseeds, so many light workers, are struggling with this. Activating the courage as well as emotionally healing those old wounds so one can fully embrace their mission is hugely important for the well-being of our planet right now, and no small task.

My own story, which I've written about in *Empowering the Spirit*, is the reason that my writing and teachings reached a relatively small number of students until I was in my 70s when I had finally broken through the old fears enough that they no longer held me back. Quite frankly, this was a lifetime I worked with for years ever since I published my first book in my forties and suddenly found myself scared to do public presentations, despite having done them multiple times prior without any fear.

As I uncovered the details of the lifetime that was holding me back, which I give more information about later in this chapter, I had to work with the inaccurate beliefs I carried of what happened after I was killed for my spiritual teachings, as well as all the emotions that were still unprocessed. This kind of trauma can follow us through several lifetimes and shows up in our human bodies at a cellular level. It becomes part of our DNA response. Although it took me several decades in this life to clear this, techniques are more available now to do this more quickly. In a sense, we no longer have the luxury of doing this the slow way. We are all needed to shine our lights now as brightly as we can.

Remembering

The most common way of accessing past-life information is through someone who channels, reads the Akashic records, or in other ways connects with higher-dimensional, nontemporal information. But unless we have an inner sense, an emotional sense of connecting to the lifetimes that are mentioned, we won't know if the information we receive is accurate (no reading is going to be accurate 100 percent of the time). While the details of other lifetime experiences may not be precise and don't have to be for us to utilize them, the themes, including the gifts and shadow elements need to be in alignment with what our inner experience was. So, although using the gifts of another person to access this information is fine, it needs to resonate with you to be useful.

Another way many of us connect with other lifetime experiences is when we meet people for the first time in this lifetime, and we can feel we have known them before. I met several women when I was in my twenties, and I had a strong awareness I had been in convents with them. It might have been over different lifetimes, as I feel I was in convents in Europe in more than one life. This was a strange awareness for me because I was Jewish this time around, so connecting with experiences I had in convents did not parallel any experiences I had in this lifetime. That was a tip-off right there that I was tapping into a different time.

I also experienced an instant connection with an ex-husband. We recognized each other immediately and had a strong psychic connection from the start. While he was not my ultimate soul mate for this life, he was an extremely important relationship that helped me recognize many of my gifts.

If you think over your own experiences, you'll realize that you have often met new people who you sensed you already knew. You might have clear scenarios about them from other lifetimes or you might not, but you will get a strong feeling that you have known this person for a long time the moment you meet them. When you realize that you are having a memory from another life, it helps you to access more memories. This is part of our expanding bandwidth. Our concept of linear time expands to include many other linear timelines, many other streaming channels that you have access to and may have been experiencing unconsciously. Now they become more available to you, should you choose to give them your attention. The other thing to stay aware of is that since this is all happening in the now in higher-dimensional time, nothing here is static or unchangeable.

Because we have been so trained to perceive these things from a narrow bandwidth, stay aware that expanding your bandwidth too fast can throw you off-kilter. You might want to start with accessing a simple memory of your soul experience, whether about other souls you've known previously or clarity about a storyline from another life. If you put out a clear intention to not get bombarded or overloaded, this will make maintaining your balance much easier.

Remember, too, that having a strong foundation is essential to staying in balance. Knowing how to maneuver in the lifetime you are experiencing currently, healing your childhood wounds, and remembering to keep grounded and to keep grounding daily will help you to expand your perceptual bandwidth without creating an internal or external crisis. You can also set a clear intention such as "I want to connect with other lifetime gifts" or "I want to remember other lifetime trauma to finally get free when I'm ready." All of this will help too.

Meditation, dreams, and guided meditation are other ways to access your memories. Guided meditation especially is also a wonderful way to shift old trauma, whether going into your cells and deactivating the part of your DNA holding the trauma, such as the meditation I've included at the end of this chapter, or through changing the emotional outcome through visualization.

The more we can remember, and the more of us who do remember living in a higher-frequency culture, whether in the Great Star Nations or places like Lemuria and Atlantis, the more we are able to use our innate 6D creative power to shift our planet. These memories confirm that there are loving, peaceful, and spiritually advanced ways to live. This in and of itself helps us release the limiting beliefs of the old paradigm. And it gives us more clarity of what we want to manifest.

When I accessed the information from the lifetime I mentioned in the section above, I also accessed information about having lived in a higher-frequency village for the early part of my life. I don't have the exact location, but it was near Greece, and I believe it was around the time when patriarchy was beginning to get a stronghold in what is now Athens. The village I was born into was idyllic. It was physically beautiful, in harmony with the natural world, and thus in divine order. Every living being was honored, loved, and appreciated, and all children, from the time of their birth, were seen at a soul level and helped to develop their natural gifts. Everyone and everything thrived. I have a very strong sense of how this felt, and some visual experience of what it looked like. I ended up leaving the village because I had traveled to Athens and became disturbed about what was going on there. I felt it was my calling to leave the village and bring my teachings to people in the city, so my husband, children, and I relocated. It didn't end well as I was openly challenging the status quo, but, of course, it was an important lesson for my soul. In remembering this lifetime, I was both uncovering a trauma that held me back in my current lifetime and gave me a chance to heal this at a deep level, while simultaneously remembering the loving, spiritually advanced world I had been born into, so I have a model of what we need to create together to shift our planet.

You, too, can access memories of a spiritually advanced world. This helps everyone and supports our individual and collective mission to usher in a new golden age. Create an intention to visit your home planet or a highly developed outpost on Earth. Your soul knows where to lead you. The more you connect with your soul, the stronger your memories, and the more you help us all. You may want to do the meditation at the end of chapter 9.

Trauma and Timeline Intervention

We are not bound to one version of reality. When we are getting what's called *bleed throughs* from traumas that occurred in other lifetimes, much like changing the ending of a dream, we can go back to the trauma story and change it. This process shifts what we experience as reality and provides us the opportunity to clear our trauma response at a cellular level so it will no longer impact us. It doesn't matter if we have all the facts. What matters is our working to clear our emotional responses. This affects whether the trauma will continue to be expressed in our DNA or not. Processing through the original feelings as well as the feelings that occur after we change the story, and adding visualization, like the meditation at the end of this chapter, allows us to stop this gene from continuing to get expressed. This lets us shut down the part of the DNA that has kept this experience emotionally alive. When it stops expressing, it no longer impacts us.

I will go into some epigenetic information in a bit so this can make more sense to you, but before I do, I want to talk about this as a multi-layered process. I also want to stress that we still grow and change in a spiral formation, so shutting down the expression of these genes doesn't mean that they will never turn on again should we need to revisit this experience for our soul development, but we will be revisiting this at a higher, more conscious octave and likely find that the process becomes a bit easier each time.

To clear the trauma emotionally typically means identifying, expressing, and releasing the energy of the anger (a natural response to violation) in a non-harmful way, while focusing on whoever and whatever created the trauma. I have written extensively about healthy expression of anger as an important step in clearing the emotional field, so I am not going to repeat this here other than to say that this is not about blame, but about standing up for ourselves. This heals disempowerment issues that affect our third chakra and helps restore our sense of self. Reconnecting with our sense of empowerment then helps us deal with whatever fear is associated with this trauma so that it will no longer immobilize us or hold us back. Any sadness connected to this experience can also be expressed and released at this point.

After the feelings are processed, looking at any limited beliefs that you may be carrying about yourself or the world that arose from the trauma can be brought into consciousness and transformed. Then the next step, which does not need to happen sequentially, is to literally turn off the trauma gene in your DNA through visualization. The meditation at the end of this chapter is designed to help you do this.

I am going to use my own experience as an example of timeline bleed throughs, as well as how to shift the end of the experience and release the feelings involved from the original timeline. As the ending of the story changes, it actually creates a new timeline.

As I mentioned above, after I published my first book, I began to feel anxious every time I had to do any kind of public presentation. It started the same day I was doing my first book talk and book signing for *Journey to Wholeness* at our local Barnes & Noble. Speaking before groups had always been easy for me before this. This new anxiety was my signal that something was arising for me that I had buried and that I needed to deal with.

As I uncovered this other lifetime trauma and its details, here's the story that unfolded. I had left my idyllic village with my husband and three children to move to this city, to fulfill my spiritual mission. Once there, I would go out into the yard that surrounded my home and large groups of people would gather. I would speak to them and inspire them to connect with their own spiritual development and to get free of what the ruling government wanted them to believe. Because I felt strongly about the mission, I was happy to do it, although I did know there would be risks. It all went well for quite a while. I believe I was able to stay somewhat under the official radar for some time.

Then one night when my husband had gone back to our village for a visit, I was dragged out of my home and thrown into a dungeon to await my execution. My three young children, one of whom was a nursing baby, were left unattended. Even writing this now, feelings of fear and grief arise, which is interesting since I've already processed a lot of anger but hadn't worked with the grief. What was most traumatizing for me was fear and concern for my children. I didn't know if the neighbors would dare to take care of them and I didn't know if my husband would get back in time for them to be safe.

At some point while working with this lifetime, I consulted an intuitive and got the information that my husband did return quickly because word got to him. He was able to safely get the children back to our village. Still, I didn't know this while facing my death, and I crossed over scared and resentful, the shock disconnecting me from my guides and my spiritual center. I felt abandoned and betrayed by my students and others who had previously supported my work. These are feelings I have been able to process through in my current lifetime about what I believed happened then.

If I go back now and change the story, it goes something like this. Word traveled immediately, and a group of people not only made sure that my children were safe and cared for until their father returned, but they also knew where they had taken me and devised a plan that they communicated to me telepathically to help me break free and be transported back to my village. As I change this story a new set of emotions arise. Now my anger can rage at the ruthlessness of those who took me from my home with no concern for these innocent children. This was exactly the consciousness I was doing my best to counteract with my teachings in the first place.

The anger is energizing, and, by expressing and releasing it in a way that harms no one, I can ultimately sense compassion for those who behaved so ruthlessly, so soullessly. It is quite an awful way to be.

When I visualize myself being reunited with my family in our village, when I allow myself to feel that my children will no longer be motherless as they grow up, and I can reconnect with my soul and my soul purpose, which can now be carried out from my village, a sense of peacefulness arises from the still point within my being. Although there is still anger that this type of brutality still exists, it now occupies a smaller part of my emotional experience. The last step for my healing is to visualize going into my cells, locating the gene that is still reacting to this trauma, and shutting it down via this chapter's meditation.

This is a process I'll have to repeat several times, seeing both my release from the dungeon and my reunion with my family to successfully keep the trauma gene shut down. Each time I do this, I shift the energy a bit more, and I trust I will know intuitively when this process is complete because there will no longer be emotions that come up other than compassion for all involved, including myself. I will have successfully processed this through 4D and come out in the energy of 5D.

Have I changed the timeline? Certainly, I've changed the timeline I'm moving forward on in my current life. If there are any vestiges of fear holding me back, this dissolves them. Can I pop back into the old timeline? Yes. But if I do, I can put more focus on repeating this healing process until it is finally done.

To help you understand how this can work in terms of shutting down the expression of the trauma gene, let's look a bit more at the field of epigenetics. Although, as far as I know, epigenetics has not yet studied past-life trauma in our genes, it has studied childhood trauma and ancestral trauma, which epigenesists know gets passed down through the genes. Through counseling and visualization, they have had success altering which genes in our DNA are actively expressing and which are not. There is no reason to believe that any past-life trauma that is still affecting us cannot be dealt with in the same way. The information below about our DNA and how it impacts us may help you understand this more.

These are excerpts from an article published in the *Arkansas Advocate*:

> DNA controls the function of each cell in your body, and epigenetic modifications to your genes change a cell's function by switching genes on or off. Every modification impacts function on a cellular level.
>
> . . . Epigenetics is like a library where the books are your DNA codes. Not every book is being read at the same time, and environmental factors like diet, stress, or support act like librarians deciding which books (genes) are open and read . . . but just like we can choose a new book to read, we can change our environment.
>
> By altering factors like introducing counseling or healthier lifestyles, we can change which books are being read. Our DNA doesn't change, but we can influence which parts are active.[1]

Be aware that in my own story, the trauma gene did not get turned on in my current life until I was doing a talk and signing on my first book, which opened the door for me to become more public, more visible. Prior to publishing the book, this gene had minimal, if any, expression. At this time, too, my children were still young, and, while I was not conscious of this past life when the anxiety first started around public speaking, I feel strongly this was also a factor I was dealing with, an unconscious concern that I might be putting them at risk.

If this gene had not been activated, I would not have been able to heal this trauma, and it likely would have followed me into future lives. I believe that my soul set up this timing to take care of this once and for all. Should I reincarnate in human form again, it is highly unlikely I will bring this gene with me or perhaps more accurately, that it will have any expression. Pay attention, and know that when you locate something like this happening within you, you have the power to shift it by dealing with the feelings, then changing the timeline (changing the story) and ultimately deactivating the part of your genes that has carried this trauma.

Collective Bleed Throughs

We seem to be currently living on a few different timelines, which is part of our confusion about what is real. An interesting example of this is the public reaction to the COVID-19 vaccine. This is a hard section for me to write since I know it will not be a popular one with many of my colleagues, but I'm committed to following my own guidance here.

Part of the public was relieved and staunchly supportive of the vaccine as the only solution to stopping the pandemic. Other parts of the public saw the vaccine as dangerous and a way to control masses of people, potentially programming them to get sick in other ways and, at best, taking away their freedom to choose what went into their bodies. Both sides were emphatic that they had the truth.

When the vaccine first came out, I went through a lot of questioning if I would get the first shot or not. I've never been pro-vaccine and chose not to get my children vaccinated until they went to school, where it was mandatory in Illinois, even for a private Montessori school. By that time, and after having consulted with a chiropractor/acupuncturist who I have great respect for, I felt they were old enough that the vaccines would not do harm in the way they might have if I had gone through the protocol when they were infants. In fairness, I do think the polio vaccine and the smallpox vaccine were important to public health and did successfully make those diseases obsolete. I also believe they were designed differently than current childhood vaccines. The older vaccines were set up to work homeopathically and did not contain additives that children's vaccines have had for the last several decades.

A few months after the COVID-19 vaccine was introduced, I was going to be flying, and, although I had been doing a lot of natural things to strengthen my immune system, I did not want to take a chance when traveling that I'd contract the virus and subject others to it on my trip. I kept going back and forth, stuck in my indecision about whether to get the vaccine. Then I read an Akashic record reading that talked about the vaccine being what we believed it to be. For instance, if we felt it was dangerous, we should not get it. If we felt it would not cause us harm and that it would provide some protection, then it would be fine.

I researched the mRNA vaccine, and it made good sense to me. I think the idea is brilliant, but that it ultimately should not be put into the body. Rather, it should be programmed to work outside of the body with the information transmitted to people's immune systems energetically. Of course, one would have to trust the programmers to only use it to create immunity, and not for some negative purpose.

What I learned in my research was that the mRNA was not supposed to stay in my body but rather be flushed out within a short period of time after having programmed immunity in my cells. I decided to just do it. I drank a lot of water afterward, visualized it leaving my body, and had what I thought was no negative reaction to it. Still, I wasn't sure that I would bother to get a second shot, especially since side effects were more likely. I figured the first one would give me enough protection for my upcoming trip, and that was all I needed.

Shortly after the injection, I started having heart palpitations. And just when I was due to be able to have the second round, news was released that this was a side effect of the vaccine. I reported my symptoms to the CDC (Centers for Disease Control), quite sure this was what was going on for me. However, a few days later it dawned on me that the heart palpitations might not have anything to do with the vaccine but rather with the supplement I was taking for my thyroid. I remembered that my doctor said if I was taking more than my body needed, heart palpitations could occur. I stopped the supplement, and my heart went back to normal immediately. It turned out my thyroid was getting better, which was later borne out by a blood test. I still never went back for a second round of the COVID-19 vaccine because my travels were over, I rarely went to public places, and I felt there was no need to put anything extra into my body again.

I share all this to give you a background of where I was coming from on this issue. I had friends who were vehemently opposed to the vaccine and others who were convinced of the importance of it for public health. I was in the middle of the road here. Also, energetically the intensity of people's views fed the current polarity on our planet, and I didn't want to participate in this.

While all the hullabaloo was going on, I heard something that really connected for me. In the later stages of Atlantis when the society was sorely out of balance, a vaccine similar to the mRNA vaccine was developed and harmed a lot of people. Apparently, it was designed to do this, and I think it might have contributed to our star DNA strands beginning to shut down. I also think that part of the anti-vax intensity around COVID, at least in the spiritual community, came from people who were carrying a trauma gene from this experience in Atlantis. This was a collective bleed through where people were convinced that the danger of this current vaccine was based on something that happened on a different timeline but had remained unconscious and deactivated for them until this controversial vaccine was released in their current timeline.

This is not to say that the vaccine was not harmful for some people. And perhaps it did alter some DNA despite what I read, although intuitively that is not the hit I get. I'm sure there has been research and statistics on side effects that have been suppressed. But I know of hundreds of people who did get the vaccine—many got the boosters as well—who have never gotten sick. Some are spiritual teachers who have not in any way had their gifts suppressed. And I've personally heard through the grapevine only two stories about people who were harmed, one having a stroke and the other who died. I also know folks who have had serious long-term side effects from getting COVID-19 in the first place. If the other timeline had not been affecting our collective consciousness, things perhaps would have unfolded differently.

More than likely, there are many other collective bleed throughs I'm not aware of that do affect us. It is important for us to realize that this can occur and to use it as a possible factor when we have intense triggers and we are trying to figure out what may or may not be real.

Choosing Our Future

If we can change our past 3D timelines, we can change our future ones as well. But to do this successfully, we need to be energetically in a neutral state to reach into the quantum field or, more simply, into 6D to choose the timeline we most want. The best way I can describe what I mean by neutrality is a feeling of total openness where the body is in a relaxed state, and we are free of emotional triggers and ego agendas. While we are choosing a desired outcome, we are choosing it from a place of nonattachment, simply trusting the flow.

Imagine, if you will, of being in the center of a wheel with numerous spokes. Each spoke leads to a possible future. If you choose one from a place of unconsciousness, which humans often do, more than likely the spoke that you will travel will take you to a future created from your fears, old wounds, and old patterns. If instead, you choose a spoke path from a higher-dimensional state of consciousness, from a neutral state, allowing the wisdom of your heart to lead you, you will find that you can manifest a life that matches your heart's desires.

The more you can visualize, feel into, and energize a consciously chosen future with nonattachment, the more you intensify the likelihood that it will manifest and that this will be the reality you live. Remember, though, not to bypass awareness of the rogue cells. As humans with trillions of cells, there are going to be some that hold trauma genes that have not been fully shut down. This does not need to stand in the way of our ability to create and choose loving and peaceful futures for ourselves and the planet, but it does stress the importance of staying in conscious awareness and noticing when feelings re-arise.

As a practice, I recommend beginning with something relatively small but important to you. A recent example that I observed and worked with in myself went something like this. I was awake in the middle of the night, still in bed and in a kind of meditative state. My heart was feeling very open, and my body was fairly relaxed. I decided to put out clear intent that for the remainder of writing this book, I would be in an inner state of ease and allow the remaining chapters to flow out effortlessly.

As I began to visualize this, I immediately noticed a tightening in my solar plexus. That was a clear sign that my rogue cells were afoot and that old-paradigm beliefs wanted to take over my process and create more of a struggle. A deeper look revealed beliefs such as "If it's too easy, it won't be any good." And other beliefs like "This would be impossible," "I'm not capable of letting this happen," "It can't be that easy," as well as other beliefs that were variations on both themes.

I could feel the struggle of the old beliefs wanting to interfere and take charge of creating my future reality. Clearly, I was not fully in neutral because there was an emotional charge from them. I knew that by noticing my inner reflexive responses, I was already helping to disempower these old dysfunctional beliefs. I also knew that the more clearly I could define these beliefs, the easier it would be for me to calm them down so they would have less and less influence on the outcome. Remember that everything is energy. My heart was putting out the energy of loving neutrality where I could trust this book was ready to be finished and that I already contained everything I needed to make it happen. My solar plexus was giving me a signal that not all of me was resonating with this. I knew that calming down the old beliefs de-energizes them so that even if they are not 100 percent aligned, they will stay significantly weaker than the energy of creating ease that my heart was emitting.

The stakes in this example are relatively small. I had signed a contract; I knew the book would be completed. It could be enjoyable or stressful. I could continue in a state of ease or give the old beliefs the power to create stress. Either way, only my short-term inner experience was on the line. Thus, it is a perfect way to learn more about how I create my reality and to become more consciously skilled at it.

I didn't expect myself to do it perfectly. I knew that I might or might not experience stress again about getting the book done. As I was writing this part, the writing was flowing, and my solar plexus was calm. If I'm writing another day and feel the stress, so be it. I can stop, breathe, calm those old beliefs down once again, and carry on. What I felt confident I could do is have a sense of ease predominant in my process going forward. It did not have to be at 100 percent to work. It just had to be stronger than my inner resistance.

I encourage you to begin with something relatively small: something you would like to see happen or experience, but whether you successfully create it or not, all will still be okay. This helps you connect with both the inner sense of neutrality necessary to be successful at this, and simultaneously become more astute at noticing any counterreactions. Doing this will both give you practice and help you develop the expertise needed to consciously create more of your reality going forward.

The more of us who learn to consciously create our future, the closer we become collectively to creating New Earth. The intensity of old beliefs such as "peace is impossible" has been energized for millenniums, and we need to hone our creation skills to counterbalance them. Since all future timelines already exist, choosing and energizing the ones we most want is part of our curriculum as we continue to learn to leave the old painful realities behind.

✴ MEDITATION ✴
Cellular Journey to Deactivate Our Trauma DNA

Allow your eyes to soften and put all your attention on taking deep centering breaths. As you exhale release any distractions, any concerns, any tension. Just let that all flow out with the breath. On the inhale imagine that you are drawing in tiny golden spirals of light filled with love and consciousness and allow those tiny spirals to spread to every cell in your body. Keep focusing on your breath as you begin to feel a sense of calm and deep relaxation.

Now imagine you are in a beautiful meadow. The sky is a vibrant blue, the sun warms your hair and skin. You listen to the birds chirping, singing, and calling to one another. You drink in the beauty of the wildflowers surrounding you and of the lush green grass. You breathe in the fragrances wafting through the crisp air.

As you walk through the meadow, you come to a temple, perhaps one you have come to before in these meditations. You realize that this is your sacred temple and take a moment to look at its color and shape, to touch the outer walls, and feel their texture and temperature. When you are ready, walk into the temple. You might want to light some candles that are there for you. Then spend a few minutes exploring this space.

You notice the staircase off to one side and begin to go up the stairs until you come out on an upper deck. There's a comfortable mat waiting for you. Go ahead and lie down on it. Take a moment to soak in the beauty of the sky above you. Feel your cells vibrating more quickly and your frequency getting higher.

Now imagine that you can use your consciousness to travel inside of your body. You might enter through your mouth or travel through the space between the molecules on your skin to move into your body. Once you enter, find a cell that calls to you and spend time inside it examining your DNA. You might find that there are parts of each of the strands that are lit up and other parts that seem to have no energy.

Look over the lit-up areas. Notice that some give off a beautiful radiance where just looking at these areas opens your heart and your access to joy. Then you may see some that are unpleasant looking, perhaps due to their color or some undefined quality. Those are trauma areas holding both ancestral and other lifetime wounds, as well as wounds from your current lifetime.

Create an intention to become aware of which area most needs your attention right now in your life. It might be wounds that keep you feeling victimized or stuck or that interfere with your sense of financial security or with your trust to fully enter a love relationship. It may be wounds that make it too scary for you to fully show your gifts to the world. Use your intuition for guidance and stop before the area that most reflects these wounds.

You have the power to deactivate this part of your DNA. You can do this with a magic wand that shows up for you, through your mental focus, through touch, or through any other way that comes to you. Go ahead and deactivate this trauma/wound area—just let it release its energy and then flicker out.

Now let yourself know that you are safe to live your life without this wounding and that as you deactivate the old traumas from your cells, this helps you create this change. Breathe into this awareness and know that now you have more inner space to light up your star DNA as you are ready.

Slowly get up from your mat, and walk back down the temple stairs out to the meadow and allow your awareness to come back into the room you are in. Wiggle your fingers and toes to help you come back into your body. You may want to revisit your cells again and again, to make sure that this DNA stays deactivated.

Take some time to journal on this experience.

Note: Find this meditation on my YouTube channel, Wisdom Within Us, in the "Meditations to Raise Your Frequency" playlist.

Journal Questions to Ponder

1. Are you aware of feeling uncomfortable emotions or emotional triggers from something that happened years ago? Have you been able to process these feelings so they occur less and less frequently? Why or why not?
2. What beliefs might you still have that choosing a timeline you want to live in now is impossible?
3. Do you have information about other lifetimes that your soul has lived? If so, how have you accessed them? In what ways have they been useful to you?
4. What interests and experiences did you have as a child that inform you of your sacred purpose in this lifetime?
5. Are you aware of other traumas from other lifetimes that are affecting

you now? If so, write out the storyline, notice any emotions that arise, and then go through the process of changing the story of the experience. Include, how has that lifetime impacted you in this one.

6. Take a moment to choose a future for yourself that reflects something you want to happen but will be fine if it doesn't. Focus on it and call up any old beliefs and resistances to creating this. Then write about it.

PART THREE

Pathways to New Earth through Empowerment and Compassion

8

Steps to True Empowerment: The Antidote to Control

Those of us waking up, activating courage, and holding compassion for all as we step into the unknown are being challenged to trust ourselves and our inner wisdom. We are being asked to do our part to co-create and support the transition to make our planet the evolved, loving place it is meant to be. We realize no government is going to save us. No leader is going to save us. No spiritual guru is going to save us. Even those loving guides who make up our personal light team are not going to save us. To move through the pitfalls of third- and fourth-dimensional consciousness into the evolved frequencies of 5D and 6D is totally up to us. Books like this one can help. Podcasts can help. Spiritual teachers can help. But truly they are only of value if you are ready and committed to step into spiritual adulthood, to heal any issues that may be holding you back, and to reactivate and connect with your star DNA, which allows you to utilize your wisdom and gifts to live a life of higher-dimensional consciousness, and then to contribute to creating this on a planetary level.

The more we have expanded our bandwidth, the less vulnerable we become to the cultural control games of the old consensus reality. The more often we visit the peaceful, still place within, the place where we connect with our inner truth and cosmic awareness, the place of our divine core, the less we feel confusion or fear as we confront or witness the chaos in the outer world.

Our sense of empowerment grows the more we accept that we create our lives. Committing ourselves to take whatever steps are necessary to heal old wounds and trauma frees us then to open our heart, to feel unconditional love for ourselves and others, and to feel how we are one with all of creation. This is our 5D frequency. As our compassion grows, our reactivity diminishes. The peace we seek for the outer world shows up ever more consistently within us.

Although everyone's process is somewhat unique, there are important universal elements to be aware of and to navigate through on the journey. As more and more of us embark on and travel the road to living in our 5D/6D frequencies, this evolved energy vibrates out into our global energy field and the creation of New Earth moves closer and closer.

Embodiment

Quantum physics has shown us it changes based on the consciousness it is viewed from, making reality, by its very nature, malleable. This means we need to find an inner compass that transcends this malleability. What we have believed we needed for our survival by seeking to create external security turns out not to be what we need at all. Only by connecting with our inner stillness, by tuning into the wisdom of our heart and soul, can we keep our balance in this time of external uncertainty. This is why becoming and staying embodied is so important. It is through the feedback our body provides, the sensations it gives us, that we can tell if we are on the right track.

Our bodies are quite magical. Not only do they carry an innate ability to heal, but they also connect us to our feelings. When we learn to accurately read their signals, we expand our ability to live from our heart. However, connecting with and reading the language of our bodies accurately is no easy thing. Generally, we have been trained to live in our heads, to trust the intellect, and to ignore the body's wisdom. If we were physically or sexually abused as children or had a debilitating illness, this can become even more challenging.

The ignorance of our culture, which provides us with minimal or no guidance about how to recognize and clear emotional pain (including our feelings) intensifies this. Often people have difficulty even identifying what they are feeling, and even more often don't know what to do when various feelings arise. Our Western solution to this is to use pharmaceuticals that tend to numb what is unpleasant and simultaneously can keep people disconnected from their body's signals.

There are five primary feelings we experience as humans: fear, anger, sadness, joy, and love. All the rest such as guilt and shame are conditioned or are derivatives that arise because the primary feelings aren't honored. This includes anxiety, depression, bitterness, and resentment. When the more difficult feelings of fear, anger, and sadness are not recognized, it limits a person's ability to feel joy and love.

Our feelings are fourth dimensional. As I said in chapter 7, they connect with the right hemisphere of our brain, where all time is experienced simultaneously. This is why unprocessed feelings from childhood remain active, although often outside of a person's conscious sphere through dissociation, repression, and other forms of numbing out. These unprocessed feelings interact with our 3D bodies to create anxiety and depression in numerous human variations. This makes it more difficult to navigate the journey from being 3D/4D humans to owning ourselves as 5D/6D humans or divine humans.

One might be able to bypass processing trauma for a while through opening intuitive channels, and, in fact, many severely abused children are extremely psychic and tuned into higher-dimensional worlds as this became a survival strategy for them, but living in true well-being without healing the effects of the trauma or wounds ultimately becomes unsustainable. Until we are willing to do the emotional work, we cannot clear our emotional body, and it will show up in our lives in one way or another.

As we become more proficient at honoring our feelings, which means that we can more easily identify, express, and release fear, sadness, and anger as they arise, we begin to notice that our body will give us signals to help. Although these vary from person to person, anger often shows up as shoulder tension, sadness as heaviness in the chest, heart, and throat area, and fear is typically around the solar plexus or in the abdominal area, although it can show up as agitation around the heart area as well. As for love and joy, which of course we don't want to release, but rather we want to keep experiencing; love typically expresses itself first around the heart area, with feelings of melting, relaxing, and pleasure that then can permeate throughout our body. Joy, too, seems to begin in the heart area and spreads through our cells much like love.

The actual clearing of fear, sadness, and anger—emotions that are all important to our well-being—asks that we recognize and feel them before releasing them. The process of clearing itself is not difficult and can feel good. What makes it so challenging are the beliefs and judgments we carry about ourselves and about these feelings. This creates the resistance that makes emotional clearing so difficult.

As an example, if it was scary to express anger at being mistreated as a child, an adult working to release these feelings needs to disempower the belief that they will be bad or punished if they allow themselves to acknowledge this anger. This needs to happen before they can effectively process through and ultimately release it. If as children they experienced the adults in their lives being out of control and harming others with their anger, they need to learn there are healthy, nonharmful ways of releasing pent-up anger while staying in charge of the process.

Fear, of course, is a signal that there is danger. If it is literal, in other words, if we are in immediate physical danger, fear in its pure state helps us react in a way to stay safer. Most modern adult fears, however, come from our thoughts and our unconscious, which holds unprocessed, unhealed wounds, and ancestral trauma. Learning to recognize when these fears are triggered and learning strategies to not allow them to overtake you, is key. When we connect deeply with our inner divinity, the place of stillness within that connects us to all that is, fear usually will dissipate on its own. If we fear doing something because it is new or unknown, activating courage and doing it anyway is what is being asked of us.

It is natural to feel sadness for any loss. Allowing ourselves to express this through tears and keening releases the energy that can get blocked in our aura. Many years ago, I lived out in the country across from a family of horses: a mom, dad, and colt. At one point two of the horses were relocated, and the remaining horse loudly vocalized its grief for quite a while, and then seemed to get through it. As humans, though, we often keep ourselves from expressing and releasing our grief since our culture has taught us it is undignified to sob and keen, and sometimes to even cry. This makes it difficult to fully heal from old losses, and the unexpressed sadness creates congestion in our emotional body that in turn creates murkiness in the 4D canopy.

Anger is the most misunderstood of human emotions. Its energy is almost universally misused. We rarely have models to teach us how to express it in a healthy, non-harmful way. If it has no outlet, it turns against the self and becomes depression. If it becomes an outlet for fear or sadness, it becomes distorted, scary, and often violent. If it's explosive, which is usually the result of storing it up, it creates fear in others and spews negative energy. Anger that is unexpressed or expressed in a harmful or distorted way also creates congestion in our emotional body.

When we are violated or treated unfairly, anger is a natural response. If repressed, it damages our third chakra, our sense of self, creating a belief that we do not deserve to be treated well. If it is expressed violently, or in any way that causes harm to others, whether through intimidation, physical destruction, pain, or ultimately war, its energy is distorted and continues to murk up the 4D canopy both personally and collectively, blocking access to the higher-frequency portals. If instead anger is expressed in a way that does no harm but assertively stands up for our personal or collective rights, it offers us empowerment and healing.

Joy and love are our birthright. We can feel loving and be filled with loving energy even when we go through fear, anger, or sadness. Those last three feelings are fleeting when they are processed in a healthy way, whereas love and joy are enduring. We can experience joyfulness simply by watching the sunrise or hearing a cat purr. When we are strongly connected to joy, the simple act of breathing will amplify it. The more we clear our emotional body, the more access we have to feeling both loving and joyful.

As we become more embodied, not only have we become skilled at identifying and processing through challenging feelings so that their energy does not become distorted and clog our emotional body, but there's also another important gift our human body provides: it gives us sensations that support our intuitive knowing and helps us discern if outside information is in alignment with our inner wisdom. It also helps us know if our thoughts are aligned with our soul or have been distorted by old beliefs or cultural propaganda. We can run these things through our body and notice how it feels. Does it activate a sensation of relaxation and well-being? Or does it feel chaotic, fearful, or out of balance in any way? This is also a way we can notice signals we get when our ego responds positively, but our soul does not. As we become more and more skilled at interpreting the messages our body gives us, we will become more astute at distinguishing the difference between our ego responses and our soul responses.

Because this is so subjective, it can be tricky territory. We might get a good sensation that is more connected to abdicating our power to an outside authority because it feels safer to look outward for someone to tell us what is real. That illusion of safety feels good. However, for those of us committed to doing our inner work and expanding our bandwidth, we can learn to tell when or if this is getting in the way, and then become more in tune to the subtle differences in the signals our bodies provide.

There's a particular sense of depth in the sensation we get from our inner core that we learn over time we can count on. This may take a fair amount of practice, and, of course, it may feel different for you than for me, but as you become more aware of the sensation that arises when you activate your inner wisdom, it becomes easier and easier to notice and follow.

If one is not fully embodied, you will be accessing information more through the third-dimensional brain than the higher mind, and it will be difficult for you to discern what is real for you. There is a sense of calm and peacefulness when we can get in tune with our divine core that is accessed through our embodied body sensations. This is where we connect to our inner compass and how someone like Nelson Mandela was able to withstand decades of imprisonment and keep his heart open and his humanity intact.

Another sign that we are embodied is that we feel energy move throughout our entire body. We can pull higher-dimensional energy down through our crown chakra and bring it all the way to our toes, as well as distribute it to all our cells. We can send a grounding cord from our base chakra deep into the heart of Mother Earth and bring up Earth energy through this chakra and/or the bottom of our feet to keep us grounded. This also means that we can notice where we are blocking energy, and then do what's needed to release those blocks.

Feeling love and appreciation for our physical bodies is extremely important. Freeing yourself from the cultural ideas of how we should look and appreciating the amazing things our body does for us by allowing us to see our environment, to taste our food, to walk, to hug, to exchange energy with another. Even if we are ill, there is always something that our body can do that we can appreciate, and the more we love and appreciate our body, the more it can function well for us. The more we honor our body and what it needs to be healthy and vibrant, the more embodied we become and the more we will be able to use its signals and sensations optimally to help our ascension journey.

Loving Neutrality

As I said before, as our compassion grows, our emotional reactivity diminishes. We find that we are more consistently living from a place of calm and peacefulness. Our hearts are open and leading our minds, which are quiet and without agenda. We rarely take things personally, and, if we do, we notice this quickly as well as any other emotional triggers. This allows us to process any feelings that need attention and any beliefs that need transforming, so we can ultimately let them go.

Because our consciousness is expanded, we have developed the ability to release attachment to 3D outcomes. We can view life from a higher-dimensional frequency and see there are many paths and many choices for others, all of which contain important lessons. We have released the illusion that we can or need to control anyone else, or their views. We simply commit to doing our best, to being kind, and to holding the vision of our planet operating on the foundation of unconditional love for ourselves and others, where all beings are honored, and where there is no violence, cruelty, or abuse. We no longer live in fear and anger or from the belief that the only way to get others to stop harming us is to harm them first.

Loving neutrality ultimately becomes our default drive. This is a felt sense where you notice a peaceful flow of energy throughout your body. The more you experience yourself in this state, the easier it becomes to return to it whenever you become triggered. And, of course, as humans, we will become triggered, just less and less as time goes on, and we won't get stuck in it.

Polarization is running rampant right now, and conflicting versions of reality are spewing all over the media. Both sides suggest dire consequences if one does not support their view of the world. This intensifies the energy of fear and distorted anger that is permeating our emotional atmosphere. In turn, this amplifies the murkiness in 4D, blocking some of our access to the higher-dimensional frequencies. The more of us who hold the energy of loving neutrality the more we can counteract this, and the closer we become collectively to creating a loving, peaceful, higher frequency world.

This does not mean we have no opinion, only that we are not opinionated, meaning we don't run opinionated and therefore polarizing energy. We have learned to discern what is important by listening to our inner wisdom, noticing our internal sensations, and then allowing our inner compass to guide us. This keeps us from falling prey to accepting new versions of reality that are just as false as the old ones.

What we call *conspiracy theories* are a great example of this. Personally, I don't like the word *conspiracy*. I think it triggers a sensationalist reaction whether it is accurate or not. Has information been suppressed? Of course. Is the public generally lied to, or at least cleverly misled? Yes. Are other-planetary beings involved? Probably. Are there counterforces to planetary evolution? I'm quite sure of this. However, I've observed that once people accept ideas that the culture has labeled ridiculous, they become extremely vulnerable to believing all sorts of things that are not accurate, and then they can be easily controlled in a new way. So, I put out a word of caution. Pay attention to the energy invoked by different theories. It may start with you feeling angry about being duped, but once through that anger, ask yourself, does this energy feel loving? (It may sound loving but that doesn't mean it is.) Does it feel like there is an agenda to try to convince you of something? Be especially aware if there are particular groups of people that are being targeted as "the problem." This is an age-old strategy to deflect people's attention from what is really going on. Remember too that with AI, all sorts of things can be made to look true.

When I feel emotional activation about world events and questionable theories about what is going on, I first get grounded, then breathe into my heart, allowing my capacity for love to increase. Then I visualize expanding energetically to hold a big enough container for all of it to fit in, trusting that I will be guided in a way that is productive. I might not know what is truth and what is not—as with multiple timelines, there can be many truths operating at once. Rather I can focus on what energies feel most aligned with loving, higher frequencies.

Because we are holographic, I stay with the awareness that even the actions and ideas I feel most concerned about are also something that is reflected in me, in all of us. I then can expand beyond my opinions and hold all sides in compassion whether I agree with them or not. This is loving neutrality. We don't get caught up in the details, but rather we hold higher-frequency energy, loving all existence and creation for simply being. As this energy permeates both us and the energy field of our planet, the frequency rises and support for lower-frequency motivations including war, tribalism, nationalism, and cruelty diminishes. We are all one, and we are in this together. Harming any manifestation of the Divine hurts us all. Although we need to acknowledge the darkness, we don't need to get caught up in the specifics, but rather to hold the awareness that genuine transformation occurs through love and through energizing the visions of what we wish to create in our world.

Notice when you feel loving and neutral. Notice when you don't. Be loving and gentle to yourself in this process. When you feel triggered, work with it until you can release the triggers and return to a loving but neutral state. This essentially is our being the change we want to see.

Observing Ways That We Give Our Power Away

Becoming an observer, an objective but loving self-researcher, is fundamental to our development. It allows us to know what we are feeling and what we are thinking without emotional attachment. It allows us to notice when we are triggered, reactive, or calm. The more we practice this, the more we can notice the subtler games of our egos, the subtler layers of our psyche, and the subtler cues from our emotional body as it is translated through our physical body.

I've written fairly extensively on self-observation in the first chapter of my book *Empowering the Spirit*, so I won't repeat myself here. What I'm going to focus on is more specific: to notice the ways we allow others or mainstream culture to control us by letting them manipulate us into giving away our power.

Like all growth processes, expanding our perceptual bandwidth doesn't mean 100 percent of ourselves are in alignment. What we believe after going through an awakening, as well as what we see then, can shift back once more as we are exposed to old-paradigm stimuli from our outer world. So even with expanded consciousness, there are still those rogue cells that resist new awareness because it is so foreign to the way we've been conditioned. These parts make us vulnerable to being controlled by social and personal expectations others have of us.

For instance, if we have been trained to accept the word of people who are recognized as experts, authorities, or influencers in mass culture, we may reflexively go against our own expanded inner knowing, believing that they somehow know more than we do or have found the key to living right. Versions of the old reality can seduce us because they feel familiar and safe. It can be scary to know that we are on our own. If we are observing ourselves carefully, noticing this fear helps us not get sucked into this, but rather to calm down those scared parts of ourselves instead.

Be aware, too, that people we look up to as our teachers because they have some information that genuinely resonates for us, does not mean that everything they say will be accurate. We are all fallible and learning to discern what connects for us and what does not is an essential part of this process.

If we are not connected to our inner compass, it is very difficult to discern what genuinely resonates and what does not. This is a practice, and it isn't going to be perfect nor does it need to be. But the more you can observe about what is going on inside you and what is motivating your responses, the more you will ultimately get free.

Notice the parts of you that still want to fit in, still want to be socially acceptable in whatever circles you choose to travel in or find yourself traveling in. This is a motivation for giving away our power and allowing others to control us. Essentially any time we are not being authentic, we are disconnected from our inner compass.

The best way I can describe authenticity is that we feel an inner flow, an inner alignment. There is no self-consciousness or concern about what others think or feel about us. We have no need to second guess ourselves. If people think we're strange, weird, wrong, or crazy, so be it. To quote a card from Wayne Dyer's *Inner Wisdom Cards* deck: "Other people's opinion of me is none of my business."[1] The more fully we internalize this, the greater our sense of freedom. This is especially relevant now as more and more people are waking up and finding their family and friends are not going through this with them, which can make them feel they are doing this all on their own. It is no easy feat to be leading the way, and yet this is what is happening now for so many.

If you notice you are feeling scared to hold new expanded versions of your reality, be gentle with yourself. Of course, it's scary, and perhaps confusing as well, but do your best to not let that stop you. You will begin to attract people in your life that are resonating at the same frequency that you are. You might not see all things as the same, and that's fine. Know though, that you will have support for seeing through the illusions we've been trained to believe, and support for the awareness that we are multidimensional and here to participate in a great evolutionary leap on our planet. Just keep observing, staying conscious of anything that wants to pull you back into your lower-frequency beliefs and fears, as this is where you will find you are giving your personal power away.

We also have been trained to give ourselves and our sense of personal empowerment up in close relationships, whether familial, romantic, or with friends. This is classic codependency that our culture has defined as love. We also may lack models for how to keep a strong sense of self while being deeply connected to another. The motive here is not so much about fitting in, but about feeling loved, or, more specifically, about fear that we will not be loved if we don't take care of other people and instead stay true to ourselves. It can also take the form of dominating another, making them believe they are only okay if they do and think as you wish, in order to convince yourself that they will not leave you.

Take a moment and ponder if there are any relationships where you find yourself giving away your power or trying to take another's. If there are, ponder what your motivation is. Are you afraid of being left? Do you feel you would no longer be loved if you stayed true to yourself? Have you been conditioned to believe that giving some power to a loved one is the right thing to do and that if you somehow change from the way they expect you to be, this will mean you are not loving or good enough? Once you can understand what is driving you to give away your power, you then can do what is necessary to take it back.

Reclaiming Our Power

Once we have effectively observed how we give our power away, the next obvious step is to reclaim it. If we have cleared enough emotional wounds, and transformed enough old-paradigm beliefs, this can be as simple as noticing when we are doing it, asking ourselves what needs to change, and then following through.

However, we are very complex beings with many competing motivations. If my need to fit into conventional society is still strong, to fully regain my power I will have to work through this need and muster enough courage to be different. This means being willing to take the risk that some will judge me as weird or crazy.

Usually, the part of us that is most attached to fitting in is our inner teenager. Many people experience their teenage years as painful. We may believe something is wrong with us because we are so different and perhaps because we have been shunned by our peers. Or, if we have a strong personality, we might instead create a false persona so we appear very differently than we feel inside and disempower our true self by doing so. Doing work with your inner teen on any unhealed wounds from this time in your life will help you get free of this. When we view our inner teen from an adult perspective with compassion for what they are going through and respect for who they really are beneath the insecurity or false persona, this helps shift the need to fit in.

As I've told numerous clients over numerous years when they ask me if something is normal, normal and healthy are not the same thing. We live in a culture where most, if not all the norms are dysfunctional, and then we have labeled those who follow those norms as normal, as if this were a good thing. So, giving up any concern about what's normal allows us to become continually healthier.

Fears of being unlovable or abandoned are also a common motivation for giving up power in relationships. These tend to be more challenging to shift because they often go back to an earlier time in our childhood. For those fears, doing some effective psychotherapy is the way to go. Again, the intent here is to clear out old, stuck emotions and shift old views of ourselves, transforming anything that feeds any beliefs we carry that we are not okay. As we do this, we regain more trust in ourselves and increase our ability to love ourselves, flaws and all. So many people stay in relationships where they are not expressing who they fully are because of these fears, which come down to being scared if they step into their true power and radiance, or, if they release manipulative control of another, they will be all alone.

Another motivation for people to hold themselves back from others in their lives is fear of hurting their partner, family, and friends if they end up outgrowing them. As we evolve, we need to work through and release these fears and worries. Every time we allow relationships to stop us from being in our authentic power and expressing who we truly are, we wound ourselves, and we interfere with our ability to step into our soul's mission. We also hurt those we believe we are protecting because we are not giving them the chance to see us modeling this journey for them. As we break free of these patterns, we may find we are simply needing to lead the way, and loved ones will follow. If they choose not to follow, they will be free of a relationship built on pretense, and we will be free to make deeper connections that support us at our soul level.

Ultimately, though, this is an independent journey, and we need to be prepared for what we have looked to as outer security to be swept away. It is well worth it because as we do this, we develop a sense of inner security that is never at risk from the outside world. The energies of the universe then can, and will, support us once we make this choice. And true joy and a sense of connection to all that is will be the ultimate result.

Take some time to assess your close relationships. Are they supporting your growth? Are you seen for who you truly are? Do you hold yourself back to protect others? The journal questions at the end of this chapter will help you look more deeply at how you may be holding yourself back.

No one can control us if we understand the means used for control, whether from the larger society or in personal relationships, and then refuse to play the game. This means once we understand it, we need to muster the courage to step out of the brainwashing and into who we are at a soul level. When we do, our frequency and our level of personal power become high enough that we are no longer susceptible to manipulations from outer forces. This is the way we find ourselves in a new, loving reality despite the outer chaos. This is how we change our lives and change our world.

Shadow Work

If we cannot see our shadow, we cannot truly know ourselves, and we will not be able to successfully navigate through the fourth dimension. This means we need to unearth anything about us that we have been taught not to see or learned is unacceptable. Often this includes our unique gifts, and always it includes the parts that hold the ability to act out with cruelty and venom, essentially the parts that hold the dark side of humanity.

Remember, we are holographic. There is no part of humanity, dark or light, that does not have some place within us. For most of us, those dark parts are small and have little or no power over us. They may show up with bizarre thoughts or feelings of wanting to hurt someone we think has wronged us, wronged a loved one, or wronged the world, but we would not act them out. Still, because of our conditioning, they tend to scare us, and most people will try to avoid acknowledging they exist within them.

When we avoid noticing or acknowledging our dark thoughts or desires, they can build up power in our unconscious. Although the likelihood of our doing physical harm to someone is low for most of us, what happens when we won't own these thoughts is that they can create subtle levels of harm or undermining. We cannot fully know ourselves until we are willing to notice these things about ourselves. We cannot authentically embrace our wholeness without acknowledging our shadow. Blocking this acknowledgment also opens us to unconscious projection. If I don't own my angry thoughts about something that happened to me, I may find that I project that anger onto something else or someone else: a vulnerable group, a politician, or anyone I believe has harmed others or the world. Essentially, we are disowning this part of ourselves, which means we are giving up the opportunity to create personal and planetary transformation by acknowledging and then integrating our shadow.

We may also find that collective shadow parts have entered our consciousness. They may show up as prejudice about a group of people that consciously we feel fully accepting of, even a group that we are part of. This happens because those shadow parts are in the collective consciousness, and we are all a part of this. Again, once noticed, they can lose any energy that might create harm or pain. If we judge or refuse to notice them, they can feed these qualities in the sixth dimension, which can strengthen rather than weaken their potential to do harm.

Many decades ago, I was at a conference on science and spirituality. Elizabeth Kübler-Ross was the keynote speaker, and she talked essentially about us owning our shadow, although I don't believe those were the words she used. She spoke of how within each of us was the capacity to become Hitler. This was particularly poignant because after WWII she had been part of the IVSP (International Voluntary Service for Peace) and worked to help concentration camp survivors.[2] Her point was that we needed to understand that the human psyche holds all of the human experience, dark and light. Clearly, her talk left a major impression on me. We are all capable of everything.

When I was in graduate school in Chicago in the early 1970s, I was in a small group that went to interview her for a project we were working on. This was before she became well-known, but she had already published her book *On Death and Dying*. She was working in a mental-health center on the south side of the city. Being in my midtwenties and a bit callow, my first impression was that she seemed like a wizened old woman, very nondescript and probably boring. Then she began to speak. I was mesmerized and ultimately transformed, grateful to have had the privilege of being in her presence and hearing her wisdom. Having this experience before being at the conference years later, I was already aware of her high level of consciousness and thus was able to understand on a deep level what she was communicating to us. We are all part of each other, and all humans have the potential to become the best of or the worst of humanity.

Do not be afraid of the dark. When it shows up inside you, develop skills to recognize it, process any emotions that might be feeding it, and then send it love to neutralize the negative energy it holds and ultimately transform it. Facing the dark within us not only leads us personally to wholeness, but it leads us there collectively as well.

When beings become so damaged that they no longer have any connection to their soul is when they become capable of doing great harm. Hitler, of course, is an example of this happening on a grand scale. Although I don't like the word *evil* because it carries a sensationalist resonance, once someone is soulless, it seems they are not likely to have access to the light.

Years ago, I worked with a client who came from a ritually abusive family. Her parents were leaders in a cult that not only horribly abused children but apparently sacrificed some at a young age as well. For whatever reason, rural Illinois is a hotbed for cult abuse. In my client's case, her family owned large acres of farmland so that they were able to meet at night without detection.

This client suffered great abuse both from the cult and from her father who physically and sexually abused her throughout her childhood. Her mother, who was a well-respected high school teacher, sexually abused her as well. Miraculously, she was not soulless. In fact, she was consciously trying to do good in the world by protecting abused children, but she was programmed through the cult to have various dissociative parts, and at least two of those parts participated in the cult abuse. When we started working together, she had no conscious awareness of being in the cult or of much of the abuse she had suffered and, no doubt, perpetrated. She only knew that something was really off. When someone suffers from DID (Dissociative Identity Disorder), which used to be called *multiple personality disorder*, they often lose time. What is going on when this happens is that another personality comes forward, takes the main stage, so to speak, and the core personality becomes unaware of this, only aware that time has been missing. As I learned more about how to work with DID and cult abuse, I learned how to help her become more conscious and therefore in charge of these personalities. I also helped her to bring different ones forward in our sessions so that we could heal them and ultimately integrate her so that she no longer was vulnerable to them taking over. In the process, I learned quite a bit about the dark.

It is my understanding, in reading about cult abuse and consulting with other therapists who were also dealing with cult-abused clients, that in these families, children were trained to dissociate, and various personalities were intentionally developed to carry on the work of the cult. Most of my client's cult personalities were hurt, angry children acting out their pain by abusing others. Those parts began to respond to love and reach a point where they no longer could tolerate participating in doing harm. As my client became more conscious, she was able to control this. However, there was one part that ultimately came forward, as the others healed, that would fit my definition of soulless. What I learned working with this part was that it could not tolerate the light. I would consciously beam it light filled with love and watch as it had to retreat. This taught me that we don't have to fear the dark; we don't have to fear what we have labeled evil. The dark potential within the vast majority of us will simply transform if we beam that light on it. We will not become Hitler-like. For those small number who have fully disconnected from their soul, know that the light is more powerful than their darkness. Beaming them with light is intolerable to them, and they will go away and no longer be able to do harm, at least in this reality.

Are there alien races, who, in their soullessness, are influencing what is happening on our planet? I have no personal experience that validates this, but there are credible sources that believe this to be true. What I have learned, though, is that there is no need to fear this. Beaming light filled with love will ultimately disempower them. More and more light is being beamed here from our sun and from the central suns that communicate with our sun. This will make Earth ultimately intolerable for those forces. The other piece to remember is that we create what we focus on. So, there is a fine line between seeing what is occurring from our expanded bandwidth and inadvertently empowering the dark because we are focusing on it and thus providing it with energy. If this is something you have been doing, I urge you to shift your focus to what you want to create and to learn how to use your own sixth-dimensional creative potential.

Inner Trust

From early on in our incarnation, we have been trained not to trust our perceptions. This is how our bandwidth becomes constricted in the first place. We are taught to believe only what we are told is real by our families or society at large, not what comes to us intuitively.

Breaking through this conditioning is the primary task to reclaim our multidimensional nature and live from an expanded perceptual bandwidth. The more we connect with our intuitive wisdom, the harder it becomes for us to participate in collective illusions. Ultimately, we become free agents with an ongoing practice to go within and notice how our heart and gut respond to outside information, and then to connect with our inner compass. If there is a sense that an agenda is attached to information coming from the media, alternative or mainstream, or from other's opinions, rather than from higher-consciousness neutrality, my advice is to stay away from it.

The other important point is that we don't have to know all the details of where we are going, either personally or collectively. We only need to feel into our next right step and to be able to discern if it is coming from our heart and in alignment with our embodied wisdom or if it is fear-based or anger-based disinformation intended to manipulate us. Although, as I've said before, honoring our fears and anger is essential to our well-being, those emotions are not to be used to guide us. They are not what leads our planet out from pain and suffering, war, and oppression. It is only love that can truly lead the way.

Humanity is evolving whether we see that yet in our outer world or not. The more of us who reclaim who we are on a soul level, the more of us there are to vibrate at and emit higher-dimensional frequencies while living in a 3D world. The more our numbers grow, the faster our world transforms.

✳ MEDITATION ✳
Reclaiming Empowerment and Authenticity

Allow your eyes to soften and put all your attention on taking deep centering breaths. As you exhale release any distractions, any concerns, any tension. Just let that all flow out with the breath. On the inhale imagine that you are drawing in tiny golden spirals of light filled with love and consciousness and allow those tiny spirals to spread to every cell in your body. Keep focusing on your breath as you begin to feel a sense of calm and deep relaxation.

Now imagine that you are standing on top of a beautiful mountain. The sky is a vibrant blue, the sun is warming your hair and skin. You look out over the beautiful vista, allowing yourself to drink in its beauty as you focus on the colors and shapes of the magnificent view. You can hear the birds singing and calling to one another and the tree leaves as they rustle in the breeze. The air is fresh and crisp. You might spend a few minutes touching all that surrounds you, feeling the energy of the large, beautiful boulders, of the tree trunks, of the wildflowers.

Now find a large boulder where you can stand with your back supported and your spine straight. Spend a few minutes just breathing deeply, appreciating the natural beauty that surrounds you. Then, keeping your focus on your breathing, feel yourself stand taller and taller. Say something out loud and notice that your voice is strong, clear, and resonant. You might want to belt out a song, singing at the top of your lungs, and feel this powerful energy course through you.

Think about a time when you felt yourself at your most empowered, when you felt on top of your game and deeply in alignment with your inner self. It might have been at a significant life event or something that was just momentary, either way, allow this image and this feeling to come back to you. Keep breathing into this image until you feel stronger and more and more radiant. Experience yourself this way fully connected to your spirit, totally confident in your goodness, while being loving, gentle, and nonjudgmental of your flaws.

Rub your hands together and place them over your heart using the warmth of your hands to help this area relax and fill with love. Bathe this fully empowered version of you in this love, feeling deep appreciation for who you really are.

Now I would like you to see standing before you the part of yourself that tends to abdicate your power, the deflated part that holds back your truth when dealing with people in your life or with the outside world. Lovingly observe this part and let your empowered self beam and bathe this deflated part in love.

Take a moment and dialogue with this disempowered version of who you are. Provide this part with images of ways they can behave in the future in order to not abdicate their power. Let them know that you are strong enough to protect them.

When it feels right, breathe deeply once again, and slowly on the inhale, bring this disempowered self into you. Notice how you can contain this part that holds self-doubt and fear without losing energy. Send love to yourself once again to strengthen your sense of empowerment, and then create an intention to stay in this empowered version of yourself more and more in your life.

You might want to think of a color you associate with your feelings of full empowerment. Then see yourself surrounded with this color.

Slowly come back from the mountain. Breathe deeply and feel into and ponder the experience you just had. Now slowly allow yourself to come back into the room you are in, perhaps wiggling your fingers and toes to help you more fully get back into your body. As you go through the next several days or weeks, surround yourself with objects of this color to continue living in your full power from your authentic self.

Note: Find this meditation on my YouTube channel, Wisdom Within Us, in the "Meditations to Raise Your Frequency" playlist.

Journal Questions to Ponder

1. What did you learn about expressing feelings as a child? How were feelings expressed in your family and how did you feel about this? What reactions did you get from your parents when you expressed various feelings?
2. How embodied do you consider yourself? What signals do you get from your body about your feelings? What signals do you get that let you know if something resonates with you? In what ways do you honor your body?
3. Write about your experience of the difference between reactivity and loving neutrality. What opinions do you hold that tend to stir up the energy of being opinionated? What signals do you get that you are in a place of loving neutrality?

4. Are you able to view your responses, feelings, and behavior with loving objectivity? What might you need to do to improve your skills here?
5. How frequently do you feel you are expressing yourself authentically? When you are not, what do you think makes this hard or scary for you? What might help you break through this?
6. In what relationships do you find that you give your power away rather than staying true to yourself? In what ways do you do this? What may be the beliefs you carry that drive this behavior?
7. Are you in any close relationships where you hold yourself back from your full power and radiance because you fear the relationship will end if you don't? In what ways do you do this? What fears or beliefs are you carrying that contribute?
8. What fears and beliefs are you still carrying that make it difficult for you to accept your intuitive wisdom and guidance? What helps you accept your intuitive wisdom and guidance?

9

A Joyful New World

Take a moment and think about how you feel when you are living from your highest frequency. Focus on the feeling you get when your heart is open and its vibrations of love flow through your body. Feel or imagine how the energy of joy and gratitude can permeate all you do as you go through your day.

Then imagine what it would be like to live on a planet where everyone you meet, everyone you connect with, and everyone in your world is vibrating at this frequency. No one is operating from an ego agenda. No one is operating from or reacting to old wounds and trauma. All have awakened and are living from their expanded bandwidth in the big picture of their lives, free of the old-paradigm programming.

Notice how it feels to realize that the 5D qualities of unconditional love, nonjudgment, unity consciousness, and unbridled creativity have now become the norm. The idea of judging another as somehow less than we are, or somehow wrong because of their race, ethnicity, culture, sexual orientation, gender identification, or any other qualities that the old world found uncomfortable, has become nonexistent. Each individual is free to live as their soul directs them and is honored for those choices, as long as they do no harm.

Judgment and self-judgment have been replaced by lovingly neutral objective observation.

Let yourself feel what it is like to live in this spiritually awakened world where everyone has an open and generous heart. A world where all basic needs for comfortable shelter in a clean, healthy, and beautiful environment are met. Where everyone has nutritious, vibrant food. Where all live in safety and general well-being. In this world, everyone is appreciated for their soul gifts and encouraged to pursue what they most love as a way of contributing to the overall well-being of the planet. This is a world that is peaceful and stress-free. This is a world that has been created by people vibrating at their 5D/6D frequency.

Crime, mental illness, addictions, and disease are a rarity and are lovingly and humanely dealt with focusing on healing the source, not the symptoms. Our interconnection with all that exists in creation is honored. This has allowed us to reclaim the balance and bounty of the Earth. We no longer do anything that can harm her. Food is grown in fertile soil and and without chemicals. Vibration and resonance are used to increase food production. If animal products are still eaten, the animals have all been treated with kindness, both in their life and their death.

The climate has rebalanced. There are no intense storms or earthquakes. None of Earth's resources are used without her permission. To those of us living on this planet, the idea of Earth not being treated as a living being makes no sense.

Energy is free and produced by aligning the electromagnetic currents that run through all creation, using the gravity of the Earth to harness the energy of the cosmos, and the energy of the cosmos to harness the energy of the Earth. This provides us with everything needed for heating, cooling, technology, transportation, and any other needs of this sort that arise.

We have the capacity to create this world. This is not a pipe dream. We have been programmed to believe this is impossible, but that is simply a lie of the old paradigm. We free ourselves from this the more we raise our frequency and see out of our higher-dimensional eyes.

We have lived in worlds like this before. Can you remember?

As We Transition

Frequency, in all its myriad variations, creates material reality. Everything we see on Earth existed first in the frequencies of the sixth dimension. This New Earth, which already exists on a future timeline and in its energy form in 6D, is created from these higher-consciousness frequencies. The more of us who raise our vibration, the more quickly this world will manifest.

And as I've said before, part of what happens in this transitionary process is that our frequency will tend to go up and down. Noticing what raises our frequency, what opens our heart more fully, what connects us with our soul helps on days when we are not naturally vibrating at this level. Being gentle with ourselves on these days is equally important, as feelings and judgments that we are not doing it right will lower our vibration and make raising it again more difficult.

The way to gauge our progress is to observe if we are increasing the amount of time we are generally in higher frequency. Notice how good this feels when you are. Notice, too, what triggers take you down, and what strategies work to offset the triggers.

Personal challenges, whether around money, relationships, health, or work certainly can trigger us. But those of us living in the big picture know that all these things are part of an Earth school curriculum to help us grow and heal. We can cheer ourselves on through each challenge or succumb to the stress and distress. And it is fine to do both, as long as we don't get stuck in self-pity or victim consciousness.

My best transitional strategy is to keep my sense of humor as I watch my old lower-vibrational beliefs step into the foreground. For instance, despite my intent to make writing this book easy and joyful, pretty much every morning after I'd wake up, I'd find myself concerned that I wouldn't be able to write anything. Even in this last chapter, this still occurred. Yet somehow the words always showed up somewhat effortlessly on the page. Shaking my head and lovingly laughing at myself keeps this all from getting heavy and standing in my way. We all still must deal with our human foibles. We are all on some level still bumbling through as we walk the evolutionary path. Seeing the comedic parts lightens the energy of self-judgment and brings a more joyful feeling even when we notice we are not operating from a higher frequency.

Then there are the collective triggers. The old world is not dying gracefully, and knowing of the suffering of so many is certainly one trigger that can keep us stuck in the fear and anger of the old frequencies. Learning to activate feelings of compassion whenever we hear, read, or see suffering without letting it drag us into the energy of pain is a practice we all need to develop.

I handle this by not looking at any videos or photos of what is going on because I know that if I see them, this will make disconnecting from the pain much more difficult and that taking on this pain will not help anyone. Instead, I hold everyone involved in compassion and send out daily prayers. Thinking of people starving, especially children, breaks my heart, and each time I eat, I not only express gratitude for my food but ask that all beings around the planet have access to this food.

Connecting with our soul mission, with what our souls have brought us here to do, and then doing our best to carry this out is another important part of dealing with the current suffering. We then are using the pain and sadness of the world to strengthen our motivation to be a more active part of the New Earth birth team.

Remember, too, that it is the transition stage of the birthing process that is the most difficult, and it happens right before the birth.

Keep holding the vision of the old, low-frequency world receding as more and more people around the globe reclaim their true selves and operate from their fifth- and sixth-dimensional energy. This is why we are here now, and it is our birthright.

The Future of Screen Technology

As we move into the future there are likely to be two different screen-technology timelines. Those of us who have embraced and are leading the ascension path understand the challenges that are being created with the addictive and seductive nature of screen time, and how technology can be misused to produce false realities to keep people caught in lower frequencies. With the development of AI, this now has reached a whole new level of sophistication. There's an old bumper sticker that says, "Don't believe everything you think." Wise words. Now we need an adaptation that says, "Don't believe everything you see." Learning how to discern when we are being manipulated by false images, and when we not, is both challenging and essential as we continue on this journey.

Those who are not on an ascension path are vulnerable to being overtaken by AI, especially those who have no tools to discern the dangers. For them, artificial intelligence could play a large role in limiting their perceptual bandwidth, keeping their frequency low, and fostering screen-time addictions that disconnect them from nature and from their inner core. This leaves them easy to manipulate by whoever is running the tech narrative.

Used properly, of course, technology has great attributes. It provides us with remarkable opportunities to connect with people around the planet, to share our gifts globally, to have an abundance of information at our fingertips. Used with consciousness, technology makes numerous things in our lives easier.

From our 5D frequency, we'll become more able to detect what information has integrity and what doesn't. We will also be in internal balance so not vulnerable to misusing this form of technology, understanding that it is a useful tool and needs to be used skillfully.

As we transition to the new world, we will need to address how to no longer exploit the resources from Mother Earth that are currently needed to create our devices, and how to create these devices so they last for long periods of time and not pollute her with more waste. This is a short-term fix, a transitional fix, which with collective intent, can occur soon.

Ultimately, though, as we continue on our ascension path, we will be consciously creating everything from frequency. Devices, in their current form, will become obsolete. We will be transmitting and receiving information in totally new ways. This may occur on both technology timelines, but the energy with which the transmissions occur, and the level of consciousness with which these transmissions will be received will be quite different on each timeline.

At some point, I sense the 3D and 5D reality timelines may fully split, with each no longer interacting with the other. Crossing timelines may no longer be an option. Those who choose to remain on a 3D timeline may no longer be able to shift in their current incarnation. Until then, the timelines will be more permeable as our vibratory speed continues to go up and down.

Other Technologies

Each planet that is home to conscious beings who operate from their 5D frequencies or higher has unique ways of aligning with their planet's physical properties to fulfill their energy needs, transportation needs, health, food production, and the like. Some advanced civilizations will use a lot of technology and others will use little while still creating a high quality of life for everyone.

Lemuria and Atlantis are good examples of how this played out here. The Lemurians were into simplicity and were able to produce much of what they needed through manifesting their thought forms. Their need for technology was minimal. This was because as a feminine-based society, their focus was more about their internal richness than their external experience. Atlantis, on the other hand, was more dynamic and more external because of its more masculine nature. I think that many of the Indigenous tribes around our globe were descendants of the Lemurians, whereas the more technologically advanced societies, ancient Egypt, and the like, descended from the Atlanteans.

Lemurians were naturally peaceful and loving and embraced the natural world of this planet without ambition or desire for grandeur. Their shelters were simple but beautiful and comfortable. Their temples and meeting places incorporated the natural elements that were close by. They lived simply, in harmony with the Earth and each other. Even though they were a feminine culture, they still brought in the energy of the sacred masculine, using it for structure and organization and for the actions needed to carry out their visions.

Atlanteans, too, created from thought forms but chose to design a more technologically elaborate society because they were more masculine. At their height, they were balanced with the energy of the sacred feminine, which brought a high level of psychospiritual development. I think it's fair to say that their declines happened when this balance was broken.

Whenever this occurred, their technology and its use became out of balance as well.

Coming from a different solar system than ours, both Lemurians and Atlanteans would have had to recalibrate to the vibrations of our sun. Atlantis, when it was in balance, had breathtaking structures. They were all created from sacred geometric forms, and if my memory serves me correctly, because of the high frequency of the population, the structures themselves vibrated at this frequency. It was as if they were shimmering versions of the denser constructions that showed up as temples in ancient Egypt and which are still standing today.

Atlantis also apparently had a centralized power satellite that bounced energy into crystal receptors that would then distribute the power wherever it was needed. However, this centralization left them vulnerable, and the story I've heard is that some opposing forces destroyed the satellite, taking their energy grid down suddenly, which threw the society into chaos. I suspect that the power grid destruction was part of the second fall.

What is most relevant for our new world is to realize we have the ability to create all the energy that people need on our planet without harming the planet. And this energy can be abundant and available to all. I feel certain there are souls here and souls coming in who will not only remember what has been created before in our advanced civilizations but will have the 5D creativity to take the lessons learned and adapt the knowledge from the past into something that will work even better for us now. As we reclaim our internal health and the gifts that balancing the energies of the sacred masculine and the sacred feminine bring, we will have the wisdom to develop and use technology in a way that harms nothing and that improves the quality of life for everyone.

When I did a meditation around being in ancient Egypt while it was still functioning in 5D, I saw that people were able to transport themselves slightly above the ground, kind of like a hovercraft, but without the craft. Although this doesn't seem like a viable replacement to cars, trains, planes, or buses, it does allow our imagination to expand enough so that something quite different can be birthed. And then, of course, there's the idea, thanks to *Star Trek*, that for long distances, we just tele-transport. Yogananda, in his book *The Autobiography of a Yogi*, spoke of one of his teachers who could bilocate. All sorts of magical things become possible when we step into the 5D/6D paradigm.

What I believe is most important right now in this transition is for us to realize that all of the above and more are possible. It is all waiting in the sixth dimension, and the more we stay aware and begin to collectively hold images like this, trusting they can manifest here, the sooner they will.

Unbridled Creativity and Collective Unfoldment

The more we activate our 5D frequency, the more strands of our DNA become operative, and thus the more access we have to the creativity and visions we need to produce this joyful, loving, spiritually awake planet. Although unbridled creativity is one of the primary characteristics of 5D, remember the actual creation, the actual manifesting comes through interacting with 6D.

Remember, too, that in 6D, it is not just physical things that have their energetic blueprint there. This dimension holds energetic representations of all qualities as well. So, concepts like peace, equality, compassion, and inspiration all reside there energetically and all can show up more fully into our lives through focused intent. There is so much collective brilliance waiting to be harnessed and brought into our physical world. Because of the narrowly conditioned bandwidth we've been programmed with, humanity has not yet broken free enough to strengthen the collective will needed to bring these to fruition, but this is now changing. We are on the brink.

All around our planet there are more individuals waking up, opening their heart, healing their wounds, and holding a higher frequency to reclaim who they really are than has occurred here for well over twelve thousand years. The power of this collective awakening is not to be minimized. It is unstoppable, and when the time is right, it will roll across our globe and create the planet we have all been longing for.

The solutions are already in our global energy field, held by different individuals throughout our world. The energy to manifest these solutions is building. Living in a joyful world filled with loving, thriving people is at our doorstep waiting to be welcomed into being.

And So It Is

Imagine waking up one morning and finding that the door has been thrown open, the planet transformed. Suffering has become a thing of the past. Out your window, the children in the street are dancing and singing with abandon. Trees, flowers, and vegetation are everywhere. Adults wander by radiating health and contentment on their way to gather with others to collaborate on making their contributions to their world. Families, now configured by adults of all physical genders, all skin tones and ethnicities, and holding the common features of open, loving hearts and awakened spirits, stroll by with the very little ones.

Perhaps you take a deep breath, inhaling the beauty of the scene before you, inhaling the joy of living in a conscious, loving world. You take a moment to feel how you have transformed inwardly and are now a lighter brighter version of how you once were. Gratitude springs up spontaneously. A sense of ease and relaxation travels through your body.

You can still remember when humanity was riddled with disease, with the energy of fear, suffering the effects of war, cruelty, and injustice. You remember the feeling of being in constant struggle, of anxiety, of depression. Perhaps you shake your head in amazement that this now is a thing of the past.

You think about the transformation. How people all over the planet stepped up to shine their reclaimed consciousness around the globe. How they came forward with a frequency so powerful and loving that the old forces could not stop them. How, together, they held a common vision of a world where all beings were valued and honored for the divine spark within. With their once dormant strands of DNA now reactivated, they used their manifestation prowess for the good of all.

You remember how the atmosphere shifted, radiating peace. You saw more and more people awaken. The planet herself was brought back into balance. Earth's new reality was finally birthed.

And so, dear reader, hold these visions. Fill them with your own wisdom. Keep opening your heart, bathing yourself in love, then send this out to all. It is time once again to usher in a golden age across this planet. Together we will bring this to fruition.

In the words of John Lennon:

"You may say I'm a dreamer, but I'm not the only one. I hope someday you'll join us, and the world will live as One."

✴ MEDITATION ✴

Stepping into a Higher-Frequency World

Allow your eyes to soften and put all your attention on taking deep centering breaths. As you exhale release any distractions, any concerns, any tension. Just let that all flow out with the breath. On the inhale imagine that you are drawing in tiny golden spirals of light filled with love and consciousness and allow those tiny spirals to spread to every cell in your body. Keep focusing on your breath as you begin to feel a deepening sense of calm and relaxation.

See yourself now on a beautiful, wooded mountain path. As you walk up it, you become fully aware of the vibrant blue sky above, of the sun warming your hair and skin. You listen to the birds singing and calling to one another, and the sound of your footsteps crunching the fallen twigs. Smell the freshness of the air, the fragrances carried in the crisp breeze. Touch the trunks of the trees as you pass them to feel the life force energy they hold. Perhaps they will share some of their wisdom with you.

As you go farther up the path, you see before you a waterfall of golden light that you must pass through to continue. Walk into this waterfall and stop for a few moments allowing the golden light to wash away any fears, any concerns, any stale, lower-frequency energies, leaving you open, lovingly grateful, and fully refreshed. Walking out onto the other side, you see a beautiful grove of tall trees and people shimmering with light, standing in a circle inside the grove. They beckon to you to join them. You realize that you, too, are emitting this light, and as you join the circle a sense of coming home washes over you. You have entered New Earth and been welcomed. As you stand together with the others in the circle, you realize that your vibration has sped up to resonate with their frequency. You experience your heart becoming more open than ever before and your sense of well-being stronger than you have ever experienced.

The person standing next to you points to another opening beyond the grove, and you see a vibrant village. If you feel called, go ahead and walk into the village. You'll see that there are groups of people who are gathering to manage and solve various issues of day-to-day life. Some are working with health care, some education, some distribution of resources, some with energy production.

There are numerous groups dealing with all aspects of this society. Perhaps you are drawn to one group in particular. Go there and both listen and contribute your ideas.

Spend as much time as you choose in this new world. Know that as you do, you are helping to bring it onto our planet.

At some point, bring yourself back to the grove, through the waterfall of golden light, and back to where you began this journey. Breathe deeply and feel the change that has occurred in your energy. Then slowly bring your awareness back into your room, wiggling your fingers and toes to help you get fully back.

Journal on your experience and as you go through your day-to-day life remember to energize the creation of the world you have visited.

Note: Find this meditation on my YouTube channel, Wisdom Within Us, in the "Meditations to Raise Your Frequency" playlist.

Journal Questions to Ponder

1. What are your visions of a loving, spiritually awake planet?
2. What beliefs do you carry that these visions can't manifest?
3. What beliefs do you carry that these visions will manifest?
4. Do you use screen time as a distraction to keep yourself from doing what you've come here to do? Does this interfere with carrying out your mission in the world?
5. When you think about your gifts and talents, how would you choose to participate in both creating and being part of this loving, spiritually awake world?

Acknowledgments

As I start this acknowledgments page, the words that come are "It takes a planet," as this is how it feels when I think of all the remarkable students and friends from around the world who have shared their gifts and wisdom with me, enhancing and supporting my work.

Thank you to all the wonderful people at Inner Traditions. Every one of you has been great, and it is so nice to be working with you yet again. A very special thank you to Jon Graham, who emailed on a Sunday to let me know my contract was accepted rather than waiting to be back in his office. Thank you to my wonderful project editor, Beth Wojiski, for her focus and support to help this book shine. And thank you, too, to my friend and neighbor Linda Star Wolf for connecting me to this amazing publishing house in the first place. This book and *Activating Your 5D Frequency* wouldn't have gotten out into the world without your support.

Special appreciation to Nadi Hana, who passed away suddenly as this book was going into production, but who I know is still playing a major role in sharing her gifts from the other side. Nadi, I could not have completed the sacred geometry section of this book without your classes and without your feedback as I was writing this. Thank you so much.

Thank you to my Pleiadian soul sister, Eva Marquez, for all your help with the light language section. I couldn't have written it without you and have so much appreciation for the wise, radiant soul that you are.

Thank you, Barbara Hand Clow, for your ongoing enthusiasm about this book and for the brilliant and accessible way you have brought the wisdom of the 9D Vertical Axis into modern consciousness.

Thank you to my dear friend and soul sister Tammy Billups for all your guidance and love through this process. And to my other MasterHeart sisters Carley Mattimore and Stephanie Red Feather. Along with Tammy, your love, support, and brilliance activated this book coming forth for me. I love and appreciate you all dearly.

Thank you to readers Ruby Falconer, Linda Schrieber, and Janice DiGiralamo. Ruby, this book would not have been completed without that early and essential guidance from you. Linda, I so appreciate your attention to detail. And Janice, my dear friend of numerous decades, your feedback and encouragement kept me going.

To Shama Viola, without whose amazing oracle reading it's unlikely this book would have come into fruition as quickly as it did, I still have the word *persevere* on my altar.

Thank you to Caroline Oceana Ryan for coming through toward the end of this process with your wisdom on the golden light and the golden triangles in Sol and your thoughtful and generous sharing of your material.

Thank you to my wonderful assistant Becky Wheeler for all the ways you lighten my load, giving me more space to write this book, and for the beautiful rendition you created of the Expanded Bandwidth in chapter 1 (fig. 1.1). Your many gifts keep amazing and delighting me, Becky.

I send so much appreciation to my favorite photographer, Brittany Bey, who came through yet again capturing my soul through her camera.

And thank you with all my heart to my wonderful soul mate and life partner, Dennis, for his ongoing love and support of me and my gifts. Forty-five years later, we're still having fun, and I still adore you.

Notes

Chapter 1. The Big Picture

1. Maurice Doreal, trans., "The Emerald Tablets of Thoth: Preface," Crystalinks website.
2. Tom T. Moore, "Atlantis and Lemuria: The Lost Continents Revealed," *Conscious Community Magazine* website, October 12, 2020.
3. Stephanie Red Feather, *Empath Activation Cards: Discover Your Cosmic Purpose* (Bear & Company, 2021), 78.
4. Joe Vitale and Ihaleakala Hew Len, *Zero Limits, The Secret Hawaiian System for Wealth, Health, Peace, and More* (Wiley, 2008), 23.
5. Vitale and Len, *Zero Limits*, 23.

Chapter 2. A Deeper Look at Sixth-Dimensional Consciousness

1. "Episode 1: Masters of the Net," *Sacred Geometry series*.
2. Sanaya Roman, *Soul Love: Awakening Your Heart Centers* (H. J. Kramer, 1997), 70.
3. Roman, *Soul Love*, 71.
4. "Domino Theory: Cold War Misconception about Communism's Spread," Daily Dosed Documentary website.
5. Barbour, Julian, *The End of Time: The Next Revolution in Physics* (Oxford University Press, 1999), 46.
6. Barbara Hand Clow and Gerry Clow, *Alchemy of Nine Dimensions: The 2011/2012 Prophecies and Nine Dimensions of Consciousness* (Hampton Roads Publishing, 2010), 80.
7. Hand Clow and Clow, *Alchemy of Nine Dimensions*, 91, 92.

Chapter 3. The Creation of Our Personal Reality

1. Nicki Scully and Linda Star Wolf, *Shamanic Mysteries of Egypt: Awakening the Healing Power of the Heart* (Bear & Company, 2007), 45.
2. Scully and Star Wolf, *Shamanic Mysteries of Egypt*, 45.
3. *Hallelujah: Leonard Cohen, a Journey, a Song*, directed by Dan Geller and Dayna Goldfine (Sony Pictures Classics, 2022).
4. Lauren O. Thyme and Sareya Orion, *The Lemurian Way: Remembering Your Essential Nature*, 2nd ed. (Lauren O. Thyme Publishing, 2017), 19–22.
5. Thyme and Orion, *Lemurian Way*, 20, 21.
6. Barbara Hand Clow and Gerry Clow, *Alchemy of Nine Dimensions: The 2011/2012 Prophecies and Nine Dimension of Consciousness* (Hampton Roads Publishing, 2010), 72.
7. Hand Clow and Clow, *Alchemy of Nine Dimensions*, 72, 73.

Chapter 4. We Really Can Change the World

1. Lizzie Widdicombe, "What Can We Learn from the Germans about Confronting Our History?" *New Yorker* website, October 21, 2019.
2. Sarah Souli, "Does America Need a Truth and Reconciliation Commission?" Politico Magazine website, August 16, 2020.
3. Souli, "Truth and Reconciliation."
4. Kendra Cherry, "Understanding the Milgram Experiment in Psychology," Very Well Mind website, updated August 13, 2024.
5. Susan Pike, "Poison Ivy Has a Role in Our Ecosystem Despite Being a Nuisance," Lifestyle section, Foster's Daily Democrat website, updated September 3, 2015.
6. Lauren O. Thyme and Sareya Orion, *The Lemurian Way: Remembering Your Essential Nature*, 2nd ed. (Lauren O. Thyme Publishing, 2017), 94.
7. Caroline Oceana Ryan, *Messages from the Spirit of Abundance: Channeled Guidance from the Spirits of Prosperity and True Wealth* (self-pub., 2023), 12.
8. Hand Clow, Barbara, *The Pleiadian Agenda: A New Cosmology for the Age of Light* (Bear & Company, 1995), xix.

Chapter 5. Sacred Geometry and Other Languages of Light

1. Linda Tucker, *The Mystery of the White Lions: Children of the Sun God* (Hay House, 2010), 44.
2. Tucker, *The Mystery of the White Lions*, 45.
3. Evan Železny-Green, "Serving My People and the Earth Mother: Bear Tribe Medicine Society," InterMountain Histories website.
4. Lauren O. Thyme and Sareya Orion, *The Lemurian Way: Remembering Your Essential Nature*, 2nd ed. (Lauren O. Thyme Publishing, 2017), 20, 21.
5. J. J. Hurtak, *The Book of Knowledge: The Keys of Enoch* (Academy for Future Science, 1996), 100.
6. Hurtak, *The Book of Knowledge*, 97.
7. "Episode 1: Masters of the Net," *Sacred Geometry: Spiritual Science* series, hosted by Robert Gilbert, season 1, episode 1, Gaia TV, 2022.
8. "Sacred Geometry Shapes," Healing Stones blog, Cosmic Cuts website.
9. Shakti Gawain, *Living in the Light: A Guide to Personal and Planetary Transformation* (Nataraj Publishing, 1995), 69–70.
10. "The Great Central Sun," The Star Science website, July 6, 2021.
11. *Encyclopaedia Britannica Online*, s.v. "Black Hole," Science section, updated November 27, 2024.
12. "The Central Galactic Sun," Solar Ministry UK website, accessed December 7, 2024.
13. Caroline Oceans, Ryan, personal communication with Judith Corvin-Blackburn, March 22, 2024.
14. Richard Rudd, *The Gene Keys* (Watkins Publishing, 2013), xxxii.
15. iStock photo by ArtVector.

Chapter 6. Sacred Architecture, Sacred Sites, and the Frequency of Our Structures

1. John Michell with Allan Brown, *How the World Is Made: The Story of Creation According to Sacred Geometry* (Inner Traditions, 2009), 39.
2. Barbara Hand Clow and Gerry Clow, *Alchemy of Nine Dimensions: The 2011/2012 Prophecies and Nine Dimension of Consciousness* (Hampton Roads Publishing, 2010), 93.

3. Michell with Brown, *How the World Is Made*, 64, 65.
4. Skye Sherwin, "8 Brilliant Definitions of Beauty, from Aristotle to Aguilera," BBC Radio 2's Faith in the World Week, BBC website, 2016.
5. Fukagawa Hidetoshi and Tony Rothman, *Sacred Mathematics: Japanese Temple Geometry* (Princeton University Press), 2008.
6. John Keats, "Ode on a Grecian Urn," Poetry Foundation website, accessed December 7, 2024.
7. Tasha Shayne, "Decoding the Actual Age of the Great Sphinx," Gaia website, December 24, 2020.
8. Vladimir Antonov, "The Emerald Tablets of Thoth the Atlantean," trans. Mikhail Nikolenko, Atlantis and the Atlanteans website, accessed December 7, 2024.
9. Eva Marquez, *Activate Your Cosmic DNA: Discover Your Starseed Family* (Bear & Company, 2022), 41.
10. Linda Star Wolf and Anna Cariad-Barrett, *Sacred Medicine of Bee, Butterfly, Earthworm, and Spider: Shamanic Teachers of the Instar Medicine Wheel* (Bear & Company, 2013), 4, 5.
11. Mona Rain, "What Is an [Incan] Apacheta?," *Chacaruna Healing* (blog), Chacaruna Healing website, accessed December 7, 2024.
12. Eva Marquez, "Oneness Movement—Connecting Starseed Ground Crew with Crystals Set into Earth's Crystaline Grid," Eva Marquez channel, streamed live on October 24, 2022, YouTube video, 21:06, YouTube website.

Chapter 7. Time, Timelines, and Timelessness

1. Sara Johnson, "Understanding Epigenetics: How Trauma Is Passed On through Our Family Members," Commentary, *Arkansas Advocate* website, July 5, 2023.

Chapter 8. Steps to True Empowerment: The Antidote to Control

1. Wayne W. Dyer, *Inner Wisdom Cards* (Hay House, 2001).
2. Elizabeth Kübler-Ross, *The Wheel of Life: A Memoir of Living and Dying* (Scribner, 1997).

Bibliography

Barbour, Julian. *The End of Time: The Next Revolution in Physics.* Oxford University Press, 1999.

Beattie, Melody. *Codependent No More: How to Stop Controlling Others and Start Caring for Yourself.* Spiegel & Grau, 2022.

Billups, Tammy. *Animal Wayshowers: The Light Workers Ushering the 5D Consciousness.* With a foreword by Linda Star Wolf. Bear & Company, 2022.

Cooper, Diana. *Discover Atlantis.* Findhorn Press, 2007.

Cori, Patricia. *The New Sirian Revelations: Galactic Prophesies from the Sixth Dimension.* Bear & Company, 2023.

Corvin-Blackburn, Judith. *Activating Your 5D Frequency: A Guidebook for the Journey into Higher Dimensions.* Bear & Company, 2020.

Corvin-Blackburn, Judith. *Empowering the Spirit: A Process to Activate Your Soul Potential.* Healing Concepts Publishing, 2013.

Corvin-Blackburn, Judith. *Journey to Wholeness: A Guide to Inner Healing.* Healing Concepts Publishing, 1996.

Emoto, Masaru. *The Hidden Messages in Water.* Atria Books, 2005.

Hand Clow, Barbara, with Gerry Clow. *Alchemy of Nine Dimensions: The 2011/2012 Prophecies.* Hampton Roads Publishing, 2010.

Hand Clow, Barbara. *The Pleiadian Agenda: A New Cosmology for the Age of Light.* Bear & Company, 1995.

Hornecker, John. *Quantum Transformation: Guide to Becoming a Galactic Human.* Life Sciences Center, 2012.

Hurtak, J. J. *The Book of Knowledge: The Keys of Enoch.* Academy for Future Science, 1996.

Marquez, Eva. *Activate Your Cosmic DNA: Discover Your Starseed Family from the Pleiades, Sirius, Andromeda, Centaurus, Epsilon Eridani, and Lyra.* Bear & Company, 2022.

Marquez, Eva. *Embody Your Cosmic DNA: Become Multidimensional Find Your Soul Mate.* Eva Marquez, 2023.

Mattimore, Carley, and Linda Star Wolf. *Sacred Messengers of Shamanic Africa: Teachings from Zep Tepi, the Land of First Time.* Bear & Company, 2018.

Michell, John, with Allan Brown. *How the World Is Made.* Inner Traditions, 2009.

Newton, Michael. *Destiny of Souls: New Case Studies of Life Between Lives.* Llewellyn Publications, 2004.

Red Feather, Stephanie. *Empath Activation Cards: Discover Your Cosmic Purpose.* Bear & Company, 2021.

Red Feather, Stephanie. *The Evolutionary Empath: A Practical Guide for Heart-Centered Consciousness.* Bear & Company, 2019.

Roman, Sanaya. *Soul Love: Awakening Your Heart Centers.* H. J. Kramer, 1997.

Ryan, Caroline Oceana. *New Earth Journeys: The Collective Speak on Dealing with Personal and Global Crises.* Independently published, Ascension Times Publishing, 2021.

Scully, Nicki, and Linda Star Wolf. *Shamanic Mysteries of Egypt: Awakening the Healing Power of the Heart.* Bear & Company, 2007.

Sherwin, Skye. "8 Brilliant Definitions of Beauty, from Aristotle to Aguilera." BBC Radio 2's Faith in the World Week. BBC website, 2016.

Star Wolf, Linda, and Anna Carriad-Bennett. *Sacred Medicine of Bee, Butterfly, Earthworm, and Spider: Shamanic Teachers of the Instar Medicine Wheel.* Bear & Company, 2013.

Thyme, Lauren O. *The Lemurian Way: Remembering Your Essential Nature.* Lauren O. Thyme, 2nd edition, 2017.

Tucker, Linda. *Mystery of the White Lions: Children of the Sun God.* Hay House, 2010.

Vitale, Joe, and Ihaleakala Hew Len. *Zero Limits: The Secret Hawaiian System of Wealth, Health, Peace, and More.* John Wiley & Sons, 2007.

Yogananda, Paramahansa. *Autobiography of a Yogi.* Self-Realization Fellowship, 1946.

Index

Activate Your Cosmic DNA (Marquez), 95, 159
activating starseed memories, 5, 118–21
Activating Your 5D Frequency (Blackburn), 2, 15, 19, 90, 117
activations (workshops), xii–xiii
adulting, 23–26
Air Temple, 163–64
Alchemy of Nine Dimensions (Hand Clow), xi, 15, 66
Alcyone, 95–96, 140
ancestral architecture, 149–52
anger, 28, 73, 121, 134, 189–90, 205, 206–7
apachetas, 165–67
Arcturians, 95
Aristotle, 155
Atlantis. *See also* Lemuria
  about, 13
  ancient languages rooted in, 130–31
  awareness of, 93
  connection to, 94
  falls of, 13, 42
  imbalance and destruction, 119–20
  masculine energy, 94
  memories of, 12
  sacred geometry and, 130
  technology and, 93, 230–31
  vaccine, 194
auditory light language, 138
authenticity, 213, 221–23
authentic power, 215–16
authoritarianism, 107
avatars, 20

balance
  about, 21
  Buddhism and, 136
  of dualities, 135–37
  ecological, 114–16
  empowerment and, 134
  evolutionary journey and, 61
  feminine and masculine and, 26
  feminine and masculine energy, 135–36
  5D/6D frequency and, 226
  grounding and, 185
  heart and mind, 26
  higher-dimensional consciousness and, 61
  magic of, 115–16
  rebalancing and, 116, 148
  within and without, 26–28

Index

bandwidth
  contracting, 98
  expanding, 63–65, 91–92, 101, 109, 202–3, 207–8
  narrow, perceiving from, 185
Barbour, Julian, xiv, 65–66, 72, 177
beauty, 155–57
beliefs, old
  becoming resistances, 55, 108–9
  calming, 55, 196–97
  collective chaos and, 145
  future reality and, 196
  working with, 19, 80, 82, 118–19
belief systems
  collective, 33
  disempowering, 179
  lower-frequency, 24
  opposing, 27, 33
  transforming, 183
bleed throughs
  about, 187
  collective, 192–95
  timeline, example, 188–89
blue star, 138
Blue Star Medicine Wheel, 161
The Book of Knowledge: the Keys of Enoch (Hurtak), 130–31
breath and breathing, 31, 62, 71, 143–44, 148, 151, 163, 207, 210–11, 234

Cariad-Barrett, Anna, 164
carrier waves, 69
cave allegory, 12
Cellular Journey to Deactivate Our Trauma DNA meditation, 197–99
change(s)
  collective, 22, 73
  fear of, 105–6, 108–9
  nature and challenge of, 108–11
  resistance to accepting, 27
  suffering and, 106, 108–9, 113
chaotic energy, 139
chemicals and toxins, 154
clutter and disarray, 152
codependency, 53, 84, 213
Cohen, Leonard, 88–89
coherence, 69–70
collective agreement, 106
collective beliefs
  change and, 22, 111
  power of, 33
  wars and, 50
collective bleed throughs, 192–95
collective change
  about, 73
  fear and, 107
  as threatening, 22
collective intention
  about, 32–33
  old belief systems and, 33
  power of, 34
  reweaving, 34–36
collective resistance, 30, 108–9, 121
collective shadows, 5, 111–14, 217
collective triggers, 228
collective unfoldment, 232–33
commitment, 55–56
Connecting with Your Soul Vision meditation, 37–39
consciousness
  balance and, 61
  heart-based, 12, 21
  higher-dimensional, balance and, 61
  separation, 17–18

6D, 16, 51, 68, 178
trauma, 10
victim, 52–56
conspiracy theories, 210
Cory, Patricia, 108
COVID-19 vaccine, 192–94
creation
within energy field, 25
5D and, 128
through thought forms, 13
creativity, 51, 65, 128, 156, 173, 225, 232–33
Croteau, Bob, 168–71
crystals, 172
cultural beliefs, 73, 104, 106, 107
Cygnus, 140–41

dark shadow, 63–64, 86
da Vinci, Leonardo, 155
Destiny of Souls (Newton), 180
DID (Dissociative Identity Disorder), 219
dimensional descent, 1, 11, 14–15, 96, 107, 149
dimensionality, xii, xiv, 65. *See also* multidimensionality
disempowerment, 10, 53, 67, 179, 182, 188
divine 5D/6D human
about, 14
perspective, 16–17
sacred sites and, 172
understanding, 15–19
Divine Mind, 44, 131, 141, 173
DNA
dormant, reactivating, 10
the Fall and, 11–14
junk, 9
light codes, 8–9, 140, 141

star, 20–21, 51, 110, 117–19, 144, 194, 197–99, 202
trauma, 110
trauma gene, turning off, 188, 190–91
twelve-strand, 8–9, 11–12

Earth Temple, 162
ecological balance, 114–16
Egypt, ancient
energy of, 92
as 5D society, 41–42, 232
frequencies and wisdom of, 13–14
Karnak, 96
sacred sites, 157–59
8D (eighth dimension), 45
embodiment
about, 203–4
bodily energy movement and, 208
body acceptance and, 208–9
information access and, 208
intuitive knowing and, 207
processing feelings and, 204–7
sense of depth and, 207–8
Embodying Our Cosmic DNA (Marquez), 137
emotional body
in blocking access, 16
clearing, 51, 84, 100, 205, 207
congestion in, 206, 207
fourth dimension and, 15
healing, 46, 164
as out of alignment, 18
emotional triggers
neutrality and, 195, 209
noticing, 36, 61
utilizing, 36–37

Empowering the Spirit: A Process to Activate Your Full Soul Potential (Blackburn), 63, 182, 183, 212
empowerment
  about, 6
  balance and, 134
  creative, 56
  embodiment and, 203–9
  giving power away and, 211–14
  inner trust and, 220–21
  light codes and, 9
  loving neutrality and, 209–11
  personal, 17, 52, 133
  reclaiming power and, 214–16
  reconnecting with, 188
  relationships and, 215–16
  shadow work and, 216–20
  steps to, 202–24
  we create our lives and, 203
End of Time, The (Barbour), xiv, 65–66, 177
energetic blueprint, 2, 18, 48, 87, 132, 149, 167, 233
environments
  about, 152–53
  awareness of, 154–55
  beauty and, 155–57
  chemicals and toxins, 154
  structures, 153
epigenetics, 190–91
evolutionary process, 2, 5, 61, 105, 153, 157, 178

Fall, the, 11–14
fear
  about, 205–6
  attachment to, 32
  of change, 105–6, 108–9
  disempowerment and, 182
  freedom and, 22–23
  harmfulness of, 133
  of our power, 98
  resistance and, 27, 108–9, 139
  stepping into leadership and, 89–90, 91
  surrender and, 69
  through anger, 134
  war and, 50
female conditioning, 58
Fibonacci spiral, 132
the field of plenty, 47
Fire Temple, 163
1D (first dimension), 47
4D
  blocks, clearing, 51
  canopy, 15–16, 178
  collective wound, 18
  consciousness, 178
  frequency, 15
  wound, 18
5D
  collective familiarity with, 65
  creativity and, 128
  frequency, 12, 115
  physicality of, 15
  qualities, 2
  unconditional love, 62–63
5D/6D frequencies
  Indigenous cultures and, 129
  manifestation and, 35
  operation from, 179
  world created by, 226
5D/6D society, 159
fragmentation vs. harmonization, 139–40
freedom, 22–23, 213

frequency matching, for manifestation, 96–100
future
  choosing, 195–96
  old beliefs and, 196
  screen technology and, 229–30

Gawain, Shakti, 136
Gene Keys (Rudd), 142
Gilbert, Robert, 131–32
global peace meditations, 35, 116
golden age, 121–22
golden pyramids, 141–42
Great Pyramid, 157, 158
Grof, Stanislav and Christina, xiii
grounding, 173, 185, 208, 210–11
"Ground Crew, the," 172

Hand Clow, Barabara, xi–xv, 2, 15–16, 41, 96, 118, 122, 149
heart-based consciousness, 12, 21
heart openness, 48–49, 84
higher-dimensional reality, creating, 116–17
Hollis Renewal Center, apacheta, 167
Holotropic Breathwork, xiii
Hurtak, J. J., 130–31

imbalance, 134, 135
"I'm not up to it," 54–55
Indigenous cultures, 129–30
inner trust, 220–21
Instar Medicine Wheel, 164, 167
intention
  about, 32–36
  collective, 32–34
  paying attention and, 34

rogue cells and, 31–32
sacred sites and, 173
intuitive knowing, 207

journal questions
  awakened world, 236
  big picture, 39–40
  change, 125
  empowerment, 223–24
  personal reality creation, 103
  sacred architecture and sacred sites, 176
  sacred geometry, 146–47
  sixth-dimensional consciousness, 77
  time and timelines, 199–200
Journey of Souls (Newton), 180
Journey to Wholeness: A Guide to Inner Healing (Blackburn), 16, 188
joyfulness, 29–30, 56, 84, 207
judgment(s), 29, 33–34, 51, 61, 72–73, 98, 137, 225–26, 236
junk DNA, 9

ka
  about, 48–49
  amount of, 88
  embodying, 87–88, 89
  energetic blueprint, 84, 132
  energetic configurations, 132
  existence of, 87
  frequency matching for manifestation and, 100
  meditation, 101–3
karma, releasing, 182
Karnak, 96
Kübler-Ross, Elizabeth, 217–18

languages, ancient, 130–31

leadership, 89–91, 117
Lemuria. *See also* Atlantis
   about, 13, 92
   energy of, 92
   fall of, 93
   feminine energy, 94
   gold light and, 120
   imbalance and destruction, 119–20
   memories of, 12
   sacred geometry, 92
   technology and, 230–31
Len, Dr. Hew, 36–37
ley lines, 92
lifetimes, 180–84
light codes, DNA, 8–9, 140, 141
lightening up, 143
light language. *See also* sacred geometry
   auditory, 138
   forms of, 137–39
light polarization, 85–86
light workers, 20, 123, 183
love. *See also* self-love
   codependency and, 84
   conditional, 64
   creation and, 115
   holding, 24, 151
   motivation of, 51–52
   sacred geometry and, 139
   soul, 44, 62–63, 65
   unconditional, 11–12, 15, 23–25, 50, 62, 86, 101, 117, 203
   your enemy, 107
loving neutrality, 209–11

male conditioning, 57–58
manifestation
   5D/6D frequencies and, 35
   frequency matching for, 96–100
   hidden motivations and, 82
Marquez, Eva, 95, 137, 159, 172
meditation(s)
   Cellular Journey to Deactivate Our Trauma DNA, 197–99
   Connecting with Your Soul Vision, 37–39
   global peace, 35, 116
   Meeting Your Ka, 101–3
   Messages from Metatron's Cube, 145–46
   neutrality and, 72
   Planetary Healing: Planting Portals of Light, 122–25
   Reclaiming Empowerment and Authenticity, 221–23
   Rogue Cell Dialogue, 74–77
   on sacred geometry, 144–45
   Stepping into a Higher-Frequency World, 235–36
   this book, 6
   Visiting Advanced Civilizations, 174–76
Meeting Your Ka meditation, 101–3
Messages from Metatron's Cube meditation, 145–46
Metatron's Cube, 144, 145
Milgram Experiment, 113
money frequency, 97
multidimensionality, 11, 15, 41–43, 100, 159
music frequency, 97–98
Mutwa, Credo, 129

neutrality
   coherence and, 70
   emotional triggers and, 195, 209

empowerment and, 209–11
loving, 209–11
meditation and, 72
New Sirian Revelations, The (Cory), 108
Newton, Michael, 180
Nine-Dimensional Human, 43
nine dimensions, 42–47
9D
about, 42
frequency, 45
Vertical Axis, xii, 2, 5, 44–45
norms, 4, 90, 108, 215

On Death and Dying (Kübler-Ross), 218
Oneness, 25, 45, 65, 94, 141, 172
organization, this book, 5–6

past, our, 91
past-life experiences
author examples of, 180–82
gifts of, 184
instant connections and, 184–85
means of accessing, 185–86
remembering, 184–87
spiritually advanced world, 186–87
perceptual bandwidth, 9–10
personal intention, 31–32
personal reality
about, 78–82
accessing our past and, 91–96
creating, 81, 83
frequency matching and, 96–100
health and, 79
intersection with others' journeys, 83–84
ka and, 87–89
leadership and, 89–91

purpose and, 79
relationships and, 79
6D and, 81
taking charge of, 80–81
unconscious intent and, 81
phi ratio (Golden Mean), 132
Planetary Healing: Planting Portals of Light meditation, 122–25
Plato, 12, 13, 72, 150
Platonia, 72
Platonic solids. *See also* sacred geometry
about, 132
cube (hexahedron), 48, 133
dodecahedron, 48, 133
elements and, 133
icosahedron, 48, 133
illustrated, 48
octahedron, 48, 133
tetrahedron, 48, 133
3D patterns from, 128
used in integrity, 133
Pleiadian Agenda, The, (Hand Clow), xii, 96, 118, 122
Pleiadian alignment, 172
Pleiadians, 15–16, 41, 95, 140
power
acceptance of, 58–60
authentic, 215–16
of collective intention, 34
fear of, 98
observing ways we give away, 211–14
reclaiming, 214–16
of surrender, 68–72
pyramids, 157–59

quantum field, 69–70
quantum physics, 108, 203

"Reality Splitting," 122
rebalancing, 116, 148. *See also* balance
Reclaiming Empowerment and Authenticity meditation, 221–23
reclaiming our power, 214–16
reclamation journey, 1–2
Red Feather, Stephanie, 31, 166, 167
relationships
    collective wound and, 10
    empowerment and, 213, 214, 215–16
    internal imbalance and, 135
    personal reality and, 79
resistance
    collective, 30, 108–9, 121
    creation of, 98, 205
    embracing, xiv
    fear and, 27, 108–9, 139
    guilt and, 59
    practicing with, 71, 197
Revelations Trilogy, xiii
right hemisphere, brain, 177–78
Rogue Cell Dialogue meditation, 74–77
rogue cells, 32, 98, 196
Roman, Sanaya, 62
Rotary Sundial installation, 168–71
Rudd, Richard, 14, 142
Ryan, Caroline Oceana, 120–21, 141–42

sacred architecture
    about, 148–49
    ancestral, 149–52
    beauty and, 156
    geometric patterns, 149
    harmony and well-being, 150–51
    living in, 151
    mathematics, 150
    as microcosm, 150

sacred feminine, 26, 58, 68–69, 134–35, 232–33
sacred geometry. *See also* Platonic solids
    about, 4, 5
    Atlantean, 130
    connecting with, 131–35
    Lemurian, 92
    male and female energy and, 134–35
    meditation, 144–46
    9D Vertical Axis and, 44–45
    6D and, 4, 131
sacred masculine, 26, 134–35, 231–32
sacred sites
    about, 157
    Air Temple, 163–64
    ancient, 157–60
    apachetas, 165–67
    creating, 171–74
    creation types, 161
    Earth Temple, 162
    Egypt, 157–59
    Fire Temple, 163
    Goddess Sekhmet statue, 164–65
    Instar Medicine Wheel, 164, 167
    instructions for creating, 173
    modern, 161–71
    Scotland, 160
    Sunflower installation, 168–71
    types of, 172
    Venus Rising Association of Transformation, 162–65
    visiting, 157–59
    Water Temple, 164
sacred sound, 128–29, 130
sadness, 49, 82, 90, 188, 205, 206
Saint Francis of Assisi, 24
screen technology, future of, 229–30

2D (second dimension), 47
Sekhmet statue, 164–65
self-consciousness, 213
self-doubt, 25, 56, 58, 90, 111
self-love, 28, 54, 58–60, 61. *See also* love
self-observation, 212
self-responsibility, 52–56
separation consciousness, 17–18
sex-role conditioning, 57–58
shadow
   avoiding, 217
   collective, 5, 111–14, 217
   dark, 63–64, 86, 219–20
   emotional triggers, 37
   experiences, working with, 183
   global, 112
   identifying and honoring, 64–65
   parts, integrating, 15–16, 26, 46, 51
   personal, 111
   thoughts and feelings, 72–73
shadow work, 216–20
Shamanic Breathwork, 163
Sirians, 95
Sirius star system, 140
6D
   comprehension of, xii
   creation through thought forms and, 13
   energetic blueprint, 18, 48, 87, 149, 167, 233
   energy configuration, 49–50
   as evolutionary key, 1–6
   importance of, 65–68
   light forms, 45, 47–48
   New Earth energy blueprints, 2
   qualities in, 49
   as quantum field, 3, 69–70
   sacred geometry and, 4, 131
   soul configuration, 48
   structure of, 47–50
   3D and, 18, 34, 51
   visualization, xiv, 47
   as world of forms, 3
6D consciousness, 16, 51, 68, 178
social growth, 104–5
soul love, 44, 62–63, 65
Sphinx, 157–58
standing stones, 160
star ancestors, 12, 95. *See also* Atlantis; Lemuria
star DNA, 20–21, 51, 110, 117–19, 144, 194, 202
starseeds
   about, 20
   awareness expansion, 120
   identification as, 95
   memory activation, 5, 118–21, 183
Star Wolf, Linda, 161–64
Stepping into a Higher-Frequency World meditation, 235–36
structures, 153. *See also* sacred architecture
suffering, 78, 106, 108–9, 113, 139, 149, 228
Sun Bear, 130
Sunflower installation, 168–71
surrender
   challenge of, 72
   coherence and, 70
   ego and, 72
   as energetic state, 69
   energy of, 144
   fear and, 69
   as journey strategy, 144
   manifestation and, 18, 71

technology
　Lemuria and Atlantis and, 93, 230–31
　screen, future of, 229–30
Temple of Hathor, 159
3D
　collective reality, 34
　controlling from, 51
　imbalance, 114
　as impermanent, 23
　reality, 3
　6D and, 18, 34, 51
　timelines, 180
3D egoic self
　holding in your heart, 84–87
　loving relationship with, 85–86
　old conditioning of, 85
Thoth, 14, 150, 158
thoughts
　as energy, 67
　fears from, 205–6
　frequency, 96–97
　magical triangles of, xiv
　noticing, 34, 61–64
　shadow, 64, 72–73, 137
Thyme, Lauren O., 120, 130
time
　about, 5
　expansion, 177
　linear, 185
　perception of, 178
　as simultaneous, 179–80
timelines
　changing, 190–92
　soul and, 180
　3D, 180
　understanding, 179
"Tower of Song," 88

transitionary process, 227–28
trauma consciousness, 10
trauma DNA, 110, 197–99
trauma gene, turning off, 188, 190–91
trauma(s)
　about, 5
　bleed throughs, 187, 192–95
　clearing, 187–88
　collective, 59–60
　creation of, 10
　from other lifetimes, 182–83, 184
　processing, 204–7
　timeline intervention and, 187
triggers, 227–28
trust, inner, 220–21
"Truth and Reconciliation," 111–12

unconditional love, 62, 86

Venus Rising Association of Transformation, 162–65
Viola, Shama, 180
Visiting Advanced Civilizations meditation, 174–76
visualization, xiv, 59, 186–90, 196
Vitale, Joe, 36–37

war concept, 50, 66–67, 116
Water Temple, 164
way-showers, 20, 61, 89
witness self, 63
writing this book, 4, 50, 55–56, 66, 70, 80, 90, 120, 133

yin/yang symbol, 136

Zero Limits (Vitale and Len), 36–37

About the Author

Judith Corvin-Blackburn, LCSW, DMin, is an award-winning author, internationally known teacher, transpersonal psychotherapist, and shamanic minister, who has been inspiring people to step into joy, purpose, and inner authority for more than forty-five years. Her passion is to guide and empower individuals to reclaim their true soul nature so that collectively we can transform planet Earth into the loving, peaceful, creative place it is meant to be.

Coming of age in the 1960s, and having had a profound, life-changing spiritual awakening in the mid-'70s, Judith has spent much of her adult life guiding people to heal old wounds from this lifetime and others, to reconnect with their heart's wisdom and their soul missions, so that together we can manifest a spiritually awakened planet based on unconditional love for all beings.

She is the author of four books: *The 6D Ascension Journey, Activating Your 5D Frequency, Empowering the Spirit*, and *Journey to Wholeness*.

In addition to offering private transpersonal psychotherapy sessions, she offers online and Zoom classes to empower one's spirit, embrace our starseed nature, and to activate our higher-frequency potential. She also teaches a Global Shamanic Multidimensional Mystery School.

Her home is in the beautiful Smoky Mountains, where she lives with her husband, Dennis, and Athena, their cat who adopted them while they were taking a walk.

Learn more about her at empoweringthespirit.com.

Check out her YouTube channel, Wisdom Within Us, for numerous free meditations.